CANADIAN ANNUAL REVIEW OF POLITICS AND PUBLIC AFFAIRS 2005

Canadian Annual Review
of politics and public affairs
2005

EDITED BY DAVID MUTIMER

Published with the support of York University by
University of Toronto Press
Toronto Buffalo London

ISBN 978-1-4426-4385-7

Printed on acid-free, 100% post-consumer recycled paper with vegetable-based inks.

A cataloguing record for this publication is available from Library and Archives Canada.

University of Toronto Press acknowledges the financial assistance to its publishing program of the Canada Council for the Arts and the Ontario Arts Council.

  Canada Council   Conseil des Arts
for the Arts   du Canada
 ONTARIO ARTS COUNCIL
CONSEIL DES ARTS DE L'ONTARIO

University of Toronto Press acknowledges the financial support of the Government of Canada through the Canada Book Fund for its publishing activities.

This book was published with the support of York University.

Copies of the Canadian Annual Review published annually for 1989 and 1991–2004 are available.

Contents

Contributors

MELVIN BAKER, Archivist/Historian, President's Office, Memorial University of Newfoundland

EMMANUEL BRUNET-JAILLY, Assistant Professor, School of Public Administration, University of Victoria

PETER EDWARD BUKER, Assistant Professor, Department of Political Studies, University of Prince Edward Island

KRISTIN BURNETT, Assistant Professor, History Department, Lakehead University

KEN COATES, Adjunct Professor of Political Studies, University of Saskatchewan

ROBERT DRUMMOND, Associate Professor, Department of Political Science, York University

ROBERT EVERETT, University Secretariat, York University

ROBERT G. FINBOW, Associate Professor, Department of Political Science, Dalhousie University

JOSEPH GARCEA, Associate Professor, Department of Political Science, University of Saskatchewan

CHRIS HENDERSHOT, compiler, Calendar and Obituaries; doctoral candidate, Department of Political Science, York University

CAREY HILL, independent researcher, Ottawa, Ontario

HAROLD JANSEN, Assistant Professor, Department of Political Science, University of Lethbridge

SERENA KATAOKA, doctoral candidate, Department of Political Science, University of Victoria

GEOFFREY LAMBERT, Professor, Department of Political Studies, University of Manitoba

WARREN MAGNUSSON, Professor, Department of Political Science, University of Victoria

DAVID MUTIMER, Editor, *Canadian Annual Review of Politics and Public Affairs;* Associate Professor of Political Science, York University, and Deputy Director, York Centre for International and Security Studies.

PETER NEARY, Professor, Department of History, University of Western Ontario

GREG POELZER, Associate Professor, Department of Political Studies, University of Saskatchewan

DANIEL SALÉE, Professor of Political Science and Principal, School of Community and Public Affairs, Concordia University

CHRISTOPHER SPEARIN, Assistant Professor, Department of Defence Studies, Canadian Forces College, Toronto

SHANNON STETTNER, Managing Editor, *Canadian Annual Review of Politics and Public Affairs* (carppa@yorku.ca).

RICHARD WILBUR, Fundy Promotions, St. Andrews, New Brunswick

Canadian calendar 2005

4   The Canadian junior men's hockey team defeats Russia six to one at the IHHF World Junior Championship to win Canada's first gold medal since 1997.

5   Statistics Canada reports a marked improvement in housing conditions during the late 1990s in Canada's twenty-seven largest urban centres. However, the report also indicates that in 2001 one in every six urban households fell below one or more housing standard.

7   Statistics Canada reports that an estimated 34,000 jobs were created in December 2004. This increase pushed the unemployment rate down to 7 per cent, which was its lowest point since May 2001. For the year, 228,000 jobs were created, which is a slightly lower percentage increase than in 2003 (1.4 per cent compared to 1.8 per cent).

8   Canada's Disaster Assistance Response Team arrives in Sri Lanka to provide humanitarian assistance in the aftermath of a massive earthquake and subsequent tsunami in late December 2004.

10   Mahmoud Abbas succeeds Yasser Arafat as leader of the Palestinian Authority.

–   Statistics Canada reports that the value of building permits for November 2004 totalled $5 billion, an increase of 9.3 per cent from October 2004.

–   The federal government announces that it will provide $425 million for disaster relief to the tsunami-affected areas of Southeast Asia.

12   Statistics Canada reports that the soaring Canadian dollar and a drop in the volume of imported goods resulted in a near-record trade surplus for Canada with respect to the rest of the world in November 2004.

13 Statistics Canada reports that Canada's GDP per capita was 83 per cent of that of the United States GDP per capita between 1994 and 2002.

14 Citizenship and Immigration Minister Judy Sgro resigns amid allegations of impropriety during her re-election campaign. She is later cleared of any wrongdoing.

15 Army Specialist Charles Graner Jr. is sentenced to fifteen years for his role in the Abu Ghraib prisoner scandal.

16 Prime Minister Paul Martin begins a nine-day trip to the tsunami-affected areas of Southeast Asia.

18 Statistics Canada reports that the number of undergraduate and master's degrees and undergraduate certificates and diplomas issued rose for the third consecutive year in 2001. However, the report also indicates that the number of doctorates granted fell to its lowest level since 1995.

–   Statistics Canada reports that each additional year of parental education directly increases the likelihood of their children attending university. Data was collected from the 1991 and 1995 School Leavers surveys.

19 Statistics Canada reports that the twelve-month consumer price index fell to 2.1 per cent in December 2004, down from 2.4 per cent in November.

20 Norman Kwong is appointed lieutenant-governor of Alberta.

21 CIBC World Markets Inc. warns that Canadians are 'are sitting on a time bomb of consumer debt.' According to the bank, personal lines of credit increased 30 per cent in 2004.

25 The sixtieth anniversary of the liberation of Auschwitz is marked by a gathering of world leaders at the site of the largest of the Nazi concentration camps.

26 Statistics Canada reports that wage rates in Canada have remained relatively stable since the 1980s, with only minor changes in the proportion of persons holding either a high-paid or low-paid job.

31 Close to 11,000 Iraqis residing in Canada cast their ballots in Iraq's first parliamentary elections since the U.S.-led invasion in March 2003.

–   Statistics Canada reports that the GDP increased 0.2 per cent in November 2004.

FEBRUARY

1   Ernie Eves, the Progressive Conservative MPP for Dufferin-Peel-Wellington-Grey, retires from Ontario provincial politics after twenty-four years of service.

2 Harjit Singh, the man at the centre of the Judy Sgro immigration controversy, is deported to India.

3 Nortel Networks files suit against three former executives who were fired because of an accounting scandal, in order to recover nearly $13 million worth of bonuses.

4 Statistics Canada reports that the unemployment rate for January remained steady at 7 per cent.

7 Statistics Canada reports that the value of building permits reached record levels in 2004, with $55.4 billion worth of permits issued, representing a 9.1 per cent increase over 2003. The value of permits for December 2004 increased 1.6 per cent from November, to $5.1 billion.

8 Jean Chrétien testifies before the Gomery inquiry that although mistakes were made, he still believes the sponsorship program made a genuine effort to promote national unity.

– A peace summit in Egypt concludes with Ariel Sharon and Mahmoud Abbas announcing a truce between Israel and the Palestinian Authority.

– Julian Fantino, Toronto's chief of police, is appointed the new commissioner of emergency management for Ontario.

9 Walmart closes its store in Jonquière, Quebec, only six months after employees obtain union certification.

10 Prime Minister Paul Martin testifies before the Gomery inquiry that he had little input into how the special unity fund was dispersed by the sponsorship program.

14 The federal government and Newfoundland and Labrador sign a deal that would see a more equitable distribution of revenues from offshore energy resources.

– Former prime minister of Lebanon Rafik Hariri is killed by a bomb blast.

15 Statistics Canada reports that during the 1990s one-quarter of firms closed their doors after one year in operation, one-third ceased operations after five years, and one-fifth survived for ten years.

16 The Kyoto Protocol goes into effect but Canada continues to deliberate how to proceed with its own plan to reduce greenhouse gas emissions.

– The House of Commons begins debate on same-sex marriage legislation introduced by Justice Minister Irwin Cotler.

– Statistics Canada reports that people from moderate- to low-income families were no less likely to enter university in 2001 than in 1993, despite increasing financial burdens including rising tuition costs.

- Gary Bettman, commissioner of the National Hockey League, cancels the 2004–05 NHL season as a labour dispute with the players continues.
17 Statistics Canada reports that $53.4 billion worth of Canadian securities were purchased by foreign investors in 2004, which represents the largest ever yearly investment by foreign investors.
22 Statistics Canada reports that in January the twelve-month consumer price index fell to 2 per cent, a decrease of 0.1 per cent.
23 Finance Minister Ralph Goodale announces a federal budget that includes billions of new spending initiatives for the military, cities, and a national daycare program, tax cuts, increased equalization payments, and a surplus.
24 Canada opts out of the American National Missile Defence project.
- A massive student strike begins in Quebec. At its peak, more than 230,000 post-secondary students are on strike in protest of proposed budget changes to student funding in the province.
25 Statistics Canada reports that Canadian corporations recorded $204 billion in operating profits in 2004, a record high, up 18.8 per cent from 2003 levels.
- Following its blessing of same-sex marriages, the Anglican Church of Canada is asked to voluntarily withdraw from the Anglican Consultative Council.
28 Statistics Canada reports that real GDP rose 2.8 per cent in 2004. Economic growth slowed 0.4 in the fourth quarter and the GDP rose 0.2 per cent in December.

MARCH

1 UNICEF releases a report finding that close to 15 per cent of children in Canada live at or below the poverty line, placing Canada nineteenth out of twenty-six of the world's wealthiest countries. The report goes on to state that this percentage has remained relatively unchanged in Canada for the past fifteen years.
- Ontario passes legislation to ban the acquisition and breeding of pit bull terriers in the province.
3 Four RCMP officers are killed in a raid on a suspected marijuana grow op in Mayerthorpe, Alberta.
7 Statistics Canada reports that the value of building permits fell from its record high in December to $4.5 billion in January, an 11 per cent decrease.

8 Frank McKenna assumes the position of Canada's ambassador to the United States.

9 Canadian mining company Noranda announces its takeover of Falconbridge to become one of world's largest base metal mining companies.

10 *Forbes* magazine releases its billionaires list for 2004. The list includes seventeen Canadians, an increase of one from 2003.

11 The federal government launches a $39-million lawsuit in the Quebec Superior Court against Lafleur Communications, Groupaction, Everest, and Polygone, the four advertising firms at the centre of the sponsorship scandal.

– Jetsgo, Canada's third largest airline, files for bankruptcy protection and ceases operations, leaving an estimated 17,000 passengers with worthless tickets.

14 A $9.9-billion oil sands expansion is announced by Suncor.

16 Ripudaman Singh Malik and Ajaib Singh Bagri are found not guilty of conspiracy to commit murder in the 1985 bombing of Air India flight 182.

17 John Tory, leader of Ontario's Progressive Conservatives, easily wins a by-election in the riding of the Dufferin-Peel-Wellington-Grey, giving him a seat in the provincial legislature.

– Statistics Canada reports that national net worth topped $4.3 trillion, or $132,500 per capita, at the end of the fourth quarter in 2004.

– Statistics Canada reports that foreign investors purchased $1.8 billion of Canadian debt instruments in January.

18 Statistics Canada reports that between 1991 and 2004 demand for labour switched from the high-tech sector to the housing and resource sectors.

22 Statistics Canada reports that in 2001, 47 per cent of Canadian households spent more than their pre-tax income, a 12 per cent increase from 1982 levels. More troubling, per capita debt doubled between 1982 and 2001, with mortgage and consumer debt being the most immediate cause of this doubling.

23 Statistics Canada reports that the twelve-month consumer price index rose 1 per cent in February, to 2.1 per cent.

24 Prime Minister Paul Martin announces the appointment of nine new senators. The appointees are Roméo Dallaire, Art Eggleton, Lillian Dyck, Jim Cowan, Elaine McCoy, Grant Mitchell, Robert Peterson, Nancy Ruth, and Claudette Tardif.

– An immigration panel denies American Jeremy Hinzman and his family refugee status in Canada. Hinzman, a former paratrooper, fled the United States as a conscientious objector to the war in Iraq.

29 The president of Enron Mortgage is sentenced to six years in prison for his role in one the largest mortgage scams in Canadian history: investors lost $182 million.

31 Alberta announces that it is officially debt-free.

– Canada's Competition Bureau finds no evidence of collusion in the fixing of gasoline prices.

APRIL

2 Striking Quebec post-secondary students reach a deal with the provincial government that will see a $428-million investment over four years, officially ending the five-week student walkout.

– Pope John Paul II dies after a twenty-six-year papacy.

4 One of Canada's wealthiest persons, Edward Bronfman, dies at the age of seventy-seven.

5 An Ontario judge rules that is unconstitutional for the Province of Ontario to arbitrarily cut services for children with autism when the child reaches six years old.

– The United States government announces a plan that by 2008 will require Canadians to have passports or another secure document in order to gain access to the country.

6 Statistics Canada reports that the value of building permits in March rose substantially, to $5.06 billion, an increase of 13.5 per cent from February.

– Prince Rainier of Monaco passes away.

7 Statistics Canada reports that a new study of obesity finds that Canadians who are overweight are more likely to continue to gain weight than they are to lose weight. According to the study, of Canadians who were overweight in 1994–95, one-quarter had become obese by 2002–03.

8 Charles, Prince of Wales, and Camilla Parker Bowles wed in the United Kingdom.

– Statistics Canada reports that the unemployment rate inched down to 6.9 per cent in March. Fewer people searching for work was cited as the main reason for the decrease.

12 Kelly Ellard is found guilty in the 1997 beating and drowning death of Victoria teenager Reena Virk.

14 Statistics Canada reports that energy export and investment powered Canada's economic growth in 2004. According to the report, economic growth was evenly distributed, with no province or major industry recording a loss.

16   The burned body of twenty-year-old Charlene Gauld is dis-
     covered in the town of Hay Lakes, Alberta. Gauld is the eighth
     Edmonton-area sex worker to be murdered since 1989.

19   A report from the federal government reveals that Canada will fo-
     cus its foreign aid on the world's twenty-five most impoverished
     countries. Critics believe this will further delay Canada's commit-
     ment to increasing foreign aid to 0.7 per cent of its GDP.

–   German cardinal Joseph Ratzinger is ordained as Pope Bene-
     dict XVI.

–   The twenty-fifth anniversary of the beginning of Terry Fox's
     Marathon of Hope is marked with the unveiling of a monument in
     St. John's, Newfoundland and Labrador.

20   Statistics Canada reports that Canadians aged seventeen years and
     younger were the victims of a disproportionate number of reported
     sexual and physical assaults in 2003. The report indicates that one-
     fifth of all violent crimes in Canada, including six out of ten sexual
     assaults, were committed against Canadian youth, who represent
     21 per cent of the Canadian population.

22   Statistics Canada reports that in 2002 the top 10 per cent income
     earners in Canada accounted for 52.6 per cent of federal income
     tax payments. Advancing incomes and smaller reductions in taxa-
     tion rates account for this 6.6 per cent increase from 1990 levels.
     Accordingly, middle- and low-income earners' proportion of fed-
     eral income tax revenue fell during this period.

–   Molson Canada purchases Creemore Springs Brewery in Ontario.

–   Statistics Canada reports that under pressure from rising gas prices,
     the consumer price index rose 0.2 per cent in March, to 2.3 per cent.

24   Syria ends its twenty-nine-year military presence in Lebanon.

25   Statistics Canada reports that between 1981 and 2004, the propor-
     tion of employed Canadian adults holding university degrees rose
     from 14 to 24 per cent. However, this increase in education was
     not reflected in wage increases, as the number of adult employees
     being paid $10 per hour or less (in 2001 dollars) decreased only
     1 per cent (from 17 to 16 per cent) over this period.

26   An agreement in principle is reached by the Liberals and New
     Democratic Party, with the NDP agreeing to support Liberal bud-
     get plans as long as a $4.6-billion boost in social program spend-
     ing over two years is included in the budget.

–   The CIA ends its search for weapons of mass destruction in Iraq.

29   Statistics Canada reports that real GDP advanced 0.3 per cent in
     February.

MAY

1   A 15 per cent surtax on U.S. imports of cigarettes, oysters, live
     swine, and some types of fish goes into effect. The surtax is in
     retaliation for the United States' failure to comply with the World
     Trade Organization's ruling against the Byrd Amendment.

3   Statistics Canada reports that according to a new study using data
     from the National Longitudinal Survey of Children and Youth,
     between 1998–99 and 2000–01 an estimated 12 per cent of boys
     and 13 per cent of girls reported having sexual intercourse by the
     ages of fourteen and fifteen. Furthermore, data from the 2003 Ca-
     nadian Community Health Survey reveals that 28 per cent of
     fifteen-to-seventeen-year-olds reported having had sexual inter-
     course at least once. The 2003 CCHS also revealed that 80 per
     cent of twenty-to-twenty-four-year-olds reported having had sex-
     ual intercourse at least once. Finally, the 2003 CCHS reveals that
     three out ten young persons who had sex with multiple partners
     did not wear a condom during their most recent sexual encounter.

–   Statistics Canada reports that the 2003 CCHS reveals that in 2000–
     01 an estimated 3.7 million Canadians could be considered to be
     living in a 'food insecure' household. The study also found that
     40 per cent of low- and lower-middle-income households reported
     having experienced some degree of food insecurity in 2000–01.

4   The Canadian Navy releases a report that finds 'no fault' in the
     death of Lieut. Chris Saunders aboard HMCS *Chicoutimi* during
     a fire on the submarine.

5   Statistics Canada reports that the value of building permits in
     March increased 4.9 per cent to $5.27 billion. This marks the sec-
     ond highest value of permits ever recorded.

–   Statistics Canada reports that in 2003 the median total income for
     individual Canadians fell 0.6 per cent, to $23,600.

6   Statistics Canada reports that the unemployment rate fell 0.1 per
     cent in April, to 6.8 per cent, which is the lowest recorded level
     since December 2000.

8   Canadian veterans mark the sixtieth anniversary of VE Day at a
     ceremony in the Netherlands.

–   Steve Nash becomes the first Canadian-born player to receive the
     National Basketball Association's Most Valuable Player Award.

10   Despite losing an opposition censure vote 153 to 150, the federal
     Liberals maintain that they will continue to govern, calling the
     vote a procedural matter and not a vote of confidence. How-

ever, the Liberals announce that the opposition parties will have three days at the end of May in which to introduce formal non-confidence motions.

12 Statistics Canada reports little growth in after-tax income in 2003 for virtually all Canadian families, for the second straight year. This comes after five previous years of strong growth.

17 Belinda Stronach, MP for Newmarket-Aurora, crosses the floor to join the Liberal Party and is appointed Minister of Human Resources.

– British Columbians re-elect Gordon Campbell and the provincial Liberals with a much reduced majority. A referendum on reforming the electoral system in British Columbia fails to achieve the necessary 60 per cent of the vote required for mandatory implementation.

– Statistics Canada reports that foreign direct investment in Canada rose 3 per cent in 2004, compared to a 10 per cent increase in Canadian direct investment abroad.

18 Queen Elizabeth begins her twenty-first official visit to Canada in Regina, in order to celebrate the centennials of Saskatchewan and Manitoba.

– In an effort to thwart counterfeiting, a new ten-dollar bill goes into circulation.

19 For the first time ever, the Speaker of the House of Commons breaks a tie, in a confidence vote on an amendment to the federal budget. The 153–152 vote ensures that the Liberals will continue to be Canada's governing party.

– Statistics Canada reports that from 1920 to 1990, increases in the mandatory time that youths must stay in school have resulted in a 12 per cent increase in average annual income for every extra year a person spends in school.

20 Statistics Canada reports that rising gasoline prices continue to influence the twelve-month consumer price index; it edged up 0.1 per cent in April, to 2.4 per cent.

26 The Liberal minority government survives a second confidence vote on a budget amendment designed to garner support from the NDP.

– Statistics Canada reports that operating profits for Canadian corporations advanced 3.4 per cent, to $51.4 billion, for the first quarter of 2005.

30 The Canadian Red Cross formally apologizes for its role in Canada's 'tainted blood' scandal during the 1980s and 1990s, during

which more than 1,000 Canadians became infected with HIV and close to 20,000 contracted hepatitis C.

31 Gurmant Grewal, Conservative MP for Surrey Central, releases tape recordings of alleged attempts by the Liberal Party to buy the votes of two MPs before the confidence votes on the budget earlier in the month.

– Statistics Canada reports that real GDP increased 0.6 per cent in the first quarter of 2005.

JUNE

1 Statistics Canada reports that between 1996 and 2001 the number of jobs located farther than five kilometres from city centres increased by 733,200, compared with a 156,000 increase for jobs located within five kilometres of city centres. Although economic activity remains concentrated in the cores of cities, these numbers demonstrate a significant change in commuting patterns in urban areas.

2 Canadian Foreign Affairs Minister Bill Graham offers an apology and handshake to Maher Arar for Canada's role in Arar's detention and subsequent torture in Syria.

3 Statistics Canada reports that between 1 April 1999 and 31 March 2004, of the 25,000 adults who served and completed time in Saskatchewan's correctional services, 57 per cent were of Aboriginal descent. This number is drastically disproportionate, as Aboriginal peoples constituted only 10 per cent of Saskatchewan's adult population in 2001.

6 Pat O'Brien, MP for London-Fanshawe, resigns from the Liberal Party of Canada to sit as an independent in the House of Commons, citing his opposition to same-sex marriage legislation.

– The International Criminal Court announces that it intends to undertake an investigation into the occurrence of war crimes in the Darfur region of Sudan.

– Statistics Canada reports that the value of building permits fell 2.6 per cent, to $5 billion, in April.

9 The Supreme Court of Canada rules that a ban on private health care in Quebec is unconstitutional. The court found that the ban contravened Quebec's charter of rights if and when public health care failed to provide services in a timely manner.

10 Both the president and the chief technology officer of embattled Nortel Networks resign, citing 'divergent management styles,' after a clash with CEO Bill Owens.

— Statistics Canada reports that employment was up 0.6 per cent for the first five months of 2005. However, the unemployment rate remained steady at 6.8 per cent as more people began looking for work.

11 The G8 reaches a deal to forgive US$40 billion in debt owed to the World Bank and the International Monetary Fund by the world's poorest countries.

13 Cineplex Galaxy becomes Canada's largest chain of movie theatres with its $500 million purchase of rival Famous Players.

15 Statistics Canada reports that a new study reveals that as of 15 April 2004, one-third of women and children seeking accommodation in shelters to escape abuse and other health and economic issues had previously sought residence in shelters.

— The first ever same-sex wedding on a Canadian Forces Base is performed at CFB Greenwood in Nova Scotia. This follows a 2003 ruling that granted formal equity to gay and lesbians in the Canadian Forces.

21 Statistics Canada reports that the annual average number of work hours fell by seventy hours, or 1.4 hours per worker, per week between 2000 and 2003. According to the Labour Force Survey this overall decrease is surprising; 8.1 per cent growth in employment with only a 4.3 per cent increase in total hours worked is unprecedented.

22 TD Waterhouse USA is purchased for $2.9 billion by Ameritrade. TD Bank retains a stake in the company, which will be known as TD Ameritrade.

23 The twentieth Anniversary of the Air India bombing is marked by Prime Minister Paul Martin in Ahakista, Ireland. Martin declares a national day of mourning.

— Statistics Canada reports that according to a new study, living conditions for Aboriginal people residing in urban centres in 2001 have improved significantly over the past two decades. However, this study also finds significant differentials between Aboriginals and non-Aboriginals residing in western Canadian cities, with non-Aboriginals continuing to experience better overall living conditions.

24 Conservative leader Mahmoud Ahmadinejad wins Iran's presidential elections.

28 The Canadian Forces undergo a major command restructuring with the standing up of Canada Command.

29 The House of Commons passes legislation giving same-sex couples in Canada the right to legally marry. The legislation passed with a vote of 158 to 133.

- Statistics Canada reports that according to data from the National Mortality Database, firearms-related deaths decreased by more than one-half between 1979 and 2002.
30 Automaker Toyota announces a plan for a second assembly plant in Woodstock, Ontario. The company intends to invest $800 million in the new plant, creating thousands of new jobs.

JULY

1 Canada celebrates its 138th birthday.
2 The Live 8 event to raise awareness of global poverty involves ten free concerts in nine different countries, including a concert in Barrie, Ontario.
4 Karla Homolka is released after serving a twelve-year sentence for her role in the abductions and murders of Kristen French and Leslie Mahaffy.
6 Statistics Canada reports that in 2004 an estimated 500,000 children between two and seventeen years (8 per cent of the total) were obese, which is a 5 per cent increase over 1978–79 numbers. The number of obese adults in 2004 was estimated to be 5.5 million people, or 23 per cent of the adult population, which is a 9 per cent increase over 1978–79 numbers.
7 A coordinated series of explosions kills fifty people in London, England, during the morning rush hour.
- Statistics Canada reports that the value of building permits fell 2.1 per cent, to $5 billion, in May.
- Statistics Canada reports that 94 per cent of Canadians felt safe from being a victim of crime in 2004, which is up from 86 per cent in 1993 and 91 per cent in 1999.
8 Statistics Canada reports that the unemployment rate fell to 6.7 per cent in June. This number equals the lowest rate in close to thirty years, which occurred in June 2000.
11 The former chief of the Assembly of First Nations, David Ahenakew, is stripped of the Order of Canada a week after being convicted of promoting hatred, for comments he made about the Jewish community in 2003.
13 A tentative agreement is reached between the NHL Players' Association and the league. Surprisingly, the agreement includes a salary cap.
14 Following a series of court battles, the USDA reopens the Canada–U.S. border to the import of Canadian cattle products. The border had been closed since May 2003.

- Statistics Canada reports that according to data from the 2004 General Social Survey, 7 per cent of women and 6 per cent of men had encountered spousal violence sometime during the previous five years.
21 Statistics Canada reports that the rate of crime in Canada fell 1 per cent in 2004; however, the national homicide rate increased 12 per cent.
24 American cyclist Lance Armstrong wins a record seventh straight Tour de France.
29 Wendy's announces plans to make up to 18 per cent of Tim Hortons stock available for public purchase.

AUGUST

2 An Air France plane landing in severe weather at Toronto's Pearson International Airport skids off the runway, causing the craft to burst into flames. All 300 passengers and crew escape safely.
- CIBC settles a $2.4 billion lawsuit related to the Enron scandal in the United States. As a result the bank reports its largest-ever quarterly loss and cuts 900 jobs.
4 Journalist Michaëlle Jean is chosen by Prime Minister Paul Martin to be Canada's next Governor General.
- The Supreme Court suspends for twelve months a June ruling that found that a ban on funding private health care in Quebec is unconstitutional.
6 The sixtieth anniversary of the Hiroshima atomic bomb attack is marked in Japan and several Canadian cities.
8 The sixtieth anniversary of Nagasaki atomic bomb attack is marked in Japan and several Canadian cities.
- Statistics Canada reports that the value of building permits rose 1.5 per cent, to $5 billion, in June.
12 Rising fuel costs prompt WestJet and Air Canada to increase ticket prices.
15 A lockout of 5,500 CBC employees begins.
17 Israeli soldiers begin forcibly removing Jewish settlers from the Gaza Strip as Israel begins its withdrawal from the territory.
25 Hurricane Katrina begins to pound the Gulf Coast of the United States. Coastal Louisiana, including the city of New Orleans, and Mississippi are the hardest-hit areas. Poor evacuation planning and slow disaster response only exacerbate a situation that results in the deaths of more than 1,600 people and displacement of one million people.

xxviii / CANADIAN CALENDAR 2005

26 Statistics Canada reports that surging gasoline prices are again to blame for a 0.3 per cent increase in the twelve-month consumer price index, from 1.7 per cent in June to 2 per cent in July.

31 A stampede at a Shia shrine in Baghdad's Kadhimiya district, to which more than one million pilgrims had flocked, leaves 1,000 people dead.

– Statistics Canada reports that the real GDP advanced 0.8 per cent in the second quarter of 2004.

SEPTEMBER

1 Statistics Canada reports that post-secondary students in Canada will pay on average 1.8 per cent more for tuition in 2005, the smallest increase in more than a decade.

7 Statistics Canada reports that the value of building permits fell 3 per cent in July, to $4.9 billion.

8 Statistics Canada reports that Canadians spent $16.1 billion on alcohol in the fiscal year ending 31 March 2004. This number represents a 4.9 per cent increase from the previous year. Beer continued to dominate, accounting for 50.7 per cent of sales.

– Chinese President Hu Jintao makes his first official state visit to Canada.

9 Statistics Canada reports that 28,000 jobs were added in August, bringing the total for the past twelve months to 234,000, which is a 1.4 per cent increase from the previous year.

18 Parliamentary elections are held in Afghanistan. Voter turnout is significantly lower than for the presidential elections held earlier in the year.

20 David Radler, a former executive for Hollinger Inc., pleads guilty to mail fraud. He receives a reduced sentence in exchange for his cooperation with prosecutors.

22 Statistics Canada reports that rising gasoline prices pushed the twelve-month consumer price index to 2.6 per cent in August.

23 Hurricane Rita batters the Gulf Coast of the United States only a month after the devastation wrought by Hurricane Katrina.

26 PFC Lynndie England is sentenced to three years in prison for her role in the abuse of prisoners in Abu Ghraib prison in Iraq.

27 Michaëlle Jean is sworn in as Canada's twenty-seventh Governor General, becoming the first women of Haitian descent to hold the position.

– Statistics Canada reports that tuition fees quadrupled for medical school and tripled for law school in Ontario during the 1990s.

28 David Dingwall resigns as CEO of the Royal Canadian Mint
    amid allegations of improper spending practices.

–   Republican house leader Tom Delay resigns following indictment
    on charges of conspiracy to violate Texas election law.

–   Statistics Canada reports that Canada recorded the second-highest
    population growth of G8 countries between 1994 and 2004, with
    net immigration primarily accounting for the growth.

OCTOBER

4   Hurricane Stan wreaks havoc in Mexico and Central America,
    triggering a mudslide in Guatemala that kills 1,400 people in the
    village of Panabaj.

6   Statistics Canada reports that the value of building permits rose
    10.2 per cent, to $5.4 billion, in August, which represents the
    highest level on record.

–   Statistics Canada reports that after a thirty-year low in 2003, the
    homicide rate rose in 2004 to 622 reported cases. Edmonton,
    Montreal, Vancouver, Winnipeg, and Calgary account for three-
    quarters of the increase.

7   In response to legislation that would impose a new contract and
    wage freezes, 40,000 teachers in British Columbia begin an ille-
    gal strike.

–   A mysterious respiratory disease that resulted in the deaths of
    more than a dozen people at the Seven Oaks Home in Toronto is
    identified as legionnaires' disease.

–   Statistics Canada reports that the unemployment rate dipped 0.1
    per cent, to 6.7 per cent, in September.

8   A powerful earthquake rocks India and Pakistan. The resulting death
    toll is reported to be anywhere between 20,000 and 90,000 people.

11 Inco announces a $12-billion friendly takeover of Falconbridge,
    which will result in creation of the world's largest nickel-produc-
    ing corporation.

–   Statistics Canada reports that 999,400 students registered in uni-
    versity in Canada in 2003–04, which is a 6.1 per cent increase
    from the previous year.

12 Statistics Canada reports that consumption of energy derived
    from fossil fuels increased 1.4 per cent in 2004. This is the third
    consecutive year that the demand for energy derived from fossil
    fuels has risen in Canada.

13 Statistics Canada reports that according to data from the Longitu-
    dinal Survey of Immigrants to Canada, 80 per cent of immigrants

between the ages of twenty-five and forty-four were employed at least once within the first two years of their arrival in Canada.

19 The trial of Saddam Hussein begins in Baghdad and then is adjourned until the end of November.

– Hurricane Wilma becomes the twenty-first named storm of the 2005 Atlantic hurricane season, tying a record set in 1933.

24 Rosa Parks, whose refusal in 1955 to give up her seat on a bus to a white man ignited the civil rights movement in the United States, dies at the age of ninety-two.

– The teachers' strike ends in British Columbia.

25 Iraq ratifies a new constitution, which clears the way for election of a full-term parliament to be held in December.

26 Raymond Lévesque, a poet and singer-songwriter, refuses to accept the Governor General's Performing Arts Award because of his support for Quebec sovereignty.

– An audit clears David Dingwall of any wrongdoing during his tenure as CEO of the Royal Canadian Mint. The audit requires Dingwall to repay $2,500 but finds no evidence of improper office spending.

27 The inquiry into the Maher Arar affair reads a report that finds accounts of Arar's torture in a Syrian jail to be accurate and notes that he still suffers from the after-effects of this abuse.

– Issues of contaminated water on the Kashechewan First Nation reserve results in evacuation of 1,100 residents. The federal government promises to relocate the community over the next five to ten years.

– A group of seventeen co-workers in Alberta claim a record $54.2 million Lotto 6/49 jackpot.

31 Statistics Canada reports that the GDP advanced 0.5 per cent in August, up from the 0.2 per cent advance in July.

NOVEMBER

1 The Gomery inquiry releases an interim report that cites former prime minister Jean Chrétien and his chief of staff, among others, for improprieties in allocating funds from the federal sponsorship program.

4 Statistics Canada reports that the unemployment rate reached its lowest point in three decades as it edged down 0.1 per cent to 6.6 per cent with the addition of 69,000 jobs, almost all part-time, in October.

– Statistics Canada reports that obesity rates among children are directly tied to socio-economic status. According to a study published in the *Canadian Journal of Public Health,* the proportion of overweight children in 2000–01 ranged from 24 per cent for children with high socio-economic status to 35 per cent for children with low socio-economic status.

7   Statistics Canada reports that the value of building permits fell 5.3 per cent, to $5 billion, in September.

14 The House of Commons passes a Liberal mini-budget that commits the federal government to $30 billion in personal tax cuts.

15 André Boisclair is elected as the new leader of the Parti Québécois.

–   Toronto's Pearson International Airport raises its landing fees, making it the most expensive place in world for airplanes to land.

16 Federal finance minister Ralph Goodale announces that the government expects to have a $5.9-billion budget surplus at the end of the fiscal year, which is $1.9 billion more than initially forecast by the Liberals.

–   Statistics Canada reports that according to analysis of data from the 2002 Canadian Community Health Survey, 3.3 million Canadians fifteen years and older reported having problems either going to sleep or staying asleep.

17 The U.S. Attorney's Office in Chicago charges Conrad Black and three associates with eight counts of fraud, alleging that Black and his associates diverted monies intended for Hollinger Inc. and its shareholders.

21 General Motors announces plans to cut 30,000 employees, including 3,900 in Ontario, from its workforce.

–   Statistics Canada reports that, according to a new tracking study, the majority of young people going before Canada's youth and adult courts are one-time offenders.

23 A $1.9-billion compensation package is offered by the Liberal government to survivors of abuse in Canada's Native residential school system.

–   The federal government announces that it will not impose new taxes on income trusts, and instead promises to lower taxes on dividends.

24 Statistics Canada reports that corporations reported record-level operating profits in the third quarter of 2005, with $55 billion in profit. Operating profits have risen in thirteen of the past fifteen quarters in Canada.

25 The federal government announces a plan to provide $5 billion over five years with the aim of raising the standard of living for Aboriginal people to that of non-Native Canadians.

27 Harmeet Singh Sooden and James Loney, two Canadian humanitarian workers, are taken hostage in Iraq.

– The Edmonton Eskimos win the ninety-third Grey Cup game.

28 The Liberal minority government falls after a no-confidence vote after only seventeen months in power. The 171–133 vote is the first time a minority government has succumbed to a motion of no-confidence.

29 Prime Minister Paul Martin asks the Governor General to dissolve the thirty-eighth Parliament of Canada. A federal election is set for 23 January 2006.

– Gurmant Grewal, MP for Surrey Central, who has been embroiled in controversy since the end of May, announces that he will not seek re-election in the upcoming federal contest.

30 Domtar, a pulp-and-paper corporation, announces plans to eliminate 1,800 jobs. Domtar cites the rising Canadian dollar as the major reason for the cutbacks.

– Statistics Canada reports that the real GDP advanced 0.9 per cent in the third quarter of 2005.

DECEMBER

1 Conrad Black pleads not guilty to eight counts of fraud in a Chicago courtroom. His bail is set at US$20 million.

– Statistics Canada reports that on any given day in 2003–04 in Canada, 720 young persons were being held in secure custody and 620 youth were being held in open custody. This represents a significant decline in the numbers of young persons being held in custody since the introduction of the *Youth Criminal Justice Act.*

2 Statistics Canada reports that the unemployment rate dropped 0.2 per cent, to 6.4 per cent, in November, which is the lowest rate of unemployment in thirty years.

– Torstar and the Ontario Teachers' Pension Plan purchase a major stake in the media division of Bell Globemedia.

– Statistics Canada reports that according to the 2005 edition of *Human Activity and the Environment,* per person, Canadians produced an average of 383 kilograms of solid waste in 2002. The total of residential waste exceeded 12 million tonnes.

5 The trial of Saddam Hussein resumes in Baghdad.

– Westin Hotels across Canada go smoke-free.

6 Statistics Canada reports that the value of building permits rose 1.2 per cent, to $5.2 billion, in October.

7   After coming out on the losing side of a series of NAFTA and WTO decisions, the United States agrees to lower duties on soft-wood lumber by almost half.

9   Creditors for Canadian steel producer Stelco agree to a restructuring deal that grants them access to new equity in the corporation. As a result, the value of commonly held shares becomes virtually worthless.

10   A two-week meeting on climate change in Montreal ends with an agreement to extend the Kyoto Protocol beyond its 2012 expiration.

12   Statistics Canada reports that on average Canadian households spent $63,640 in 2004, spending more on high-tech goods, mortgages, health care, and energy. This is a 3.4 per cent increase from 2003, which significantly exceeds the 1.9 per cent rate of inflation.

14   Statistics Canada reports that greenhouse gas emissions rose, air quality trends deteriorated, and water quality pollutant standards were being regularly exceeded between 1990 and 2003 in Canada.

15   Conrad Black is charged with four additional criminal charges, including racketeering and obstruction of justice. Black pleads not guilty on all counts. His trial is set for March 2007.

–   Iraqis go to the polls to elect 275 members of Iraq's national assembly, forming the country's first permanent government since the U.S.-led overthrow of Saddam Hussein.

16   Statistics Canada reports that in 2003–04 the percentage of people being held in Canadian prisons fell to its lowest level since 1981–82, with 130 people incarcerated for every 100,000 Canadians.

17   Abdullah Khadr is arrested in Toronto at the behest of American officials. Khadr, the eldest son of Ahmed Said Khadr, an alleged al Qaeda financier, is accused of purchasing weapons for insurgent forces in Afghanistan.

19   Afghanistan opens its first elected parliament in thirty years.

20   Mark Bourque, a retired RCMP officer, is shot and killed in Haiti. Bourque was in Haiti as part of a Canadian police contingent providing security for an election to be held in January 2006.

–   Statistics Canada reports that the twelve-month consumer price index fell 0.6 per cent, to 2.0 per cent, in October.

21   Statistics Canada reports that the combined life expectancy for men and women rose to 79.9 years in 2003.

22   22 Placer Dome, Canada's second-largest gold miner, accepts a $10.4-billion takeover bid by Barrick Gold, Canada's largest gold miner.

CANADIAN ANNUAL REVIEW OF POLITICS
AND PUBLIC AFFAIRS 2005

EDITOR'S INTRODUCTION:
THE YEAR IN REVIEW

Canada entered 2005 in a way it had not experienced in a quarter of a century – with a minority parliament, its first since Joe Clark's short-lived Progressive Conservative government. Minority politics dominated, as it seemed unlikely at the year's start that the Martin government would survive even until spring. While it did manage to last out the year, the government was fighting yet another general election campaign as 2005 drew to a close. The markers on the road to the January 2006 election were the dominant political stories of the year: the minority Liberals managed to avoid defeat on their budget through frenetic deal-making and a well-timed crossing of the floor; the Gomery Commission into the so-called sponsorship scandal delivered its report; and the government was allowed to survive long enough for an historic meeting of first ministers and Aboriginal leaders in Kelowna, B.C.

The government presented its 2005 budget on 23 February, the eighth consecutive balanced budget at the federal level since the deficit-slashing exercises of the now prime minister in the mid-1990s. The very healthy fiscal position, involving a massive budget surplus and projections of surpluses for the foreseeable future, allowed Finance Minister Goodale to deliver a range of popular spending initiatives in an attempt to insulate the budget from possible parliamentary defeat. It provided measures that were supported by the various interest groups affected and played to concerns of the federalist opposition parties. The headline was a large infusion of money for the Canadian Forces, $12.8 billion over five years to increase troop strength and for equipment. Such largesse was supported by the official Opposition, the newly merged Conservative Party, as were cuts to both personal and corporate taxes. For the left there was a $1-billion-a-year commitment to a national child-care program, $5 billion for environmental programs largely designed to meet Canada's Kyoto commitments, extra money for foreign aid, and a transfer of gasoline tax revenues to cities.

However, the political climate in which the budget was debated kept turning against the government as revelations of corruption mounted in the ongoing Gomery inquiry. On the basis of the military spending and tax cuts, the Harper Conservatives had been supporting the budget, support that would have assured its passage. But by April the Conservatives had decided that the Liberals had lost the 'moral authority to govern' and sought to defeat the government on the budget. The Liberals then turned to the NDP in an attempt to pass the budget and continue to govern. On 26 April the government brought forward a second budget bill that amended the first and had been agreed on with the New Democrats. The amendments included a number of new or enhanced spending commitments on key NDP issues (housing, the environment, higher education, and foreign aid) and removed the promised tax cuts for large corporations. In a series of votes in June the budget package was accepted, culminating in a late-day vote on 24 June in which the government, with the support of the NDP and the Bloc, took advantage of Conservative absences to close the debate. It was, in Peter MacKay's words, 'a well-orchestrated connivance.'

By June, however, it seemed evident that the Conservatives did not have the votes in the House to defeat the government that they thought they had in April. The most significant reason for the adverse numbers was one of the more sensational defections in Canadian political history. On 17 May, in the middle of the contentious debates over the budget bills, Belinda Stronach crossed the floor from the Conservative Party to the Liberal Cabinet. The year before, Stronach had finished second to Stephen Harper in the first leadership contest of the newly merged party of the right; she had, indeed, been instrumental in bringing the merger to pass. Furthermore, she was at the time of her defection the romantic partner of the Conservatives' number two, Peter MacKay, who found out from the media that he had lost something more than a colleague and a key parliamentary vote!

Parliamentary defections are always important in a minority parliament, and in 2005 there were several in addition to Stronach's, marking key moments in the year's politics and policy; for while the year was dominated by its parliamentary and electoral politics, there were significant matters of policy as well. In December 2004, in response to a reference by the government, the Supreme Court had ruled that the federal government did have the authority to define marriage. With this judicial affirmation in hand, on 1 February the Martin government introduced Bill C-38, which would legalize same-sex marriages, although it would not require religious institutions to marry same-sex couples. The Conservatives opposed the bill at every turn and a number of Liberals rebelled as well; nevertheless, on 28 June C-38 was passed and same-sex marriage became legal in Canada. The bill cost the Liberals a member – Pat O'Brien crossed to sit as an independent over the issue – and the NDP denied Bev Desjarlais re-nomination because of her opposition.

The Liberals had also previously lost David Kilgour to the ranks of independent MPs in April, over the issue that would ultimately dominate the year's politics: the sponsorship scandal and the Gomery inquiry. The year began with Justice Gomery defending his impartiality against former prime minister Jean Chrétien; an end-of-year interview in the *National Post* had seen him make comments he later agreed were 'ill-advised.' Having resisted Chrétien's calls for his dismissal, Gomery reconvened his public hearings in February to examine the highest-profile of his witnesses: Chrétien himself; the former minister of public works and then ambassador to Denmark, Alfonso Gagliano; and the former finance minister, now prime minister, Paul Martin. Martin's appearance on 10 February marked the first time in 130 years that a sitting Canadian prime minister had given sworn testimony before a public inquiry. While Martin's testimony was historic and Chrétien's the most entertaining, with his golf ball show-and-tell, it was the testimony of the head of Groupeaction, Jean Brault, that appears to have been the most politically damaging. Brault's testimony was initially subject to a publication ban, but in early April Gomery lifted the ban and Canadians learned that Brault had told the inquiry that he had been repeatedly asked for donations to the Liberal Party in exchange for sponsorship money. Brault's revelation led quickly to Kilgour's defection and to the Conservatives' *volte-face* on the budget.

There was continued legal wrangling over both the scandal and the inquiry throughout the year, with charges laid by the RCMP against several of its key players and attempts being made by witnesses to keep their testimony private. Politically, however, the key moment came on 1 November, when Justice Gomery tabled the first volume of his report. The report cleared the prime minister, Paul Martin, of personal blame but painted a damning picture of the party he now led: 'The public trust in its system of government was subverted and betrayed, and Canadians were outraged, not only because public funds were wasted and misappropriated, but also become no one was held responsible or punished for his misconduct.' On 24 November the leader of the Opposition, Stephen Harper, tabled a motion of no-confidence in the government. The motion was passed by the Conservatives, NDP, and Bloc on 28 November, triggering an election called for 23 January.

The vote on the no-confidence motion was delayed because on the same day it was introduced, Prime Minister Martin was meeting with his provincial counterparts and leaders of Canada's First Nations in Kelowna, B.C., the first meeting of its kind in Canada's history. It was billed as designed to 'strengthen relationships and close the gap' that separates First Nations from the rest of Canada. The agreement reached at the meeting, 'to take immediate action to improve the quality of life for the Aboriginal peoples of Canada in four important areas – health, education, housing and relationships,' came to be known as the Kelowna Accord, and it marked the culmination of a significant year in Canada's relationship with its Aboriginal peoples. First of all, on 23 March, Bill C-20 – the *First Nations Fiscal and Statistical Management Act* – became law. C-20 created four new First Nations institutions that were designed to provide the bureaucratic capacity for First Nations to tax property and thereby generate an independent source of governing revenue. Then, on 21 October, the Supreme Court ruled that the churches that had run residential schools shared responsibility for abuse of Native children with the federal government. This ruling in turn paved the way for an agreement among the Assembly of First Nations, church groups, former students, and the government on a compensation system, including formation of a Truth and Reconciliation Commission. The degree to which these developments would be as momentous in practice as they appeared in prospect, however, at year's end rested, as with so much else, on the outcome of the election forced immediately after the Kelowna meeting.

Prime Minister Martin had promised not only to work to improve First Nations government but also to provide a 'new deal' to the third level of Canada's broader governing structure: its cities. In 2005 he began to deliver on that promise, although the delivery was not as extensive as some people, particularly from the largest of Canada's urban areas, had hoped. The budget did include a direct transfer of revenue from the federal gasoline tax to municipalities, although it was targeted for 'environmentally sustainable infrastructure projects.' The new deal also involved some structural and procedural changes, including creation of a department of infrastructure and communities to replace the Cities Secretariat; the finance minister had also consulted with municipalities before the budget and promised to continue to do so in the future. What concerned the leaders of major cities, however, was a broadening of the mandate of the new deal to include much smaller communities, which the large urban centres were worried would direct attention and resources away from the particular problems they faced.

There were very few ripples in the country's politics at the provincial level in 2005. The economy was in generally fine shape, particularly in the resource-rich provinces of the West and East. On the east coast, the struggle between the provinces and Ottawa over revenues was finally resolved with the Atlantic Accord of 14 February, which allowed Newfoundland and Nova Scotia to keep offshore oil and gas royalties without affecting their equalization payments in the medium term. In the West, Alberta and Saskatchewan enjoyed the hundredth anniversaries of their becoming provinces of Canada, and both were awash in resource riches.

Only British Columbia held a general election in 2005, but it was a significant election in at least two senses. It was the first in the province's history to be held on a legally fixed election date rather than at the pleasure of the premier, as is Westminster parliamentary tradition. Premier Campbell's tying of his own hands on the timing of the election did not unduly harm him; he returned to power with a clear majority, if not nearly so large as the seventy-seven out of seventy-nine seats he held at dissolution. Perhaps even more significant in the long term, however, was that a referendum was held in conjunction with the election on introduction of a British Columbia variant of the single transferable vote system. If approved, BC-STV would mark an even more dramatic departure from the traditions of Westminster parliaments than fixed elections. The BC-STV proposal was not accepted in the referendum, but only because of the very stringent conditions that had been imposed for its success. Passage required an overall majority of 60 per cent and a majority in 60 per cent of the constituencies. It received majority support in 97 per cent of constituencies but fell agonizingly short of its second requirement, receiving an overall vote of 57.69 per cent. Premier Campbell promised a second referendum, given the widespread support. PEI also consulted voters about changing its voting system, but its plebiscite on mixed-member proportional voting, an even greater departure from Canadian traditions than STV, was supported by only 36 per cent of those who turned out to vote, and they represented only 30 per cent of eligible voters.

While attention was focused very much at home, there were international issues and developments of importance to Canada's public policy in the year. In 2004 Canada had reduced its troop commitment to the ISAF in Afghanistan, and in the spring of 2005 it announced that its base in Kabul, Camp Julien, would close. However, this by no means marked the end of Canada's involvement in Afghanistan; rather it was part of a significant shift in the role the Canadian forces were playing.

In August Canada took control of the Provincial Reconstruction Team (PRT) in Kandahar province. The PRTs are what Canada calls a 'whole-of-government' operation, involving the Department of Foreign Affairs and International Trade and CIDA as well as the Canadian Forces, but Canada also took on a more directly military leadership role in the province. NATO was increasing its presence in Kandahar, which is one of the most violent regions in Afghanistan, and Canada was slated to take the lead in this build-up, with deployment of 2,000 troops by February 2006 and a Canadian general, David Fraser, taking over the regional command.

The shift in Canada's military involvement in Afghanistan would be overseen by a new chief in Ottawa, as the government announced in January that General Rick Hillier would become Chief of Defence Staff (CDS) effective 4 February. He was replacing General Ray Henault, who had been selected to serve as head of the NATO Military Committee in Brussels. Hillier's was an interesting appointment, as it violated the convention that would have seen the navy provide a CDS after Henault. However, Hillier had significant relevant command experience, having led multinational forces in both Bosnia and Afghanistan. As its chief he had also just overseen a significant transformation of the army, so the government saw him as an ideal candidate to lead the restructuring of the forces as a whole. He started on that task immediately, beginning the process of standing up four new commands that would serve as the foundation of a reorganized military: Canada Command, Special Operations Forces Command, Expeditionary Forces Command, and Operational Support Command.

The military changes, particularly the enhanced combat role in Afghanistan and the increase in defence spending, were welcomed by the U.S. government, which might have been part of the point, in order to offset Canada's decision on Ballistic Missile Defense (BMD). Canada had played a long and cautious game with the United States over its missile defence plan, never either formally joining or formally staying out. With the change at the top of the Liberal Party in 2003, it had appeared that Canada was headed towards formal acceptance of the U.S. program. Indeed, the announcement that Canada would not participate appeared to undercut the position of the Canadian ambassador. However, once again the exigencies of a parliamentary minority led the Martin government, as the NDP, the Bloc, and many Canadians were vocally opposed to Canada's involvement in the American BMD.

Farther afield, Canada appeared to miss an opportunity to take a leadership role in the global fight against poverty and development of the world's poorest continent, Africa. The G8 meeting was held in Gleneagles, Scotland, in 2005, and the host, U.K. prime minister Tony Blair, sought to put Africa at the heart of the agenda. In support of a commitment to African development and poverty reduction, celebrity activists, led by Bob Geldof and Bono, organized a series of concerts called Live 8. Their goal was to mobilize people globally to sign a demand for action to be presented to the G8 leaders in Gleneagles. While the summit produced an impressive communiqué – unusually, one that was actually signed by the eight leaders – Canada's contribution was criticized by the rock-stars-turned-global-activists. In particular, Bono expressed disappointment in Paul Martin, whom he had famously endorsed when the latter was running for the Liberal leadership.

The (mis)treatment of Canadians abroad continued to be an issue through 2005. In 2003 Zahra Kazemi, a Canadian journalist who also held Iranian citizenship, was arrested in Iran. In the course of a short incarceration Kazemi died, apparently from abuse at the hands of her captors, although some Iranian officials suggested it was the result of a stroke. In January Iran announced that the case would be heard by a court of appeal, and there was some hope in Canada that a proper investigation and accounting would take place. However, on 11 April Iran rejected both Canada's call for an independent autopsy and even any further investigation, effectively shutting down the process of justice. Canada retaliated diplomatically, though its sanctions fell short of breaking off diplomatic ties. Canada did introduce a resolution at the autumn session of the U.N. General Assembly condemning Iran's human rights practices, which was adopted by the Assembly.

Closer to home, Canada's own treatment of its citizens was under scrutiny, as the O'Connor Commission's inquiry into the ordeal of Maher Arar continued throughout the year. Arar was a Canadian computer engineer who was detained by the United States while in transit through New York's JFK airport and was subsequently subjected to 'extraordinary rendition': sent to Syria in secret, where he spent eight months being tortured in a Syrian jail. The Commission was seeking to determine what had happened to him, and in particular what, if any, was the role of the Canadian government and security agencies in his detention and torture. The Commission had to struggle to fulfil its mandate because the United States and Syria both declined to cooperate and the documents provided by the Canadian government were heavily censored. Nevertheless, the documents that were made public in April, as well as testimony to the Commission, began to suggest that Canadian officials had behaved in at least questionable ways. Arar, however, would have to wait until 2006 at the earliest, when the Commission was due to report, to learn its judgement and the response of his government.

As the year ended, Canadians as a whole were in a position similar to Arar's: waiting for 2006 to determine their immediate fate. The country was in the midst of an increasingly nasty election campaign that was dominated by the initial findings of the Gomery Commission. Despite that, the governing Liberals appeared to be rebounding in the polls by year's end. However, on 28 December they were hit with the announcement that the RCMP was launching an investigation into allegations of leaked information around Finance Minister Goodale's press conference in November on the future of income trusts. It was a fitting end to a year that had been dominated by the petty politics of minority parliaments and the strong whiff of financial irregularities surrounding the sponsorship scandal. Canadians ended 2005 in hope that the election early in 2006 would clear the air, although it truly was much more hope than expectation.

ROBERT EVERETT

Parliament and politics

Until the night of 28 November, no Canadian government had ever fallen on a straight vote of confidence in the House of Commons. History was made when the fragile minority government of Liberal prime minister Paul Martin was defeated, firmly and finally, in just that way. With no alternative governing coalition possible, the result set the stage for an early election. As the year ended, Canadians were girding for a trek to the polls in a rare winter election called for 23 January 2006. It marked the second time in eighteen months that voters would cast ballots in a time of turbulence.

Martin's government had clung to power since June 2004, following a difficult campaign in which the vaunted Liberals barely escaped a dramatic comedown, thanks to a last-minute but merely partial pardon from the electorate. Its subsequent tenure, perilous and often paralytic, was prolonged by fortuitous and sometimes unprecedented narrative twists. The autumnal climax came when an ineluctable confluence of forces made it impossible to engineer a further reprieve. The opposition parties were emboldened by the release on 1 November of a damning report issued by the Commission of Inquiry into the Sponsorship Program and Advertising Activities, conducted by Justice John Gomery. Asked to investigate who and what was responsible for the egregious mismanagement of a national unity program during the 1990s, Justice Gomery found clear evidence of 'political involvement in the administration' of the program that tied back to the Liberal Party (*Globe and Mail,* 3 Nov.). He enumerated countless examples of slipshod oversight of advertising accounts during the regime of Liberal prime minister Jean Chrétien (who was absolved of direct culpability but found to be negligent nonetheless). Several individuals at the heart of the scheme already faced criminal charges or had admitted to corruption.

Gomery's public condemnations foreclosed any further cooperation from the opposition parties. Although Martin had appointed the commission after succeeding Chrétien, he was never able to distance himself or his rebranded government from past sins. Liberal support tumbled on the heels of the report's publication, and all three opposition parties – the Conservatives, the New Democratic Party, and the Bloc Québécois – served notice of their intention to terminate the Liberal mandate. Each expected to capitalize on the Liberals' misfortunes in the next election, even though the governing party was rebounding as the election began.

The Conservatives stood to gain the most from the dissolution of Parliament. Although its leader, Stephen Harper, had not connected with the public, the party gathered some momentum from the scandal. Real traction proved elusive for the Conservatives but polls confirmed that they were the only plausible replacement for the Liberals, if it came to that. Jack Layton and the NDP hoped to attract progressive-minded supporters of the Liberals and perhaps even eclipse their scandal-damaged rivals on the centre left of the spectrum. The Bloc Québécois, led by Gilles Duceppe, aimed to reinforce a paramount position in its home province and, in the process, invigorate the sovereignist movement.

Thus it was that the year in Canadian politics was dominated by machinations and manoeuvres leading up to the decisive tally of 28 November. Substantive issues did come to the fore, however. In a close decision, Canada became the fourth country in the world to legalize same-sex marriages, when permissive legislation passed the House of Commons and Senate during the summer. An historic agreement between Aboriginal peoples and the senior levels of government was reached at a first ministers' conference in November. The budget presented by the Liberals (and subsequently amended after negotiations with the NDP) contained funding for a national child-care program and other measures that helped define partisan debates. Some of these were foursquare in the tactical joust between government and opposition, while others were mere sideshows. In the end, the status of many was made uncertain by the Liberals' downfall.

The fall of the house of Martin

For the beleaguered minority Liberal government of Paul Martin, the first true test of its sustainability loomed in February. An authentic chance to unseat the Liberals presented itself when the 2005–06 budget was presented on 23 February. It is a tenet of Canadian parliamentary democracy that budgets (and other so-called money bills involving the allocation of funds) are automatically deemed to be matters of confidence in the government. If one or more of the opposition parties did not endorse the budget or abstain, the Liberals could be dispatched.

Flirting with fiasco

Motivated but largely uncoordinated, the three opposition parties menaced the Liberals throughout the year. The sponsorship scandal arose daily in question period when the House resumed sitting in February and thereafter. Procedural dust-ups intensified once the budget was read. But the first true embarrassment for the Liberals came when the three opposition parties teamed up to deny severing international trade from the Department of Foreign Affairs (15 Feb.). The Conservatives came on board just prior to the vote on this measure, which the NDP contended would make it more difficult to link human rights issues to trade (*Ottawa Citizen,* 16 Feb.). This was a minor setback for the government but an authentic demonstration of the latent potency of combined forces across the aisle.

Earnest skirmishing was precipitated by the 23 February budget. At first the Conservatives were disinclined to topple the government, happy as they were with the tax cuts and outlays for the military. Bloc Québécois members were adamantly and unalterably against the budget. A more cautious New Democratic Party caucus held back but ultimately found the plan wanting. This set up an unusual confluence, with the main opposition party aligning with the government and poised to help pass Bill C-43, the legislative package that gave life to the budget.

The Conservatives changed their tune, however. A defiant Harper insisted that the government's environmental framework made the budget unsupportable (13 Apr.). Revelations from the Gomery Commission hardened their resolve, and an impasse loomed. A tense confrontation was resolved when the Liberals and NDP agreed on amendments to the budget on 26 April. Changes were enrobed in a separate bill, C-48. But the government was not home free. Even united, the Liberals and NDP could not command an automatic victory. They would have to rely on independents in order to surmount the Conservatives and the Bloc.

May days

With the government's compact with the NDP in place, it was left to the other opposition parties to press. The Conservatives crafted a motion calling for the government's resignation, styling it as a matter of confidence. The Bloc agreed; it purported to direct the House Public

Accounts Committee to 'recommend that the government resign because of its failure to address deficiencies in governance of the public service.' On 9 May Speaker Peter Milliken ruled the motion in order. The motion passed 153–150, and four kindred attempts were also approved in swift succession. The government chose to carry on. For several days business came to a halt as the Opposition forced early adjournment (10–12 May). The impasse ended when the government accepted a timetable for dealing with the budget.

It all came down to votes on the second reading of the budget bills, scheduled for 19 May. Two days before this crucial rendezvous, Conservative MP Belinda Stronach moved into the Liberal camp. Suddenly the political calculus was adjusted. With Stronach in the Liberal fold, the fate of the government was in the hands of three independents. Former Liberal Carolyn Parrish lined up with the government. Her erstwhile caucus mate David Kilgour did the opposite. Chuck Cadman, elected as an independent but once a member of the conservative Reform Party and battling cancer, was still pondering and remained silent.

Only the Bloc rose against the government on Bill C-43, the main budget as it had been presented in February. Next up was Bill C-48, containing the amendments worked out with the NDP. Cadman voted with the government, creating a tie. The member from Surrey North, although a staunch conservative, felt duty bound to follow the wishes of his constituents as expressed in media-sponsored polls, and they were not warm to the prospect of an early election (*Vancouver Sun,* 20 May). It was left to the Speaker to decide. Peter Milliken, a nominal Liberal, voted in favour in order to permit continuation of Parliament's deliberations – precedent required this of him. It was the first time in Canadian history that the presiding officer had settled a confidence measure.

Relieved and ebullient, Martin deemed it a moment for parliamentary reorientation and Liberal renewal. Opposition leader Harper had a different take, warning that the 'Liberals bought a Pyrrhic victory, one that will sow the seeds of its own destruction, one that will present our party with great opportunities' (*Toronto Star,* 20 May).

Summer reprieve

Although it had survived nail-biting votes in May, the government had numerous procedural hurdles to overcome. On 14 June a total of sixteen votes was recorded on sundry matters, all of them deemed to be matters of confidence. The Liberals withstood on every count, and only one vote was close. However, more peril loomed. Bill C-43 was passed on 16 June. The amendments in Bill C-48 moved through the committee report stage on 21 June, when the Liberals and NDP had a cushion of five votes. Nine of their MPs were absent, and it was clear that the Conservatives had abandoned the effort to bring down the government. Although the House was slated to adjourn for the summer on 23 June, the government sought approval to extend the sitting in order to finalize the budget approval process. The Bloc agreed on the condition that the government also put Bill C-38, the same-sex marriage bill, through each hurdle before recessing. The Conservatives were prepared to reverse their stance on the budget if the Liberals acceded to this rider.

Debate moved into the night on 24 June. After checking with procedural experts, closeting with representatives of the NDP and the Bloc, and carefully counting numbers on the opposition benches, the Liberals employed an arcane rule by which debate on a bill could be closed off without the consent of three parties. With a brace of Conservative MPs away, the House duly resolved to vote on the budget bills. The Liberals won the day in what was, said front-bench Conservative Peter MacKay, 'a well-orchestrated connivance' (*Globe and Mail,* 25 June).

Final days

The release of the first volume of Justice Gomery's report set in motion a train of events that culminated with the government's defeat. After Gomery's pronouncements on the scandal, the Conservatives and Bloc Québécois wasted little time in signalling their willingness to defeat the government. The NDP were stoical. Layton still had it in his power to leverage the Liberals' dicey situation to advantage. The issue he chose was health care. Layton and Martin had first huddled on 25 October but could not find agreement. Greater urgency was supplied by the Gomery report, and the NDP pressed again for adoption of measures that would preclude privatization of health care, as a price for the government's longevity (2 Nov.). The government answered two days later; the NDP leader 'indicated he liked some of what he saw from the Liberals – particularly a plan to prevent doctors from practicing within the public system while simultaneously working in private clinics – but other proposed government measures to prevent the growth of health-care privatization fall far short of what is necessary' (*Calgary Herald,* 5 Nov.). Through health minister Ujjal Dosanjh the Liberals offered to prevent doctors from practising simultaneously inside and outside the public system, to better monitor transfers to provinces, and to check the spread of private involvement if it undermined the integrity of the system (*Ottawa Citizen,* 8 Nov.). It was not enough. Layton banded with Harper and Duceppe to insist that the Liberals either announce an election in January or taste defeat (12 Nov.).

The date of 28 November was chosen for the final act. It could have transpired earlier, but it was agreed that Martin should attend a first ministers' conference on Aboriginal affairs in British Columbia on 24–25 November before the government fell. Before that, an NDP resolution demanding that the government call an election for 13 February passed easily, although it was ignored by the government (21 Nov.). With the pace quickening, Harper announced the text of a final motion to be seconded by Layton: 'The House condemns the government for its arrogance in refusing to compromise with the opposition parties over the timing of the next general election,' and for its 'culture of entitlement, corruption, scandal and gross abuse of public funds for political purposes and, consequently, the government no longer has the confidence of the House' (23 Nov.). A second version, much shorter, was issued one day later. It stated bluntly that the government should be removed. The anticlimactic vote on the truncated resolution was 171 to 133. The next morning Martin presented himself at the door of Rideau Hall and asked the Governor General to authorize an election. With Madame Jean's assent, eight weeks of chilly campaigning began.

Commission of inquiry into the sponsorship program and advertising activities

Initial phases

Over the objections of former prime minister Jean Chrétien and other fretful Liberals, in February 2004 Paul Martin appointed a one-person commission to follow up on revelations contained in an earlier exposé by Auditor General Sheila Fraser on the sponsorship program launched in 1996. Designed to enhance the federal presence, the initiative was born following a Quebec referendum over the province's sovereignty that preserved the status quo by the narrowest of margins. Jittery but primed for action, the Chrétien government responded with a two-pronged approach. It consisted of hard-line insistence on an unambiguous question coupled with a higher threshold in any future referenda, together with soft-selling the virtues of national unity through promotional advertising and sponsorship of cultural events. Flagrant abuses of the program surfaced, touching off probes of high-ranking political and administrative operatives by a Commons committee, the police, and the auditor general. Chrétien's legacy was tarnished and the Liberals faced a sustained, nightmarish inquisition. Martin had quickly disbanded the program after succeeding Chrétien in late 2004. He also suspended, then fired, the presidents of VIA Rail, the Canada Business Development Bank, and Canada Post over the involvement of their Crown corporations in the affair. Canada's ambassador to Denmark, Alfonso Gagliano, was recalled from Europe as punishment for alleged misdeeds while serving as minister of public works during critical phas- es of the scandal. None of this was enough to stem an onslaught against the Liberals, and the scandal contributed to the Liberals' poor showing in the June 2004 election.

Justice John Gomery of the Quebec Superior Court accepted Martin's offer to head the commission in February 2004. His mandate involved determining how the program was managed, how private firms were selected, and how funds were used. Having established the facts, Gomery was to advise on creation, operation, and political control of similar initiatives in the future. Testimony began in September 2004. Sensational cross-examinations of advertising firm executives, Crown corporation managers, and high-level bureaucrats demonstrated that the program was run in ways that consistently disregarded internal protocols. Documents reviewed by Gomery were often incomplete or they were missing entirely, turning paper trails into dead ends. Companies repeatedly failed to fulfil contacts or profited from complex transactions that moved money quite unnecessarily into their coffers. It proved difficult not to draw harsh conclusions, even though the inquiry was only partway through the process by the end of 2004. For the presiding officer, the temptation was irresistible. In a highly publicized interview with the *National Post,* Gomery confided that he had come to share the auditor general's stated conviction that the program's administration was 'catastrophic.' He also tossed out observations on leading figures in the affair, including former prime minister Jean Chrétien and Charles 'Chuck' Guité, its colourful bureaucratic point person (16 Dec. 2004).

Gomery's candour prompted Chrétien's legal team and stoutest champions to question the judge's impartiality. They were predisposed to such antipathy, given that the commission's chief counsel, Bernard Roy, was an intimate of Chrétien's foe, former prime minister Brian Mulroney. Vulnerable to attack, Gomery spent the opening weeks of 2005 defending his objectivity but ultimately admitting that he had erred in being so forth- right with the press. However, in response to a motion for his dismissal filed on behalf of Chrétien, Gomery would concede only that his remarks were 'ill-advised and inappropriate' (*Toronto Star*). He refused to recuse himself despite causing a regrettable 'distraction' (1 Feb.).

Closing the net

Among the first witnesses of 2005 were Chrétien and Martin. Given his distemper, Chrétien was feisty and unyielding on the stand. He insisted that the sponsorship program was a vital instrument in promoting Canadian unity and acknowledged nothing more than maladministration. Appearances of cronyism were just that, and the stable of eligible firms had been necessarily narrowed to those that were pro-federalist and, by default, on friendly terms with the government. Denying any knowledge about particular contracts, the former prime minister argued that he had had neither the time nor the inclination to involve himself. Condemning the entire inquiry, he ended his day in the docket with comical but acerbic jibes at Gomery (8 Feb.).

Next up was Martin, who became the first sitting Canadian prime minister to submit to giving sworn testimony in 130 years. After a dry exposition on the role of the finance minister, which Martin had been throughout the saga, the prime minister fended off intimations that he might have played a part in doling out money or was intimately acquainted with any of the scandal's notorious personalities (10 Feb.). He was unaware of the 'unity reserve fund' on the books in 1994 and 1995 that was tapped to fund the program (and which, he said, was actually set up by the Progressive Conservative government of Brian Mulroney). A disgraced Alfonso Gagliano also took the stand in February. Although ostensibly responsible for the file, Gagliano maintained that he had been disengaged from day-to-day decision making. Distraught after four days of grilling, the ex-minister complained that his reputation had been wrongly sullied and his employment prospects reduced to nothing (4 Feb.).

With these spectacles out of the way, the Commission decamped to Montreal, where Gomery turned his sights once again on undisputed insiders and beneficiaries. In an appearance marked by frequent memory lapses, Jean Lafleur of Lafleur Communication Marketing admitted that his firm's income had been almost wholly derived from dealings with the government or Crown corporations, until he sold it to the most prominent company in the scandal, Groupaction, in 2001. It was impossible to conceal that Lafleur, his company, and employees were frequent and generous donors to the Liberal Party (8 Mar.), and shortly afterwards the federal government filed a $39-million lawsuit against Lafleur Communications and Groupaction, along with the firms Everest and Polygone, in an effort to recoup losses (11 Mar.). As sworn statements piled up, executives for these and other companies described for Gomery their lax bookkeeping standards and eager brokerage of suspect deals. To take one example, Lafleur Communication received a commission for doing nothing more than passing on a substantial cheque to Via Rail for agreeing to participate in the program.

By all accounts the most explosive evidence was supplied by Jean Brault, a senior associate at Groupaction, who had been charged with criminal fraud for his conduct (31 Mar.). Gomery placed a short-term embargo on the evidence, fearing that it would have an impact on his trial. When, concluding that Brault's testimony was unrelated to the charges, Gomery unsealed it on 7 April, Brault's startling and unsavoury chronicle sent shockwaves through the body politic. It boiled down to 'allegations of a wide- ranging scheme to trade lucrative sponsorship contracts for political donations and favours to the party' (*Toronto Star,* 8 Apr.). Brault explained that he had funnelled 10 per cent of his commissions to PluriDesign, headed by Jacques Corriveau, for the unmistakable purpose of enriching the Quebec wing of the federal Liberals. Corriveau tried to extricate himself with a tale about trading in fabricated invoices to hide lucre from envious eyes, but Gomery was unconvinced by the witness's contradictions and forgetfulness.

Martin pronounced himself offended by the revelations. In an evening telecast on 21 April, the prime minister pledged to call an election within thirty days of the release of Gomery's first report. The affair was an 'unjustifiable mess' that had stymied the work of a Parliament now 'preoccupied' with election talk. (*Toronto Star,* 22 Apr.). Opposition leaders relished their own prime-time chance to pounce. The Conservatives and the Bloc were willing to defeat the government, but at this point the NDP remained cool to the idea of pushing an election.

By the time the hearings wrapped up on 17 June, the Commission had traced, with the aid of forensic accountants, a labyrinthine scheme of padded contracts, preferential dealings, phony invoices, cash handouts, kickbacks, extravagance, profiteering, and cavalier oversight. Unsealed testimony by Chuck Guité, who had made a second trip to Gomery's precincts, contained the assertion that the scheme was '150 per cent politically driven' and that former cabinet minister Alfonso Gagliano and Chrétien's chief of staff, Jean Pelletier, were in on it. When the publication ban on Brault's testimony was lifted, it was learned that the Liberal Party had received myriad donations in exchange for commissions and contracts. How had the companies compensated for this additional expense? They overbilled the client.

By any measure, the Commission accumulated sufficient incriminating evidence to make life miserable for the Liberals. But there was more. The first individual convicted in the scandal was Paul Coffin, of his eponymous firm (1 June). Coffin received lenient punishment for pleading guilty on 19 September, and he was sentenced to two years less a day of community service (which consisted of lectures on business ethics) after pleading guilty to fifteen counts of fraud. Prosecutors appealed the sentence on 28 September. That same day, a Quebec Superior Court ruled that the trial of Jean Brault and Charles Guité should be delayed until the federal election, and put off proceedings until 1 May 2006 unless they were to be conducted without a jury. The ruling reflected fears by the defendants' lawyers that the pending release of the first volume of the Gomery Commission's report on the scandal could prejudice their case (*Globe and Mail,* 29 Sept.). Testimony by the pair was unsealed on 14 October, when Gomery decided that a ban was unnecessary after it was confirmed that the trial would be delayed to the following spring. In any event, they entered a plea of not guilty at the first stage.

First, fateful report

The first volume of Justice Gomery's report, which assigned responsibility, was released on 1 November. As summarized by the *Toronto Star* on 2 November, the major findings were

- Prime Minister Paul Martin was absolved of personal blame;
- former prime minister Jean Chrétien and his chief of staff, Jean Pelletier, must shoulder some responsibility for mismanagement of the program;
- Jacques Corriveau was a key but not solitary bogeyman who reaped personal rewards but also diverted funds to the Quebec wing of the federal Liberal party;
- one-time public works minister Alfonso Gagliano had immersed himself in partisan dealings and was culpably indifferent to the scoundrels loose in his ministry; and
- innocent bureaucrats alarmed by dishonest practices were cowed into silence by an inhospitable culture.

Gomery concluded that

Many factors contributed to what has been described as the 'sponsorship scandal': inappropriate political interference in administrative matters, acceptance by public servants of such interference, excessive concentration of power in the Prime Minister's Office, carelessness and incompetence and blatant disregard of Treasury Board policies, greed and venality. The public trust in its system of government was subverted and betrayed, and Canadians were outraged, not only because public funds were wasted and misappropriated, but also because no one was held responsible or punished for his misconduct.

It was unimaginable that any of this could help the Liberals. Martin's exoneration was some consolation and, to *Toronto Star* editorialists, a plausible 'silver lining,' for 'rarely in federal politics does something so rotten turn out so well for those with so much to lose' (2 Nov.). As for Chrétien, he formally challenged Gomery's findings on 30 November, the last day he could do so.

Election 2006

After nearly a full year of discord verging on acrimony, it is little wonder that campaigning for the 2006 election began on a sour note. In his speech on the critical non-confidence vote on 24 November, Harper chastised the Liberals for willingly associating with an 'organization that was found to have been involved in a massive corruption ring using organized crime to defraud taxpayers.' An attorney served notice that a lawsuit would be forthcoming from the Liberals if the Conservative leader repeated this supposed slur outside the protected confines of the House (25 Nov.). The run-up to the election was nasty enough, and there were predictions that it would only heat up. Gloria Galloway in the *Globe and Mail* noted that the prelude to the confidence vote 'sparked a round of pre-election mudslinging that suggests the coming campaign will set new standards of viciousness' (25 Nov.). According to the *Toronto Star,* the Conservatives were laying the groundwork for a hard-hitting campaign involving 'extreme negativity ... mudslinging and a flintier approach' to the Liberals after the end of a year's respite (31 Dec.). With voter turnout falling, it was a fair guess that Canadians would find themselves alienated by the unseemly race unfolding before them.

At dissolution the party standings were Liberals, 133; Conservatives, 98; Bloc Québécois, 53; New Democrats, 18; and independent members, by choice or expulsion, 4. There were two vacancies when the writs were dropped. Each of the three national parties represented in the House contested all 308 seats, as did the budding Green Party. The Bloc fielded a full slate of 75 candidates in Quebec. Ten minor parties were also certified by Elections Canada:

- Animal Alliance Environment Voters (running in a single riding)
- Canadian Action (34 candidates)
- Christian Heritage (45 candidates)
- Communist (21 candidates)
- First Peoples National (5 candidates)
- Libertarian (10 candidates)
- Marijuana (23 candidates)
- Marxist-Leninist (69 candidates)
- Progressive Canadian (25 candidates)
- Western Bloc (4 candidates)

Ninety independents also ventured into the fray, typically against very long odds.

Parties and platforms

Having had no time to spare between the merger of the Reform and Progressive Conservative parties and the election of 2004, the Conservatives held a delayed policy convention in Montreal that wrapped up on 20 March. Extolling the party's 'modern, moderate' course, Harper basked in the glow of an endorsement from 84 per cent of delegates. Efforts were made to shed the party of right-wing baggage and the convention resolved to abandon past opposition to abortion laws and some social programs (*Calgary Herald,* 20 Mar.). Despite such retreats, the premium put on tax cuts and a smaller state set it apart. The *Toronto Star*'s James Travers argued that the meeting 'spent more time crafting a marketable election platform than debating an alternative national vision' (14 Apr.). Thematically, the Conservative campaign was organized around change, the turpitude of the Liberals, and an appeal to 'stand up for Canada.'

Notwithstanding a modulated tone, the platform veered to the right on the ideological spectrum. Big-ticket items included tax credits for regular public transit use (paid for by subtracting approximately $2 billion from the government's environmental envelope); an instant cut in the goods and services tax to 6 per cent, with another percentile reduction in five years ($32 billion); and family credits in lieu of funding for child-care spaces ($1.3 billion), along with taxable allowances for parents of younger children ($8 billion).

Among those not running for the party again were stalwarts John Reynolds, Darrel Stinson, and Randy White, all from British Columbia. New candidates included a trio of former Ontario cabinet ministers (John Baird, Jim Flaherty, and Tony Clement, who ran for the party leadership in 2004); one-time Quebec Liberal cabinet minister Lawrence Cannon; past MPs Jean-Pierre Blackburn (Quebec), Pauline Browes, Garth Turner, and Barry Turner (Ontario); and high-profile television anchor Peter Kent.

The Liberals sought to position themselves as prudent custodians of the national purse who had presided over a long, prosperous economic run. The opening weeks the campaign ran according to script. This changed on 28 December, when the RCMP confirmed that it had mounted a criminal investigation into the alleged leaking of information to investors on the eve of a government announcement on income trusts. As the Conservatives' Jason Kenney noted, this notoriety would 'bring right back front and centre the issue of accountability and ethics in this campaign ... and a [Liberal] government operating under an ethical cloud' (*Toronto Star,* 29 Nov.). The Liberals had been ahead of the Conservatives, sometimes comfortably so, in every published poll in December until the latest controversy blossomed.

Despite the Liberals' challenges they attracted several star candidates. Peripatetic scholar Michael Ignatieff, repatriated as an historian at his University of Toronto alma mater, overcame an interloper tag to win nomination in the Toronto riding of Etobicoke South. Upon arrival on home soil Ignatieff was cast as a potential Liberal leader, even though his latter academic career had been coloured by contestations of his notion that Western democracies might have to countenance (and tightly manage) otherwise untenable 'lesser evils' in order to defeat terrorism. Other key recruits included a pair of Manitoba artists and Aboriginal activists, Ray St. Germain and Tina Keeper; constitutional authority Deborah Coyne (mother of Pierre Trudeau's daughter), who took on Jack Layton; experienced New Brunswick politician Marcelle Mersereau; and Quebec's Marc Garneau, the first Canadian astronaut and head of the Canadian Space Agency. Ignatieff's university roommate, former Ontario NDP premier Bob Rae, considered running for the Liberals but ultimately demurred. His supporters harboured leadership dreams for Rae, who after leaving behind a whipsawed partisan career had busied himself by returning to law practice and taking on special projects at the behest of the governments of Canada and Ontario. Five former cabinet members decided not to run: David Anderson, Jean Augustine (a minister of state, who made way for Ignatieff), Don Boudria, Claudette Bradshaw, and John Efford. Also on the sidelines was Marlene Catterall, a chief government whip.

During the 2005 phase of the campaign, the Grits relied on the 14 November fiscal update. They stood behind individual and corporate tax reductions costed at $30 billion. Major spending promises included support for a strategy to revive the lumber industry ($1.5 billion), tuition help for post-secondary institutions and students ($4 billion), research and innovation ($2 billion), and assorted interventions on the environment.

New Democratic Party leader Jack Layton entered his second campaign as leader with a seasoned team, absent only Bev Desjarlais (running as an independent in Manitoba after dissenting on same-sex marriage) and former party leader Ed Broadbent. After being elected again in 2004 after a lengthy hiatus, Broadbent ended his brief political comeback in order to spend more time with his ailing spouse. Among the notable NDP candidates was former Manitoba premier Ed Schreyer; his candidacy marked the first time that a Governor General had re-entered partisan politics. Toronto city councillor Olivia Chow, Layton's partner, ran for a second time in Toronto. Long-time Ontario legislator Marilyn Churley debuted in the federal arena. Novice candidate Pat Summerville was one of the party's proudest recruits. A former chief economist for RBC Dominion Securities, he was one of very few business leaders to embrace the social democratic party. Returning to the fray was Svend Robinson, a legendary MP who had been forced to step down in 2004 after being convicted of shoplifting.

For the NDP it was about 'getting results for people.' This included decreasing the lowest income rate by 1 per cent and upping the child tax credit by $250 in each of four years. Together these tax savings would amount to $26 billion. When its platform was fully announced, ambitious spending designs had the party on track to be the highest rollers. It pledged to enrich Kyoto funding by an extra $7 billion and would invest in an assortment of health-care, post-secondary, urban, Aboriginal, and non-profit daycare programs.

Bloc Québécois sights were trained solely on Quebec. The BQ entered the campaign with Gilles Duceppe still at the helm after a lightning-quick flirtation with the idea of running for the provincial Parti Québécois. He announced and withdrew within a single day in deference to Pauline Marois, saying that it was time for a woman to lead (Duceppe also lagged behind Marois in initial soundings). The

BQ fielded Jacques Léonard in the riding of Outremont. A veteran provincial politician and cabinet minister on numerous occasions beginning in 1976, Léonard sought to make inroads in a Liberal-held riding made winnable by the scandal swirling around the government. Alain Boire failed in his bid for re-nomination, while Marcel Gagnon retired. Platform details were announced on 30 November. Featured planks included funding to live up to Kyoto commitments without propping up the internal-combustion-engine economies of Ontario and Alberta. The BQ was the first to unveil a platform. The tab for promises stretching over 200 pages was $55.8 billion over three years (*Montreal Gazette,* 1 Dec.).

By dint of garnering 600,000 votes in 2004, the Green Party earned public funding as well as respect. Led by Jim Harris, the Greens built their platform around compassion, integrity, and accountability – summed up in the theme 'We can.' Environmental plans adorned a platform that also stressed the need for a rejuvenated political system and a healthier, more inclusive Canada. With greater visibility came greater scrutiny, and the media reported on complaints filed with Elections Canada over Harris's party leadership expenses and alleged mistreatment of candidates (28 Dec.). Moreover, midway through the campaign the party had still not finalized its plans for allocating funds. The Greens were once again omitted from televised leaders' debates, and they readied for legal proceedings to reverse the exclusion.

On the trail

In the weeks before the year-end holiday, the Conservatives reprised their 2004 strategy of spooning out daily dollops of platform planks. Their rolling campaign was nearly a front-page fixture. The front-running Liberals held back new items until January, as did the NDP. Public opinion surveys did not detect any significant movement in voter intentions. A series of four leaders' debates was planned. The first stop was in Vancouver on 16 December. Conducted in English, the exchanges that night were lively but seen as precursors to more combative encounters ahead.

Inevitably, and notwithstanding considerable exertions to choreograph campaigns, several unexpected issues took off during the early stages of the campaign. Three stood out. The first was gun control. On 8 December Martin proposed a universal ban on handguns in the wake of urban violence. Harper and his party – implacable foes of gun registration – advocated for tougher enforcement of existing laws (20 Dec.). The random slaying of a young girl on a Boxing Day shopping excursion in Toronto added piquancy to the debate. Martin also gambled

Voter preferences by political party (percentage support) Select Environics Research polls, by month

Party	Jan	Apr	Jun/Jul	Sept/Oct	Nov	Dec 21
Liberals	37	27	34	38	35	35
Conservatives	29	33	31	27	30	30
NDP	20	24	20	20	25	17
Bloc Québécois	11	11	11	14	14	12
Other	4	4	4	1	1	5

on awakening Canadians' ambivalent feelings towards the United States by decrying contemporary American foreign policy, which, he said, lacked a 'global conscience' (7 Dec.). He later tried to capitalize on the publication, in the right-wing *Washington Times,* of a letter by Harper that more tamely addressed the delicate state of Canadian-American relations. Late in the month the Quebec television network TVQ set up a debate between Martin and Duceppe on the generally suppressed topic of separation. Martin refused. Harper contemplated filling in but settled for accusing the Liberals of secretly coveting a victory by Quebec separatists so that they could be seen as defenders of national unity (21 Dec.).

Gaffes garnered headlines too. Conservative MPs and strategists were on a relatively tight leash, so it was left to Liberals to invite negative publicity. First a senior party advisor suggested that the Conservatives' childcare allowance would encourage recipients to 'blow twenty-five bucks a week on beer and popcorn' (10 Dec.). Then an Ontario party official compared NDP candidate Olivia Chow to a dog. The NDP did manage to inject proportional representation into the mix for a spell, and differences over Canada's presence in Afghanistan and adjudication of a dispute with Denmark over territorial claims to minuscule Hans Island brought foreign policy into the spotlight for a cameo appearance. The fleeting nature of these oddments and the barrage of pitches tossed out by the parties made it entirely possible that the sponsorship scandal and the income trust investigation would weigh heavily as voters sifted their choice.

National institutions

The cabinet

There were no major shuffles of the cabinet during the year, but some significant changes occurred nonetheless. The first to leave was Judy

Sgro, minister of citizenship and immigration (14 Jan.). Sgro was caught up in serial controversies involving her office. Allegations surfaced in November 2004 that members of her staff had filed bogus reimbursement claims for activities related to her re-election campaign in Toronto. Opposition MPs later taunted her for apparently giving preferential treatment to a campaign volunteer in an immigration application. The individual in question was originally admitted to the country on a permit to work as an exotic dancer, and the affair was dubbed 'Strippergate.' Sgro's staff were also said to have threatened to withhold ministerial permits to constituents of an MP critical of the minister.

Sgro's position became untenable when it was charged that she had offered to aid an applicant in exchange for pizza for campaign workers. (It was subsequently revealed that the accuser, one Harjit Singh, had been convicted of fraud in his native India.) It was one of the more bizarre and, in the end, cruel political scandals in Canadian history. The ethics commissioner, Bernard Shapiro, largely cleared Sgro of conflict of interest over 'Strippergate,' concluding in his summation, 'Many Shades of Grey,' that she, although not her aides, had acted appropriately (22 June). One week later Singh formally apologized to the former minister as part of a legal settlement. Sgro was replaced by another Toronto MP, Joe Volpe, but when cleared of wrongdoing, she expressed the hope that she would be restored to Cabinet in an act of closure for her.

The position of solicitor general was formally abolished as of 3 April. The incumbent, deputy prime minister Anne McLellan, took on the successor portfolio as minister of public safety and emergency preparedness, on 4 April. On 17 May, Ottawa-area MP Mauril Bélanger agreed to take on the new portfolio of minister of internal trade. In doing so he added to his already lengthy repertoire of minister responsible for official languages, minister responsible for democratic reform, associate minister of national defence, and deputy house leader.

Minister of state Joe Comuzzi tendered his resignation on 28 June over his opposition to same-sex marriage. Comuzzi, representing Thunder Bay in the Commons and responsible for the Federal Economic Development Initiative for Northern Ontario, was uncomfortable about pressure on the Cabinet to unite behind the legislation. Andrew Mitchell, already minister of agriculture and agri-food, took on Comuzzi's duties.

Newfoundland's John Efford, minister of natural resources since 2003, was replaced on a temporary basis by John McCallum, who added this portfolio to his responsibilities for national revenue (29

Sept.). Efford stepped aside in order to deal with health concerns. He had initially hoped to resume his duties and stand for re-election, but eventually gave up public life altogether.

The biggest change at the cabinet level came on a remarkable day in late spring. It was on 17 May that Belinda Stronach, MP for Newmarket-Aurora, walked away from the Conservatives to join the Liberal Party. She was named minister of human resources and skills development (inherited from Lucienne Robillard) and minister responsible for democratic renewal (taking over from Mauril Bélanger). Stronach's decision had far-ranging repercussions and is discussed in more detail below.

House makeover: by-elections, defections, and resignations

A single by-election was required in 2005. With the death of Lawrence O'Brien in December 2004, a vacancy was created in the riding of Labrador. The seat was taken by the one-time head of the Labrador Métis Association, Todd Russell, after a campaign that ended on 24 May. Russell held on to a relatively safe riding for the Liberals with 51.5 per cent of the vote. Conservative candidate and Labrador City mayor Graham Letto finished with a respectable 32.3 per cent of the vote, one of the better showings by a contender in the riding. Russell's victory provided the Liberals with a much-needed cushion in the House.

Of greater interest was the series of floor crossings that had an impact on the standings in the Commons. The Liberals lacked the critical mass to ensure victory in crucial votes, and every change affected the calculus. Two members jumped the Liberal ship. The first to go was David Kilgour, one of only two Grit members from Alberta. Fed up with the tawdry sponsorship scandal, he left the Liberals to sit as an independent on 13 April. This was not a first for Kilgour. In 1990 he had bolted from the ruling Progressive Conservative party in protest against the imposition of the goods and services tax. Kilgour did not run for any party in the next election. London, Ontario, MP Pat O'Brien also withdrew from the Liberal fold. He joined the lonely ranks of independent members on 6 June. His departure was precipitated by the failure of the Liberal government to conduct public hearings on the question of same-sex marriages.

The NDP lost a sitting member on 17 October. Bev Desjarlais, who had voted against same-sex marriage, was blocked in her bid for renomination as the party's candidate for the Manitoba riding of Churchill. She decided to serve out her final days in Parliament as an independent. Bloc Québécois MP Stéphane Bergeron gave up his Verchères–Les

Patriotes seat in order to run for the Parti Québécois in a provincial by-election (9 Nov.). He won in the 12 December runoff and succeeded former Quebec premier Bernard Landry in the provincial assembly.

The Stronach shock

By far the most momentous change came with the stunning leap to the Liberals by Conservative MP Belinda Stronach (17 May). This was no ordinary conversion. Stronach had not only contested the Conservative leadership, she had finished second to Stephen Harper when the party chose the first head for the merged Progressive Conservative–Canadian Alliance in 2004. More than that, she had played a key role in crafting the deal that brought the right-wing parties together. Leaving the party also meant severing an intimate relationship with Peter MacKay, the deputy leader of the Conservatives.

Why did she turn her back on the Conservatives? Stronach explained that she was growing uncomfortable with the social conservatism of the party. Months before her departure, Brian Laghi wrote that 'although there isn't yet much of a left-wing in the [Conservative] party, it appears to have found its champion in Belinda Stronach' (*Globe and Mail,* 21 Mar.). She felt alienated by Harper, whom she described as out of touch with Canadians and overly indebted to western Canada. It was likewise disturbing that the Conservatives had worked hand in hand with the separatist Bloc Québécois in the run-up to decisive tallies in the House. With national unity at stake, Stronach considered the Conservatives too immature to make inroads in Quebec if an election was compelled, leaving the Bloc to sweep away federalist alternatives and destabilize the political system. She also wanted to see Parliament pass budget measures that would help municipalities such as the Toronto-area suburbs she represented. So, on the eve of a potentially rending crisis, she bolted to the governing party. Stronach's enlistment was facilitated by David Peterson, a former Liberal premier of of Ontario, who acted as both go-between and mentor during backroom talks leading to her transformation.

A dismayed Harper conceded that Stronach's departure lessened the chance of a Liberal defeat, attributing her turnabout to thwarted ambitions. To be sure, Stronach was handed a plum cabinet assignment immediately upon her arrival. It was recalled too that this was the daughter of Frank Stronach, head of the powerful Magna International automobile parts corporation. The elder Stronach had been an unsuccessful Liberal candidate, was opposed to free trade, and had made his offspring president of the company he founded at an early age. Although Belinda Stronach was convinced of the need for a viable conservative alternative to the Liberals, she had not seen the Harper Conservatives as sufficiently flexible and credible.

The story dominated the news for several cycles. Coverage featured live broadcasts of her first public walkabout with the prime minister as well as full-bore punditry. Fascination with Stronach was widespread. She was both a rising political star and a home-grown celebrity, given her wealth, youthful good looks, and jet-set circle of friends and admirers. Now, with the arithmetic in Parliament looking decidedly advantageous, she took on a heroic aura, at least in the eyes of salvation-starved Liberals.

Legislating switches

Party switching became rampant enough to prompt a pair of MPs to draft private member's legislation that would discourage the practice. With Bill C-251 (defeated 23 Nov.), the NDP's Peter Stoffer intended that defectors would be obliged to step down. In Bill C-408 (introduced 17 June but not resolved), submitted by Conservative Joe Preston, a voluntary change in caucus affiliation would create a vacancy after a thirty-five-day waiting period.

Senate

The Martin government was able to make numerous appointments to the Senate during the year. Selections were announced in waves. Although a handful entered the 'Red Chamber' as members of the opposition parties, the Liberals maintained their overwhelming majority. On 24 March nine individuals were summoned to the upper chamber. The newest senators were:

- Jim Cowan, a prominent Nova Scotia lawyer, who joined the Liberal caucus;
- Roméo Dallaire (Liberal, Quebec), retired lieutenant-general, assistant deputy minister in the Department of National Defence in 1998, commander of the United Nations Assistance Mission for Rwanda, and author of an award-winning account of his experiences in Africa, titled *Shake Hands with the Devil: The Failure of Humanity in Rwanda;*

- Lillian Dyck (NDP, Saskatchewan), a prominent psychiatrist and advocate for women and Aboriginal peoples;
- Art Eggleton of Ontario, a former mayor of Toronto and Liberal cabinet minister who had been forced from ministerial office over charges of favouritism;
- Elaine McCoy, an Alberta lawyer and former candidate for leadership of the province's Progressive Conservative Party;
- Grant Mitchell, a former leader of the Liberal Party in Alberta, who had experience in both government and the private sector;
- Robert Peterson (Liberal), a leading entrepreneur in Saskatchewan;
- Nancy Ruth (Progressive Conservative, Ontario), who was recognized for her activism, especially in advancing feminist causes through the Women's Legal Education and Action Fund, the Canadian Women's Foundation, the Women's Future Fund, and the Charter of Rights Coalition; and
- Claudette Tardiff (Liberal, Alberta), an academic specializing in education who had most recently served as vice-president for external relations at the University of Alberta.

By taking on the designation 'Progressive Conservative,' Ruth and McCoy fell outside the new mainstream in conservatism. In this sense Martin appeared to be at once breaking with the tradition of appointing members of the ruling party to the Senate while tweaking the nose of Stephen Harper and the Conservatives. Stephen Harper fumed that it was 'intellectually dishonest,' since 'there is no federal Progressive Conservative Party [which is] usually a euphemism now for people who support the Liberal Party' (*Globe and Mail,* 25 Mar.). Although a member of the NDP, Dyck was unwelcome in the party's caucus because of its orthodoxy on abolition of the Senate. She was styled as an independent NDP. None of the three senators from Alberta were selected from the pool of prospective candidates designated by popular election in that province.

Another five new senators were elevated on 2 August. They were:

- Larry Campbell, a British Columbia Liberal and former mayor of Vancouver, whose career as a flamboyant coroner had inspired the popular television program *Da Vinci's Inquest*;
- Andrée Champagne, a professional actor and musician from Quebec who had served as a Conservative MP and deputy speaker of the House of Commons;
- Dennis Dawson, a public relations consultant and former Liberal MP;

- Hugh Segal, a long-time Conservative strategist and advisor in both federal and Ontario provincial politics; and
- Rod Zimmer, a Manitoba businessperson, philanthropist and Liberal.

The appointees announced on 29 August were both from Quebec. Francis Fox had been a Liberal member of Parliament and cabinet minister during the Trudeau era and served as Paul Martin's principal secretary from 2004, following an interregnum in the world of law and business. Also named was Yoine Goldstein, a lawyer and professor of law with expertise in insolvency who had served as an advisor to the Senate Banking, Trade, and Commerce Committee.

On 29 September the Martin government rounded off its appointments with the selection of Sandra Lovelace Nicholas, a New Brunswick Liberal. Nicholas was known for lobbying for Canadian legislation reinstating the rights of First Nations women and their children in Canada and pursuing her case to the United Nations Human Rights Commission. In 1992 she received a Governor General's Award in commemoration of the Persons Case.

A long-serving senator passed away in the final days of the year. C. William Doody, who was one of the few senators named by Joe Clark in 1979, died on 27 December. A former Newfoundland and Labrador cabinet minister, Doody had served as deputy leader of the government in the Senate during the administration of Brian Mulroney.

Governor General

After a twelve-month extension of her five-year term, Adrienne Clarkson's tenure as Governor General came to an end in the autumn. A household name as a public broadcaster and later a diplomat in France, she had drawn intermittent criticism for leading a life that was perceived as rather too regal. This was particularly true in 2003–04. At a time when scandals over expenses and waste were brewing, Clarkson led a delegation on the first leg of a 'circumpolar' tour to northern countries. The travels were cut short by disapproving media coverage and a building public outcry. It was also observed that the budget of her office had increased substantially during her time as the Queen's representative in Canada. One of her last acts was to dedicate the Clarkson Cup for national women's hockey supremacy (10 Mar.). This idea was inspired by the example of a predecessor, Lord Stanley, after whom the National Hockey League's championship trophy is named. Clarkson underwent successful heart surgery on 8 June, after which she was temporarily replaced by the Chief Justice of the Supreme Court, Beverly McLaughlin.

Canada's new Governor General was revealed on 4 August and took office on 27 September. At the age of forty-eight, Michaëlle Jean was one of the youngest persons to hold the post. Like her immediate predecessor, Madame Jean had been born outside Canada (in Port au Prince, Haiti) and was a professional public affairs journalist and television host. She had also taught Italian at l'Université de Montréal and acquired fluency in five languages. While pursing her career, Jean performed volunteer service among the poor and immigrant communities of Montreal. The appointment was bold but not universally praised. Jean was married to Jean-Daniel Lafond, a professor of philosophy, writer, and documentary producer who had moved comfortably in separatist circles. Staunch monarchists were appalled, but the couple gave assurances of their devotion to Canada and to federalism. The new Governor General also had to surrender the French half of her dual citizenship. At her installation, Jean spoke of the need for Canadians to see beyond themselves and urged them to translate solitudes into solidarity. The celebrations after her swearing-in were unconventionally informal and spirited.

Supreme Court

No new justices were appointed to the Supreme Court in 2005, but one year-end retirement created a vacancy to be filled by the government elected in January 2006. The departing puisne judge was John C. Major of Alberta. He had joined the court in November 1992 after serving on the Alberta Court of Appeal. Although not due to retire until early 2006, he revealed on 3 August that he would end his term before the end of the calendar year, and did so on 25 December.

Major's successor was to be selected under a new process tabled with the House Committee on Justice, Human Rights, Public Safety, and Emergency Preparedness on 7 April. The following steps were to be followed:

1. consultation with provincial and territorial leaders by the minister of justice, including attorneys general, provincial court chief justices, and legal luminaries;
2. creation of a list of eight prospective nominees;
3. public input;
4. creation of an unranked short list of three possibilities by a special advisory committee consisting of an MP from each parliamentary

party, a nominee of the provincial attorneys general, a nominee of
the law societies, and two prominent Canadians who are neither lawyers nor judges;
5. appointment of an individual on the short list by the minister; and
6. appearance by the minister before the Justice standing committee to
explain the selection process and the qualities of the individual who
has been appointed.

The committee was granted an opportunity to form a consensus
around this process but did not do so. In deference to the regional criteria for appointments to the court and in view of Major's western roots,
only candidates from Alberta, Saskatchewan, Manitoba, the Northwest
Territories, and Nunavut would be entertained in the search for a successor. Justice minister Irwin Cotler took receipt of a recommendation
on 24 November but put off action until the election, explaining that to
move more swiftly 'would be fair neither to the appointments process
nor to the candidate nor to the courts' (*Globe and Mail*, 25 Nov.).

Auditor General's reports

On 15 February Auditor General Sheila Fraser issued her third annual
status report on the government's administrative and fiscal management. Her submission to the House of Commons highlighted the vul-
nerability of the federal government's extensive databases to penetra-
tion by outsiders. 'Sensitive data, including information on the privacy
of Canadians, payroll and financial transactions, program information ... are at increased risk of unauthorized disclosure, modification,
or loss – possibly without being detected' and 'in some cases the weaknesses had been exploited and gone undetected' (quoted by the *Toronto
Star,* 16 Feb.). The government had been negligent in erecting barriers
recommended in a 2002 review of online systems that were otherwise
models of government–citizen interaction.

Fraser and her team were pleased with progress in the management
of major airports and human resources. Of more pressing concern was
Ottawa's inability to hold recipients of major grants accountable, and
it was determined that $7.7 billion doled out to foundations had been
unspent. Had the government merely collected interest on these sums
it would have improved its own balance sheet. The auditor general
also detected a flaw in allocations made by the Canadian International
Development Agency (CIDA); a higher proportion of aid was flow-
ing through grants that did not have transparent conditions attached.
Poor grades were also given to the government for the tardiness of its

risk-management approach to nuclear reactor regulation, oversight of Crown corporations, and developing sound financial decision-making frameworks across the board.

The customary spring report was published on 5 April. In it Fraser discussed problems at the passport office on the same day the United States confirmed that visitors from north of the border would require passports or some other secure travel papers. As well there were serious deficiencies in emergency preparedness, national defence initiatives, and natural resources. The report also looked into selected departmental performance reports.

Headlines pivoted around Canada's security system. Some progress had been made since Fraser offered an analysis in March 2004, but there were still 'serious weaknesses' resulting from ineffective management. In the words of Susan Riley, 'for $8 billion, taxpayers expect more than a mouthful of new acronyms, taskforces and framework agreements ... and that, so far, is a large part of what our renewed security effort has produced' (*Ottawa Citizen*, 6 Apr.).

The annual report of 22 November was prefaced by a blanket observation that the government was doing some things well. Even so, Fraser registered numerous concerns. As summarized by the *Toronto Star* on 23 November, they were:

- disregard of domestic content rules by producers accessing $800 million from Heritage Canada and agencies such as Telefilm Canada and the Canadian Television Fund, and poor efforts to seek compliance;
- incomplete training of new officers by the Royal Canadian Mounted Police, together with the assigning of specially trained personnel to mundane duties and the inadequacy of backup for officers in dangerous situations, practices that could leave the Mounties open to legal challenges;
- a shortfall in fundable projects to assist victims of the 2004 Asian tsunami and the subsequent reallocation to other priorities of some of the $223 million available to CIDA for this purpose; and
- a troubling inability of the government to confirm the accuracy of commissioned polls despite their use in public policy initiatives.

Ethics commissioner

Canada's first ethics commissioner, former McGill University principal Bernard Shapiro, was on the hot seat all year. Appointed in May 2004, Shapiro was hounded by members of the House Ethics Committee over his idiosyncratic understanding of the commissioner's role and specific decisions made – or avoided. The NDP's Ed Broadbent was particularly dogged.

On 9 June a backtracking Shapiro agreed that he could investigate the conduct of Tim Murphy, prime minister Paul Martin's chief of staff, and his boss, over allegations of wooing a Conservative backbencher. At first he had asserted that he had no such jurisdiction. Recanting, Shapiro accepted that he may have construed his powers too narrowly. This he put down to a daunting learning curve. The committee also questioned Shapiro on the hiring of Borden Ladner Gervais to investigate the activities of former Liberal cabinet minister Judy Sgro for an arresting $120,000. Repeated clashes led to a showdown on 23 June at which a motion of non-confidence was on the agenda (*Toronto Star,* 22 June). Shapiro survived, thanks to the generosity of Bloc MPs, who forgave his inexperience. Even so, the office was under both a microscope and a cloud. The group Democracy Watch filed an official complaint against Shapiro on 29 June for bias and failing to comply with his mandate.

National economy

Economic indicators

Conventional measures of economic activity in 2005 continued to show that Canada was out-performing most comparable nations, including G7 partners. The overall gross domestic product rose by 2.9 per cent. This increased output, identical to the level of growth in 2004, was concentrated in the western provinces, where the petroleum-driven economy of Alberta was particularly robust. Meanwhile Ontario, the traditional engine, lagged behind the national GDP average for a third straight year. These results underlined the transitional nature of the economy. In common with other so-called industrialized countries, Canada was losing vitality in the manufacturing sector. Losses in this area were offset by further diversification towards the so-called 'knowledge economy,' but resource extraction and export was an increasingly prominent part of the equation for Canada. Housing starts slowed modestly, with the exception of condominium construction, and were concentrated in larger urban centres.

The decline in manufacturing was attributable in part to a still-rising dollar. For the third year in a row the currency appreciated against the American dollar (by 4.8 per cent). It fared even better relative to European denominations. The dollar's strength accelerated migration of production to the emerging powerhouses of China, India, and others.

Jobs were more plentiful in 2005, with a net gain of 255,000 new full-time positions. Growth was slower than the year before. Even so, unemployment fell to 6.8 per cent, its lowest point since 1976. However, the regional cast to employment persisted. Alberta and, to a lesser extent, other western provinces remained a magnet for job-seekers. Newfoundland and Labrador and the three maritime provinces trailed in both employment and job creation. A decline in the participation rate was detected for the first time since 1996, as the first wave of the baby-boom generation entered retirement, and in some quarters there were worries about a sufficiency of skilled workers.

Inflation peaked at 2.2 per cent. The consumer price index was virtually constant around the 2 per cent mark for the third consecutive year. In the basket of goods covered by the index, an exception to the rule was energy, which climbed by 10.2 per cent, inspiring further concerns about manufacturing flight as fuel costs soared.

Trade is a perennial focus for analysts of the Canadian economy. A healthy surplus was recorded in export/import transactions with the United States, which amounted to 80 per cent of all trade. Canada was in a deficit position with the rest of the world; the gap was particularly notable in the case of China.

Budget 2005

Ralph Goodale delivered his second budget as finance minister on 23 February. Nearing the end of fiscal year 2004–05, it was certain that the government would be able to claim an eighth straight balanced budget. The surplus was of such a magnitude that the government was at last capable of redeeming a number of pledges made in past election platforms. Flush with cash into the foreseeable future, Goodale spread the wealth. As summarized by the *Toronto Star* in its edition of 24 February, the spending highlights of the budget were as follows:

- $12.8 billion over five years to expand the Canadian Forces by 5,000 troops and 3,000 reservists and to purchase new equipment;
- $5 billion over five years in gas tax revenue for cities ($600 million in 2005), based on a transfer of five cents per litre;
- $5 billion over five years for a national child-care program to create new spaces;
- $5 billion extra over five years for environment protection, and especially to meet Canada's commitments to reduce greenhouse gases under the Kyoto Accord;

- $398 million for immigration settlement; and
- $3.4 billion over five years in additional foreign aid.

Many of these policy initiatives were greeted warmly by interested groups. Spending on the military was welcomed by the Canadian Forces, defence contractors, and the American ambassador. Environmental activists heralded the commitment to reduce greenhouse gas emissions and other provisions, even as they fretted about the lack of specifics. The Liberals earned kudos from municipalities for making a good start on assisting cities, but lukewarm support from child-care advocates for its plan to increase the availability of spaces. There were suspicions that the progressive promises owed more to electioneering than to genuine resolve, but the purse strings had been loosened enough to win reasonably wide favour.

On the taxation side of the ledger, the government increased the basic personal exemption on income from $8,012 in 2004 to $10,000 by 2009. Tax-reducing annual contributions to retirement funds, capped at $16,500, would be permitted up to $19,000 in 2007, with yearly increments of $1,000 thereafter to 2010. A 30 per cent ceiling on foreign investments in pension plans and retirement funds was also eliminated. Controversially, the corporate tax rate was to fall from 21 per cent to 19 per cent in staged reductions to 2010. This was complemented by the abolishment of surtaxes on large enterprises. Additionally, Goodale announced that a special expenditure review committee had earmarked $11 billion in cuts made possible by operational efficiencies.

Responses from the three opposition parties varied widely. Gilles Duceppe, leader of the Bloc Québécois, flatly rejected the government's plan and pledged to confront the government at every turn. He reasoned that the government had offered nothing to Quebec, done little to redress the 'fiscal imbalance' between federal and provincial governments, and ignored the Bloc's repeated pleas to liberalize employment insurance. The New Democratic Party wanted time to study the plan, even though its leader, Jack Layton, confessed to feeling somewhat betrayed by the Liberals (*Globe and Mail,* 24 Feb.). Eventually the NDP concluded that it tilted too far to the right. On this score, the right-wing Conservatives seemed to concur. Opposition leader Stephen Harper was pleasantly surprised by the myriad nods to the right contained in the budget. Pet predilections such as tax cuts and military spending were particularly welcome. It may not have been a perfect document, but Harper saw nothing in it that would 'warrant two elections in a year' (*Globe and*

Mail, 24 Feb.). The Liberal government appeared to have survived a crucial test of its staying power. Outside opinion was also divided. On the dissenting side, a *Globe and Mail* editorial decried an 'incoherent,' spendthrift, and politically driven document that retained only a shell of the kind of 'fiscal responsibility' that had characterized Martin's days as finance minister (24 February).

A *tale of two budgets*

Aided by the Conservatives, the Liberals survived first reading of the budget bill, C-48. From then on the ride grew rougher. Convulsed by revelations emerging at the sponsorship inquiry and implacably hostile to the government's climate-change framework, the Conservatives pivoted against the budget. Saying that the Liberals had forfeited the 'moral authority' to govern, Harper reversed course and the government was compelled to scramble.

A lifeline was offered by the NDP. Negotiations between the government and the New Democrats resulted in an agreement to bring forward amendments in a second bill, C-43 (26 April). The new legislation contained $4.6 billion for social programs and curtailed the corporate tax breaks set out in the original budget. The *Toronto Star* of 28 April summarized the details as follows:

- an infusion of $1.6 billion for affordable housing construction, including Aboriginal housing;
- a direct transfer of $1.5 billion to the provinces for post-secondary tuition reduction;
- enhanced training under the employment insurance umbrella;
- an extra $900 million for the environment, including one cent more of the federal gas tax for public transit and an energy-efficiency program for low-income housing;
- an enrichment of $500 million for foreign aid, bringing Canada in line with longstanding pledges to reach 0.7 per cent of GDP; and
- pension protection amounting to $100 million for workers.

The Liberals also surrendered on tax cuts for large corporations: only small and medium-sized enterprises would get relief. While the Conservatives agreed to approve the main budget, they resolved to defeat the amendments. The Bloc favoured neither bill, since fiscal imbalances and fundamental employment insurance reform had not been addressed to its satisfaction. Both bills passed in June.

Autumn economic update

On 14 November Goodale presented the annual economic and fiscal update to the House Finance Committee. It was fuller than was normally the case for such statements because, said Goodale, the looming defeat of the government ruled out a February 2006 budget. His audience thought it was padded to showcase pre-election sweeteners. Goodale confirmed that the budget surplus for 2004–05 was $1.6 billion, and, after reciting a string of accomplishments, he concluded that the economy was 'doing very well and it is expected to continue to do so for the foreseeable future.' This optimism was based on signposts aiming towards GDP expansion, export growth, job creation and unemployment drops, lower interest rates, higher consumer demand, and higher investment in machinery and equipment. Inflation was also under control. The economy was tracking towards GDP increases in line with earlier expectations of about 2.5 per cent for the calendar year. Consensus forecasts called for growth of 2.9 per cent in 2006 and 3.1 per cent in 2007.

This rosy outlook could be dimmed by two primary risks. One was an erosion of confidence on the part of producers and consumers if energy prices were not checked. The other was the spectre of weakening exports if unfavourable conditions in the American economy – bulging deficits in Washington's budget and massive trade deficits – resulted in further depreciation of the American currency.

The headline news about the update focused on tax cuts. Goodale announced plans to trim taxes by increasing the basic personal income reduction for individuals by $500 in 2005, with an additional $200 in 2006. Those with incomes of less than $35,595 (that is, in the lowest tax bracket) would have their rate reduced to 15 per cent, down from 16 per cent. The rates for taxpayers in middle income brackets would see a 1 per cent saving beginning in 2010. That same year the floor of the highest income rate would be lifted from $115,739 to $200,000. The government also took the opportunity to revive changes to business taxes that had been removed from the 2005 budget at the insistence of the NDP. Under this plan the general corporate rate would be reduced in increments starting in 2008, from 21 per cent to 19 per cent. The 1.12 per cent surtax on businesses would be dropped altogether in 2008. Total reductions amounted to $39 billion, with 70 per cent of this dividend accruing to individual taxpayers.

Over the longer term, Goodale projected healthy surpluses stretching to 2010–11, in the range of $8 billion to $11 billion annually. Although unswerving in its commitment to a combination of tax cuts, priority spending, and debt reduction, the government was clearest about its plans to manage debts. In the 2004 budget Goodale had set a goal of achieving a debt-to-GDP ratio of 25 per cent within ten years. Now he laid down a more ambitious marker of 20 per cent by the year 2020. Spending measures were limited to $2.1 billion over five years for more aid to post-secondary students, $3.5 billion over a similar time frame for job training, and $1 billion in 2005–06 to the provinces and territories to use for post-secondary infrastructure.

With the Liberal government in obvious peril, opposition parties dismissed the update as an ensemble of pre-election sops. Conservative finance critic Monte Solberg wondered how, 'on the eve of an election, all of a sudden the minister and the Liberal Party gets religion on tax relief for Canadians?' (*Globe and Mail,* 15 Nov.). The media also played down the substantive import of the statement, given a super-heated political atmosphere characterized by preoccupation with party tactics. Even sympathetic sources such as the *Toronto Star* editorialized that the statement was a pre-emptive strike against the Conservatives and their tax-cutting constituency (15 Nov.).

Allocation of budget surpluses

On 7 October Goodale moved first reading of Bill C-67, an act governing the allocation of unanticipated government surpluses up to 2009–10. Any amounts in excess of the $3-billion contingency reserve (which, if unspent, would be used exclusively for debt reduction) would be applied in equal parts to cutting personal income taxes, spending on social and economic priorities, and paying down the federal debt. This tripartite formula had featured in past Liberal party platforms and previous government budgets. It was also part of the framework of Bill C-48, the amendment negotiated with the New Democratic Party that allowed the government to survive votes on the main budget of February. The bill had not been dispensed with by the time Parliament was dissolved in November.

Income trusts

Major investors had become increasingly attracted to income trusts as a way of maximizing their yields. Corporations transformed into income trusts are exempt from corporate taxes and tend to provide higher payouts than regular stock dividends, even though they can be traded like other equity holdings. By 2005 there were approximately two hundred trusts listed on the Toronto Stock Exchange, and their collective value had soared to nearly $200 billion. The conversion trend was gaining momentum. This was worrisome in some quarters, and the Ministry of Finance estimated that tax revenues had fallen by $300 million in 2004 as a consequence. On 9 September Goodale announced that his department would conduct a review of the implications of income trusts, beginning with a consultation phase expected to end by 31 December.

Shortly after the review was unveiled, the finance ministry suspended ruling on applications for income trust status (19 Sept.). This news precipitated a steep drop in the value of trusts. Seeking to ease the fears of jittery investors, Goodale stepped in with assurances that he would act swiftly once public input had been digested (1 Nov.). Later he signalled that the government was considering releasing some preliminary guidance on the matter (22 Nov.). The following day, after waiting until the markets closed, Goodale informed assembled journalists that the government had decided against taxing income trusts and would, moreover, institute a more liberal tax regime for normal stocks. The review had ended prematurely, but positively for investors.

Not surprisingly, the markets responded enthusiastically when they opened on 24 November. It also appeared that there had been anomalous movements in the prices of some trusts and stocks prior to the announcement on the 23rd. This inspired allegations that some insiders had benefited from advance notice of the government's intentions. A rapid uptick in trading could have been fuelled by providential guesswork, and it was no secret that major business media outlets had mooted the possibility of appealing action by a government in serious straits, yet the innuendo would not abate.

A few days into the election campaign, Conservative leader Stephen Harper argued that Goodale should step down from his post pending an investigation of the affair (9 Dec.). Goodale refused to do so, and Prime Minister Martin brushed aside this and other demands to sack a finance minister possessed of unassailable integrity (28 Dec.). Martin's defiance was a public response to word that the RCMP would launch, at the request of the NDP, a formal investigation into the possibility of wrongdoing before Goodale's press conference. Whether or not there had been a criminal breach of trust, the timing was terrible for the Liberals, in the midst of a campaign in which the party's probity was already a major issue.

Cross-border disputes: softwood lumber, missiles, and marijuana

A long-standing feud with the United States over softwood lumber exports continued into 2005. On 15 August the American government declared that it would simply ignore a ruling made under the North American Free Trade Agreement (NAFTA) dispute resolution mechanism that its imposition of tariffs on Canadian softwood was illegal. This unilateral action prompted Ottawa to threaten to impose trade sanctions or pursue other litigation. Some avenues were blocked when, in a surprise verdict on 30 August, the World Trade Organization found in favour of the United States. International trade minister James Peterson called the outcome disappointing but vowed to find a resolution that would not undermine an industry in crisis. Canada wanted billions in tariffs returned based on the NAFTA verdict, and emphasized that the WTO ruling had not been fully operationalized.

As a sidebar to the dispute, Washington's outspoken ambassador to Canada, David Wilkins, recommended that Canadian politicians should abandon their 'emotional tirades' and resume serious negotiations (*Ottawa Citizen*, 26 Aug.). If nothing else, his vituperative remarks briefly unified otherwise fractious federal politicians. Wilkins also accused Prime Minister Martin of harbouring anti-American sentiments that jeopardized relations (8 Oct.), an ironic jibe, given Washington's relief when Martin replaced Jean Chrétien in late 2004. Martin and American president George W. Bush were reported to have exchanged heated words about the lumber situation during an icy telephone conversation on 14 October. The American leader held out for a negotiated settlement, whereas Martin threatened to sue the United States in its own courts and even launch an advocacy campaign. As the year ended there was still no definitive conclusion to the saga, one in which Canada was actually being supported by American importers and homebuilders.

On 21 December the American Senate repealed the notorious 'Byrd Amendment' to trade legislation. A major irritant to Canada and other trading nations, the amendment allowed Washington to funnel countervailing duties directly to affected industries. The WTO ruled against this practice and Ottawa imposed duties on selected American imports in retaliation for American intransigence. Lumber lobbyists in Washington succeeded in extending the life of the restrictive practice to 2007.

Canada–U.S. relations were also impaired by decisions that threatened to spill over into trade relations. The Bush administration was mightily perplexed by legislation that would reduce the penalty for recreational cannabis possession (Bill C-17, introduced 1 November 2004) and dismayed by Ottawa's decision, after a lengthy dalliance, to abstain from continental ballistic missile defence (BMD) on 24 February. Canadian firms would not be prohibited from BMD research and development, and the Martin government reiterated its commitments to continuing and emerging defence and security frameworks. Further strain was caused when Martin criticized Washington at the Montreal climate-change conference and criticized Stephen Harper as an overly pliant partner. This prompted Ambassador Wilkins to observe that 'it may be smart election-year politics to thump your chest and criticize your friend and your No. 1 trading partner constantly ... But it is a slippery slope, and all of us should hope that it doesn't have a long-term impact on the relationship' (*Toronto Star,* 13 Dec.).

Federal-provincial dynamics

Atlantic Accord

On 14 February Ottawa, Nova Scotia, and Newfoundland and Labrador finalized an agreement on the exploitation of offshore oil, allowing the two provinces to retain royalties without diminishing equalization payments from the federal government. The gift was worth $2.6 billion to Newfoundland and Labrador and $1.1 billion to Nova Scotia.

During the election campaign of 2004 the federal Liberals had promised to enter into a deal that would allow the perennial 'have-not' provinces to capitalize on new revenue streams without sacrificing their share of equalization. Accessing both was a way in which the provinces could catch up. Martin's tardiness in addressing the issue was upsetting to the point where Newfoundland and Labrador premier Danny Williams stormed out of a first ministers' conference and lowered Canadian flags around the seat of government in St John's. Nova Scotia's John Hamm was strident and impatient, if not so melodramatic. Naturally the deal was heralded by both when it was finally struck.

Some provinces were phlegmatic about a bilateral approach and were clearly interested in gaining from differentiated federalism. Others were apoplectic. Ontario premier Dalton McGuinty accused Ottawa of ignoring rightful claims for fairness and 'putting petty politics ahead of the national interest' by cutting 'side deals' with the others (*Toronto Star,* 15

Feb.). Ontario taxpayers remained the primary contributors to federal surpluses and to payouts for less affluent provinces under the national equalization plan. Saskatchewan and New Brunswick also objected to an asymmetrical divvying up of resource revenues. Prime Minister Martin rejected the volleys. 'Sometimes provincial governments think the best way to get re-elected is to run against the federal government,' he said, and added that, while 'you have to make sure you treat every province fairly ... that doesn't mean you're going to do the same thing' (*Globe and Mail,* 14 Feb.). Ontario had taken to denouncing a supposed $23-billion gap between money flowing to Ottawa and various transfers back to individuals and the provincial treasury. Finance minister Goodale went out of his way to highlight Ontario's dividends on 13 May.

Health care

Early in 2005 the House and Senate gave speedy passage to Bill C-39, an act ratifying negotiated financial arrangements with the provinces for overall health care and to fund diagnostic and medical equipment. The bill affirmed the particulars of a 'Ten Year Plan to Strengthen Health Care' signed on 16 September 2004 at the First Ministers' Meeting on the Future of Health Care.

In a report intended to 'inform debate' on health care, the non-profit Canadian Institute for Health Information published a breakdown of health-care spending. Total outlays amounted to $130 billion in 2004, up by $95 billion over two decades. The Institute estimated that population increases were responsible for 14 per cent of the rise, inflation added another 45 per cent, and the rest was attributed to diagnostic and treatment innovations. Public funding was pegged at $95.5 billion out of the total. The residual $34.5 billion in private expenditures was split evenly between insurance and personal finances, meaning that out-of-pocket costs were approximately the same as in the American system. The proportion of costs absorbed by public funding was actually less than in bigger European jurisdictions. Some 17 per cent of Canadians reported that they had gone without drugs and dental care because of lack of affordability (*Globe and Mail,* 29 Sept.).

On 9 June 2005, in a verdict of 4–3, the Supreme Court overturned a pair of lower court rulings and asserted a constitutional right to obtain private insurance for publicly available services. The decision arose in the case of a physician, Jacques Chaoulli, and a patients' rights advocate in Quebec, George Zeliotis. Together they sought a declaratory judgement that prohibitions of private care in Quebec's *Health Insurance Act* and *Hospital Insurance Act* violated the Charter of Rights and Freedoms by putting the lives of citizens in jeopardy in the face of long waiting times in the public sector. The decision in *Chaoulli* was explosive. Jeffrey Simpson of the *Globe and Mail* called the case 'breathtaking' and argued that it was 'certainly one of the two or three most consequential [decisions] yet issued by the Supreme Court since the inception of the Charter' (10 June). He prophesied that a variety of actors would use the decision to justify moves that would undermine Canada's universality. Roy Romanow, author of a milestone 2002 study of health care commissioned by Ottawa, complained that the court had 'ventured beyond constitutional and legal principles and into complex social policy,' a trespass that put the future of public health care in jeopardy (*Toronto Star,* 17 Sept.). The federal government and Quebec joined forces to ask that the ruling be suspended. On this score the court assented, granting them twelve months for assessment (4 Aug.).

Aboriginal affairs

Kelowna Accord

On the eve of the Liberals' defeat in the House, Prime Minister Martin met with the premiers, heads of territorial governments, and Aboriginal leaders at the First Ministers' Conference on Aboriginal Affairs. The conference, held 24–25 November in the British Columbia city of Kelowna, was meant to be a watershed in relations between the senior levels of government and Aboriginal peoples. At the end the signatories had agreed to a five-year plan to inject $5 billion into programs for First Nations, Métis, and Inuit peoples. Details were put off to future negotiations. In broad strokes, as summarized by the *Globe and Mail* of 26 November, funding was apportioned as follows:

- $1.8 billion for education, focused mostly on reserves, for new Aboriginal school boards and post-secondary bursaries;
- $1.6 billion for housing and infrastructure, $600 million of which was intended for private and social housing and $400 million to improve water-treatment systems and other infrastructure;
- $170 million for 'relationships and accountability' projects such as $90 million to Aboriginal organizations to enhance their capacity to assess and propose public policy and $20 million for land claims and self-government rights; and
- $200 million for economic development.

Specific targets were set for raising secondary school graduation rates to the national average, narrowing the gap in university and college enrolment, increasing the number of physicians and nurses, and reducing the incidence of youth suicide, obesity, and diabetes. The sticking point at the end was health care. Constitutional responsibility for indigenous peoples is assigned to Ottawa, and there was concern that the provinces would not participate in funding health-related services. In a document titled 'Blueprint on Aboriginal Health,' the provinces agreed to cooperate with the federal government after acknowledging their role in providing assistance to off-reserve residents.

Emotions abounded. Phil Fontaine of the Assembly of First Nations joyfully proclaimed that the achievement had been total. The sobering reality was that the accord could be symbolic, given the uncertain environment (with the federal Conservatives wary of some trends in Canada–First Nations relations) and the vagueness of some pledges. Writing in the *Globe and Mail,* John Ibbitson warned that the goals in the accord would 'never come to pass' because they were unrealistic, but celebrated a genuine milestone because it had manufactured common cause from a 'fractious bunch' (26 Nov.). Ottawa and the province of Quebec squared off over jurisdiction, with premier Jean Charest demanding, but not receiving, a more precise statement of federal and provincial responsibilities than Prime Minister Martin was prepared to yield.

Fiscal and Statistical Management Act

On 21 March the House approved Bill C-20, the *Fiscal and Statistical Management Act.* The initiative had a long gestation, with antecedents in a 1983 House report on native self-government and the 1996 Royal Commission on Aboriginal Peoples. Closer in time, the Assembly of First Nations rejected a similar proposal to rework the financial independence of First Nations in 2002. Under C-20, and on an optional basis, First Nations would have access to a quartet of financial institutions:

- the First Nations Tax Commission (replacing the Indian Taxation Advisory Board), which was revamped to streamline taxation law sign-off by Ottawa;
- the First Nations Financial Authority, a cooperative for issuing bonds and raising capital for infrastructure;
- a First Nations Financial Management Board, responsible for establishing appropriate standards and providing professional advice prior to entry into the Financial Authority; and

- the First Nations Statistical Institute, to enhance local data analysis and integration into Statistics Canada systems.

First Nations had resisted previous legislation in this domain, but consultations on C-20 were fruitful and overcame concerns about mandatory participation.

Major policy areas

Same-sex marriage

In December 2004 the Supreme Court responded to a referral from the federal government seeking advice on legislative aspects of same-sex marriage. The court confirmed that Ottawa had the authority to define marriage, advised that the draft legislation it had reviewed was constitutional, and asserted that religious institutions were not required to marry couples against their wishes. The ruling stopped short of requiring non-discrimination, but the trend in lower court rulings in province after province had been that the inability of same-sex couples to marry was at odds with the Charter. Legislation was introduced in the House on 1 February as *An Act Respecting Certain Aspects of Legal Capacity for Marriage for Civil Purposes,* or the *Civil Marriage Act* (Bill C-38).

The government was confident that the legislation was amendment-proof, given that it had carefully exempted religious organizations from the necessity to sanctify vows. The Conservatives were not so sure. Advertising it as a non-ideological compromise, Stephen Harper put forward an amendment to recognize a plurality of civil unions but to nullify the intent of the legislation, by limiting marriage per se to the union of one man and one woman. Citing a 1996 ruling by the Supreme Court, Harper insisted that Parliament could confidently uphold this opposite-sex restriction. Justice minister Irwin Cotler disagreed. Courts throughout the decade had consistently dismissed an exclusionary definition. Enshrining Harper's amendment would necessitate invoking the 'notwithstanding' clause of the Charter (16 Feb.). On 13 April the amendment failed. Even so, thirty-four Liberals broke ranks with the government in a 132–164 split.

Conservatives continued to harry the bill at every turn. Yet on 4 May, at second reading, the House divided 168–133. Taken up by a House committee, the bill was put on a faster track to third and final reading, given a foregone result. Conservative MP Vic Toews threatened to filibuster until a score of witnesses was heard, and other members agreed to a further week's delay before reporting out (2 June). That being done, the Conservatives stalled in the House (16 June). With the support of the Bloc and the NDP, the Liberals engineered a vote on 28 June. The final vote was 158 to 133, but this was not necessarily the final word. If elected, said Harper, the Conservatives would revisit the legislation in the next Parliament. He also argued – archly, in the view of critics – that a majority of federalist MPs (that is, not those in the Bloc) favoured a more traditional understanding of marriage.

Greenhouse emissions and Kyoto

Although Canada had been quick to endorse the Kyoto Protocol in 1998, the government was slow to promulgate and implement plans to reach its targets. Signatories to the convention bound themselves to a reduction in greenhouse gas emissions by 6 per cent of 1990 levels by the year 2012. Parliament ratified the protocol at the end of 2002, shortly after the Liberal government released its original climate-change plan. Kyoto was to take effect on 16 February; with this date looming, it was not yet clear how the government planned to realize annual reduction targets of 240 million megatonnes. The 23 February budget made provision for spending on related programs, and a deal was reached with domestic automobile producers on 23 March to reduce emissions, but most of the details were still murky and mired in controversy.

In the budget the government proposed to declare greenhouse gases controlled substances that could be regulated. All three opposition parties blanched at this prospect. On 6 April the government recanted and allowed the House Finance Committee to recommend against pursuing this strategy. A more comprehensive plan was put forward on 13 April. The package contained a combination of regulatory frameworks, subsidies, and tax incentives. Spending was reframed upwards to $10 billion, with money for a $5-billion climate fund, $120 million for encouraging individuals to meet a 'one-tonne challenge' in their personal energy habits, and $3 billion for initiatives in partnership with the provinces. Reaction was mixed. Critics within the House said it was 'too late and too vague' or expressed concern about rapidly escalating costs (*Globe and Mail,* 15 Apr.).

Some environmentalists welcomed investments in alternative, renewable energy sources, but many were likewise dismayed by the desultory efforts to confer with industries on ways to cut carbon dioxide emissions. It was suggested that the plan gave a 'break for the 700 or so companies that produce nearly half of the country's greenhouse gases. Yesterday's plan calls on those companies – the so-called large final emitters – to do just 12 per cent of the job of reducing the country's greenhouse gas emissions' (*Toronto Star,* 14 Apr.). There was also alarm that environment minister David Emerson was contemplating using some of the money to purchase energy credits from countries that had exceeded their goals rather than achieving meaningful results at home. On 3 November, the province of Alberta lodged a formal action to curtail the federal government's authority.

Canada hosted a major international conference on progress towards the attainment of Kyoto objectives. Delegates from 189 countries gathered in Montreal for the United Nations Conference on Climate Change, from 28 November to 9 December. It was the eleventh meeting of its kind but the agenda took on greater urgency in light of the fact that the Kyoto protocols had come into effect in February. The agenda focused on establishing a final set of rules to govern the implementation of Kyoto and extending principles beyond the 2012 expiry date. Although a framework for verifying compliance and crediting countries was adopted on 30 November, intransigence by the United States and others threatened to scupper the effort to achieve a post-Kyoto framework. It was not until after the gavel came down that a compromise emerged. Elements of the 'Montreal Action Plan' cobbled together on 10 December included binding commitments to cut greenhouse emissions beyond 2012, when the current Kyoto Protocol expires; creation of a working group to report on progress at annual sessions of the United Nations Framework Convention on Climate Change; and seven years' grace to ratify successor agreements by 2012 (*Canadian Broadcasting Corporation,* 11 Dec.).

Personalities and controversies

Maher Arar inquiry

The Commission of Inquiry into the Actions of Canadian Officials in Relation to Maher Arar was formed in February 2004 to examine the circumstances under which a Canadian citizen was detained in New York, then sent on to Syria, where he faced incarceration and torture. The commission was asked to determine the role that Canadian officials played in Arar's mistreatment and to advise on an independent review mechanism for the Royal Canadian Mounted Police in the domain of domestic security. Hearings were presided over by Dennis O'Connor, an associate chief justice in Ontario, who had earlier headed up a provincial inquiry into the contamination of the water supply in that province's town of Walkerton.

Arar's ordeal started on 26 September 2002, when American authorities seized him from a homeward flight from Tunisia. They wrongly identified him as a terrorism suspect and, after two weeks in custody, deported him to Syria, the land of his birth. It was not until 5 October 2003 that he was permitted to return to Ottawa. While in custody, Arar was confined to inhumane quarters and subjected to torturous interrogations.

Justice O'Connor heard from eighty-five witnesses before the investigatory stage of the inquiry wound up on 14 September. The inquest was hampered by lack of cooperation from the United States and Syria and was shrouded by redacted documents and repeated applications for secrecy on the grounds of national security. A hard-pressed O'Connor was reluctant to tangle at length with the government over confidentiality matters, fearing that this would delay proceedings.

At O'Connor's behest, Professor Stephen Toope authored a twenty-seven-page factual narrative of Arar's travails, based on off-the-record interviews (27 Oct.). He had no doubt that Arar had been tortured in Syria. Calling in the Syrian ambassador, foreign minister Pierre Pettigrew demanded that his country prosecute those responsible. Toope also found that three other Canadians – Abdullah Almalki, Ahmad Abou Elmaati, and Muayyed Nureddin – were also brutalized by Syrian jailers. Arar himself continued to suffer the physical and emotional scars of his brutalization (*Globe and Mail,* 28 Oct.). O'Connor's final report was due in 2006.

The Grewal tapes

An obscure British Columbia Conservative MP, Gurmant Grewal, was at the centre of a bizarre sequence of stories that ended with his decision not to run in the 2006 election. On 6 April citizenship and immigration minister Joe Volpe referred to the ethics commissioner testimony by Grewal that he routinely asked those requesting his office's help in obtaining visas for relatives to post bonds guaranteeing their return. Grewal insisted that he did so in order to prove that a small step of this kind would cut down on spurious refugee claims and overstayed visas.

Along with his wife, Nina, also a Conservative MP, Grewal charged that the Liberals had tried to lure them into changing party affiliation or abstaining prior to critical confidence votes (19 May). Grewal said he could back up his claims and released audio tapes of conversations with Tim Murphy, the prime minister's chief of staff, and health minister Ujjal Dosanjh. Both denied offering the Grewals anything concrete but admitted holding talks. Approaches were made via telephone and three meetings were arranged between 16 and 18 May in the prime minister's suite. Liberals countered that it was Grewal who came knocking to seek protection from investigations in exchange for his defection, a version confirmed by a go-between (*Vancouver Sun,* 20 May).

Initially, only nine minutes out of four hours of recordings were made public, and they were ambiguous. In them it appeared that Grewal's price for defecting was a cabinet post, while his wife would be content with a place in the Senate. There were hints at some reward without commitment to anything concrete. When the affair surfaced, it was suggested that this matter too should be taken up by the ethics commissioner. On 31 May several spools of tape were turned over to Bernard Shapiro and the Royal Canadian Mounted Police. Grewal also released additional excerpts and transcripts.

The tapes were suspect. Experts contracted by the Canadian Press and Canadian Broadcasting Corporation detected edits in the first batch of tapes (6 June). The Conservatives were forced to admit that some segments had been excised, if only accidentally (2 June). A longer excerpt was produced, and on June 5 a new translation of a Punjabi conversation between Grewal and Dosanjh was made public. After the dust had settled, the RCMP dropped the case altogether in August.

Weeks after the first controversy erupted, Grewal announced that he was taking a 'stress leave' (6 June). This came after Air Canada confirmed that Grewal was under investigation for attempting to induce passengers on a flight from Vancouver to Ottawa to carry a package on his behalf, which would have violated security regulations. He was cleared on 17 June. The ethics commissioner exonerated Grewal on the matter of helping prospective immigrants (22 June) but advised him to stop doing so. Grewal's name surfaced again in a CBC report that some donors to his campaign had not received tax receipts and that the candidate had urged them to make cheques out to him (11 July), which would have been a criminal act. The Mounties' investigation had not ended by year's end, but Grewal declared that he would not seek re-election on 29 November.

David Dingwall and lobbying

The president of the Royal Canadian Mint, former cabinet minister David Dingwall, resigned on 28 November in the face of accusations that he had violated rules governing lobbying. Conceding that he had a 'technical compliance issue,' Dingwall rebuffed efforts by Treasury Board minister Reg Alcock to convince him to stay aboard after guiding the Mint to profitability since taking over in 2003 (*Globe and Mail,* 29 Sept.). It was yet another headache for the Liberals, heading into an election campaign during which the conduct of Chrétien-era ministers would surface on the hustings. After leaving office Dingwall had worked on behalf of two high-technology firms seeking investments from Technology Partnerships Canada. In one case he had failed to register as a lobbyist, costing his client more than $6 million. In the other he contracted for a contingency fee that was not permitted and that resulted in a loss of $15 million in funding. The furore prompted industry minister David Emerson to review other grants to determine if there had been similar transgressions (*Globe and Mail,* 29 Nov.). Conservative MPs also criticized Dingwall's office expenses. The former minister requested an exonerating audit of expenditures that the government said could be easily justified and in any event had been approved by the Crown corporation's board.

CHRISTOPHER SPEARIN[1]

Foreign affairs and defence

On the one hand, 2005 seemed to promise a reinvigoration of Canada's foreign and defence policies, as was made most clear on 19 April, when the Martin government released 'Canada's International Policy Statement: A Role of Pride and Influence in the World.' The direction outlined in this document was to counter the atrophy that many felt had afflicted Canada's international presence during the 1990s and into the new century. This would be done through an integrated approach that would mesh together, both in a holistic sense and in actual foreign activities, Canada's diplomatic, defence, development, trade, and investment strategies and capabilities. In particular, Canada's relationship with the United States would be revitalized through a renewed 'North American Partnership' that would, it was hoped, remove some of the strains that had existed between the government of Jean Chrétien and that of George W. Bush. Potentially helping this was the Bush administration's decision in April to replace its hawkish ambassador to Canada, Paul Cellucci, with David Wilkins, a somewhat more conciliatory state legislator from South Carolina.

Additionally, Canadian policymakers indicated they would funnel additional monies into focused policies to allow Canada to be more influential and effective on the international stage. This was particularly the case for defence policy, which was to be a key tool in Canada's international engagement; in the 2005 federal budget the Department of National Defence and the Canadian military received a substantial multiyear commitment valued in billions of dollars, a decision U.S. policymakers praised strongly. For defence minister Bill Graham, the government's stance suggested nothing less than a rekindling of Canadian activism: 'The Statement's policy guidance ... marks the beginning of a

1 The author would like to thank Donald Spearin for his assistance in the preparation of this chapter. Except where noted, all references are to material published in 2005.

long-term process to strengthen our military. The result will be a more relevant, responsive and effective Canadian Forces capable of meeting the increasingly complex needs of the new security environment' (DFAIT News Release 68, 19 Apr.).

On the other hand, by the end of the year, the health of the government's relationships with key constituencies necessary for effective implementation and maintenance of Canada's new international posture was harmed. Perhaps influencing most significantly the decline of these relations was the defeat of the minority Liberal government on 28 November and the subsequent election call for 23 January 2006. Most significantly, during the election campaign Prime Minister Paul Martin, despite his call for better relations with the United States, rebuked the Bush administration for its environmental policies. In response, Ambassador Wilkins's comments on 13 December were equally stark and undiplomatic: 'It may be smart election-year politics to thump your chest and constantly criticize your friend and your No. 1 trading partner. But it is a slippery slope, and all of us should hope that it doesn't have a long-term impact on the relationship' (*Globe and Mail*, 14 Dec.). Given the ongoing trade disputes and other concerns about U.S. policy, analysts such as Dr Kim Richard Nossal agreed that the prime minister's decision to bash the United States was not sound: 'it's probably pretty poor politics in the long term, simply because Bush and his administration is [*sic*] going to be in office until January 2009, which in politics is a helluva long time.... It was a sufficient cheap shot that it's unlikely that the administration in Washington is going to forget it. Then you always have to ask yourself, when is the other shoe going to fall?' (*Ottawa Citizen*, 17 Dec.). Without a doubt, 2005 closed with grave concerns about how Canada would reinvigorate its international presence and ensure a sound footing for Canada-U.S. relations should the Liberals under Prime Minister Martin be re-elected.

Foreign affairs

Human rights and poverty

Canada–Iran relations

During 2005, Canada continued its diplomatic spat with Iran. At the root of this dispute was the arrest of a photojournalist with dual Canadian and Iranian citizenship, Zahra Kazemi, on 23 June 2003. Although some Iranian officials indicated that she had suffered a stroke while in custody, the more likely story was that Kazemi was tortured and ultimately succumbed to her injuries on 12 July 2003.

As the two-year anniversary of Kazemi's death approached, Canadian officials were hopeful that Iran would accept full responsibility and bring to justice the murderer(s). Indeed, on 12 January 2005 Iranian officials indicated that an appeal regarding the Kazemi case would be heard by a court of appeal in the province of Tehran. A judge later examined the appeal behind closed doors, on 21 February. To continue the pressure on the Iranian government during this time, Canadian diplomats met with the United Nations rapporteur on violence against women in particular regard to the Kazemi case. On 14 March, foreign affairs minister Pierre Pettigrew specifically focused on the human rights situation in Iran during a speech to the United Nations Human Rights Commission in Geneva: 'Iran continues to fail to implement many of its international obligations with respect to human rights; the time has come for Iran to show its willingness to address its human rights record. The human rights violations in Iran are serious and they must stop' (DFAIT News Release 108, 15 June). Further, on 5 April Minister Pettigrew, during a telephone conversation with Iranian foreign minister Kamal Kharrazi, proposed that an independent three-party group of forensic experts conduct an autopsy on Kazemi's remains. Following this phone call, Minister Pettigrew suggested that the next move was up to Iran if normal relations were to resume between the two countries: 'The ball is now in Iran's court. Only a transparent and credible process can answer the disturbing questions that remain about Zahra Kazemi's death and the subsequent investigation' (DFAIT News Release 60, 5 Apr.). Nevertheless, Canada made one further move on 6 April, when it withdrew Canadian participation from a trade event involving Iranian businessmen.

When Iran eventually did take action, it was not to Canada's liking. On 11 April, Iranian officials rejected both the call for an independent autopsy and further investigation into the case. According to Jamal Karimirad, a spokesperson for the Iranian judiciary, the decision regarding Iranian legal jurisdiction was apt: 'Kazemi was an Iranian citizen. Although she also had Canadian nationality, under Iran's laws, an additional citizenship doesn't negate her Iranian nationality. Therefore, Iran's judiciary is competent to carry out the investigation' (*Globe and Mail,* 12 Apr.). Furthermore, Karimirad attempted to discredit Shahram Azam, a former medical doctor for the Iranian defence ministry who had indicated that he had treated Kazemi and that she had suffered various kinds of torture, including rape. For Karimirad, Azam, who had been granted refugee status in Canada and received assistance from Kazemi's family, was not reliable: 'The name of this person doesn't exist in any of the (official) documents. This person for some reason has won the confidence of the Canadian government to obtain asylum' (*Globe and Mail,* 12 Apr.). Finally, on 25 July, the Iranian judiciary terminated the appeal process launched earlier in the year.

In light of these decisions, Canada took further diplomatic steps but stopped short of recalling its ambassador to Iran or shutting down the embassy in Tehran. Several measures announced on 17 May included limiting diplomatic interaction with Iranian officials to three files: (1) the Kazemi case, (2) promoting human rights in Iran, and (3) limiting Iran's nuclear program. Cooperation on all other aspects of Canadian–Iranian relations was to be halted. Export controls were also to remain in place. Minister Pettigrew suggested that the Canadian government had to be vigilant, given the dire implications of the Kazemi case: 'Zahra Kazemi's death is far more than a consular case.... It represents a clear violation, by a state, of international human rights norms and laws. The grave circumstances of her arrest and killing have attracted sustained international attention, as well as expressions of support and solidarity in the search for justice' (DFAIT News Release 108, 15 June).

This search for justice, both direct and indirect, culminated on the international stage in two ways near the end of 2005. First, in the early fall Canada pushed hard for Iran to be censured by the International Atomic Energy Agency (IAEA) for non-compliance. In fact, Canada criticized the IAEA's board of governors for not being aggressive enough. Despite the board's reluctance, Canadian officials wanted the Iranian case to be brought to the United Nations Security Council, as required by the IAEA's statute. Second, Canada introduced a resolution in the sixtieth session of the United Nations General Assembly, co-sponsored by thirty-eight other countries and adopted on 18 November, that condemned the human rights situation in Iran. The resolution covered a number of areas: 'independence of the judiciary; intimidation and persecution of defence lawyers and legal defenders; arbitrary detentions; freedom of expression; freedom of the media; the treatment of women; the treatment of persons belonging to religious and ethnic minorities; and the execution of persons under 18 years of age' (DFAIT News Release 226, 18 Nov.).

Arar inquiry

Throughout 2005, investigations into and recriminations surrounding Maher Arar's October 2002 deportation from the United States and subsequent year-long incarceration in Syria continued. Several issues came to light during testimony presented to the Arar inquiry, which was initiated in January 2004 and led by Justice O'Connor. Some of the more than 2,300 pages of documents released by the public inquiry on 21 April pointed towards the keen interest of Canadian security officials regarding what might come out of Arar's interrogation at the hands of the Syrians. Later, in June, Canada's ambassador to Syria during Arar's captivity, Franco Pillarella, indicated that he had no proof that Arar was being harmed by Syrian authorities. This was despite the fact that the prison in which Arar was being held was notorious for its mistreatment of prisoners. Moreover, it became evident through Ambassador Pillarella's testimony that CSIS officials had travelled to Syria and, although it was never apparently operationalized, Syrian security officials had offered to involve CSIS officials in their interrogation of Arar.[2] In light of this complicity and the pain and suffering Arar had endured, Paul Heinbecker, Canada's former U.N. ambassador, accused Ambassador Pillarella of tainting Canada's entire diplomatic corps.

Other testimony revealed the actions of other Canadian officials to be equally questionable. On the one hand, on 3 June, Wayne Easter, the solicitor general while Arar was in Syria, indicated that CSIS had played no role in Arar's deportation from the United States. On the other hand, it was suggested in earlier testimony by Senator Pierre De Bané that an offer had been made to return Arar to Canada from the United States on the condition that he be kept in custody and charged, an offer that was not accepted. Moreover, on 21 May, a U.N. committee investigating the Arar case reviewed Canada's compliance with the Convention against Torture and found that Canada had erred when it let the United States deport Arar to Syria. For his part, Minister Graham, as foreign affairs minister at the time, regretted the path chosen by Canada: 'Clearly we would've preferred he'd gotten out earlier, and I'm very sorry that he was not, for obvious reasons' (Canadian Broadcasting Corporation, 2 June).

The Khadrs

The Khadrs, Canada's 'al Qaeda family,' remained in the news in 2005, with attention focused on two of the family's sons. Abdullah Khadr, the eldest son of the late Ahmed Said Khadr, an al Qaeda financier, returned to Canada on 7 December following an approximately year-long incarceration in Pakistan. A few days later, at the request of U.S.

---

2 Syria did not make similar offers to security officials from countries such as the United States, the United Kingdom, and Germany.

officials, the RCMP arrested Abdullah in Toronto on 17 December. U.S. authorities wished to bring two charges against him: 'possession and use of a destructive device to further a crime of violence and conspiracy to murder a U.S. national [i.e., U.S. soldiers] outside the United States' (Canadian Broadcasting Corporation, 18 Dec.). Abdullah's lawyer, Dennis Edney, found it suspicious that his client had been detained upon his return to Canada rather than dealt with through U.S.-Pakistani channels: 'One would have thought that, if Mr. Abdullah Khadr was the bad person they suggest he is, he would have been dealt with in Pakistan ... The Americans would have brought him over to the United States and indicted him. That didn't happen' (ibid.). On 23 December Abdullah was denied bail pending his extradition hearing, for fear that sympathizers might facilitate his escape from the country.

As for Omar Khadr, the only Canadian in U.S. custody at Guantanamo Bay, Cuba, U.S. officials announced in November that he would face a military tribunal. The charges – murder, attempted murder, and aiding the enemy – were linked to the 2002 killing in Afghanistan of Sergeant Christopher Speer and the injury of Sergeant First Class Layne Morris. It was alleged that Omar, who was fifteen at the time, had thrown a grenade during a battle in an al Qaeda compound; he was the only survivor of this attack. Omar's mother, Maha Elsamnah, contended that Canada had not done enough: 'The Canadians have not been trying anything. Ottawa is allied to the Americans, so what do you expect?' (*Toronto Star,* 9 Nov.). Issues of concern were ensuring consular visits, the right to Canadian counsel, and/or preventing Omar from being subject to the death penalty. In regard to these concerns, Dan McTeague, the parliamentary secretary for Canadians abroad, asserted that Canada had not neglected Omar's plight: 'We continue to seek firm assurances. This is not the first time – there have been meetings, of course, letters from my minister ... previous letters at high levels seeking assurances from the U.S. that Mr. Khadr, who of course was a juvenile at the time of the alleged offences, won't be subjected to the death penalty' (*Toronto Star,* 9 Nov.).

Sudan

The situation in Sudan improved somewhat in 2005, and Canada played a positive role. In Nairobi, Kenya, on 9 January, the government in Khartoum and the Sudan Liberation Movement/Army signed a peace agreement that ended the long-running conflict in the south of the country. In April, during the Oslo Conference to Consolidate Peace in Sudan, Canada pledged CDN$90 million over two years to help solidify the fledgling peace agreement. As expressed by Senator Mobina Jaffer, Canada's special envoy for peace in Sudan and its representative in Oslo, all parties, international and within Sudan, needed to step forward and take responsibility: 'the international community has come together at this critical time and has pledged significant support to help consolidate the peace in Sudan. The Government of Sudan and the SPLM/A must follow through on their stated commitment to build a sustainable peace in Sudan' (DFAIT News Release 64, 12 Apr.). As well, Canada responded to U.N. Security Council Resolution 1590, issued on 24 March, which authorized a six-month-long military and police deployment to southern Sudan. On 11 April the Department of National Defence announced Operation Safari, which would see thirty-one military personnel travel to the region to serve in the United Nations Mission in Sudan (UNMIS). Brigadier-General Greg Mitchell was to be the UNMIS deputy force commander. Minister Graham indicated that such a contribution was appropriate, given Canada's past concerns regarding conflict in Sudan and its experience with United Nations missions: 'Canada is recognized in the international community for the expertise and experience we bring to peace support operations.... Canadian Forces personnel deploying to Sudan will undoubtedly make an invaluable contribution to this important UN mission' (DND News Release 05.029, 11 Apr.).

The troubles in the Darfur region of western Sudan continued to take their toll on civilians in 2005. Since the start of hostilities in 2003, 180,000 people had lost their lives and a further two million had been displaced. On 4 April Canada contributed CDN$500,000 to the International Criminal Court (ICC) in response to U.N. Security Council Resolution 1593 (issued 31 Mar.), which referred the Darfur case to the ICC. Canada was the first country to make a voluntary contribution to this specific investigation. In July, under Operation Augural, which had been launched in 2004, the Canadian military provided the African Union Mission in Sudan (AMIS) with 105 armoured vehicles to help in its efforts. Approximately eighty military personnel travelled to the region to stage the vehicles and provide training. This operation was part of a larger CDN$170-million aid package announced by Prime Minister Martin on 12 May, meant to advance the peace process and support the efforts of AMIS. Furthermore, the prime minister formed a special advisory team, including Senator Jaffer, Ambassador Robert Fowler (the prime minister's personal representative for Africa), and Senator Roméo Dallaire, that travelled to the afflicted region. This team also provided Canadian support to the African Union–led peace talks regarding Darfur in Abuja, Nigeria.

Many prominent Canadians, such as former foreign affairs minister Lloyd Axworthy, former United Nations ambassador Paul Heinbecker, and retired Major-General Lewis MacKenzie, argued that Canada should be more assertive in Sudan, given the plight of its civilians. Senator Dallaire, however, defended Canadian policy, indicating that it was much more substantial than what he had encountered while serving as the United Nations peacekeeping commander in the midst of the Rwandan genocide: 'Canada demonstrated a leadership pledge in providing tactical and operational capabilities to the African Union in order to do the job. Everything that I was looking for 10 years ago was coming in spades with Canada leading, particularly providing one of the most significant force multipliers for the force on the ground, which is mobility and protection, that is to say helicopters and armoured vehicles' (*National Post,* 16 June). As well, allowing Africans to take the lead on regional problems was something African leaders had been wanting since the 1990s, and it was an aspect agreed to by the G8 during their 2002 summit in Kananaskis, Alberta. Ambassador Fowler made it plain that Canadian policy was in keeping with this stance: 'During the four years in which I have acted as the Prime Minister's personal representative for Africa, Africans have made it excruciatingly clear to me that they are determined to be responsible for managing threats to peace and security in Africa. Put bluntly, they don't want western soldiers imposing, yet again, their peace on Africa. They have, however, asked for our assistance, and they're getting it' (*Globe and Mail,* 17 June).

Another factor to note is that Canadian governmental activism on the Sudan file occurred in the context of a Liberal minority in the House of Commons. David Kilgour had been a Liberal member of Parliament for Edmonton for approximately fifteen years, but in April he chose to leave the party and sit as an independent. This decision, which meant that he and a small handful of other independent members of Parliament held the balance of power in the midst of votes of confidence, had been spurred by a number of factors. With respect to Sudan, Kilgour argued that '[t]he Prime Minister's refusal to do anything substantive was the straw that broke my Liberal camel's back' (*National Post,* 19 Apr.).[3] When Prime Minister Martin personally met with Kilgour and Canadian policies were subsequently introduced in the wake of Kilgour's decision, charges of the prime minister's cynically clinging to power were forthcoming. Senator Dallaire, however, was quick to defend the prime

---

3 Kilgour had previously served as a secretary of state for Africa.

minister and indicate the merits of the Canadian position: 'I think that would be a real perverse statement to say that because of the complexity of the situation in Parliament that that might be a catalyst for (helping in) Darfur ... You'd really have to be warped to think of some link like that' (*Ottawa Citizen,* 5 May).

G8 summit

In the lead-up to their July summit at Gleneagles, Scotland, G8 leaders worked to dispel the notion that they were indifferent to global poverty. Although past annual G8 summits had resulted in declarations and common approaches towards increasing aid, especially to Africa, actual resulting policies and commitment of funds were not as ambitious. Moreover, the international Live 8 concerts, meant to place pressure on G8 leaders, were scheduled on 2 July, a few days before the start of the summit. On 11 June, in order to ensure a positive lead-in to the summit, the leaders decided to write off the debt owed by the world's eighteen poorest states.

By the summit's end, the G8 leaders had agreed to a communiqué with considerable scope. To indicate further the group's resolve, the summit's host, Prime Minister Tony Blair, insisted that the leaders sign the communiqué, an unusual step in G8 diplomacy. In this communiqué the leaders agreed to increase aid specifically to Africa by US$25 billion a year by 2010. In total, the world's poor countries would receive US$50 billion by the 2010 benchmark. Additional plans were put in place to counter HIV/AIDS and malaria in the developing world. Another measure was a US$3-billion aid package to assist the struggling Palestinian economy.[4]

Likely more than one catalyst contributed to this increased G8 activism. From one standpoint, Sir Bob Geldof, one of the Live 8 organizers, was convinced that public exposure of the issue to those who either attended the concerts or watched them on television or the Internet was key: 'Africa and the poor of that continent have got more out of the last three days than they have ever got in any previous summit. They got that because 3 billion people demanded that it should be so' (*Toronto Star,* 9 July). From another standpoint, using aid to address the underlying

---

4 Success, however, was not achieved with respect to reducing farm subsidies and import barriers in G8 countries that limited the competitiveness of developing-world agricultural products. Similarly, although President Bush agreed that global warming was the result of human activity, the G8 did not develop a common approach on climate change.

reasons for terrorism was important, especially in light of the terrorist attacks against London's transportation system that occurred during the summit, claiming the lives of fifty people. Prime Minister Blair suggested that the G8's approach was one step towards countering the threat of terrorism: 'There is no hope in terrorism nor any future in it worth living and it is hope that is the alternative to this hatred. So, we offer today this contrast with the politics of terror' (*Victoria Times-Colonist,* 9 July).

Despite the increased G8 attention and determination, Prime Minister Martin was singled out for criticism. Sir Bob Geldof and Bono, lead singer of the rock band U2 and a co-organizer of the Live 8 Summit, were involved in the summit's proceedings in order to maintain publicity and pressure. Although Bono had, in fact, provided a celebrity endorsement to Prime Minister Martin's candidacy for Liberal Party leader in 2003, he was upset that the prime minister had not committed Canada to contributing 0.7 per cent of its gross national product to aid by 2015: 'No, I'm not satisfied and I'm gonna kick his butt ... I think he made a mistake ... Canada has lost its chance to lead' (*Toronto Star,* 9 July). Although Prime Minister Martin was sympathetic to Bono's pleas, he felt it irresponsible to make a such a dramatic policy leap that might be nothing but a hollow gesture in the end: 'We will ultimately (reach) the 0.7 (level) but we're not going to do it ... until we can basically say to Canadians: "Here's how we're doing it, here's when we're going to do it and there's no caveats, no conditions, we're just doing it"' (*Halifax Daily News,* 7 July).

Kidnappings in Iraq

On 26 November, four members of Christian Peacemaker Teams (CPT) – a Briton, an American, and two Canadians – were kidnapped in Baghdad, Iraq. The CPT had a mandate to reduce violence the world over; it had in the past monitored elections in Iraq and provided advocacy for Iraqis detained in the Abu Ghraib prison. Despite these credentials, the kidnappers – a group named the Swords of Righteous Freedom – accused the CPT workers of being spies and conditioned their freedom on the release of all Iraqi detainees by 8 December. Otherwise, the group threatened that it would execute the four Westerners.[5] For its part, the CPT indicated that the kidnapping of its workers could be directly linked to U.S. and British policy: 'We are angry because what has happened to our teammates is the result of the actions of the

---

5 In the eighteen months prior to the kidnapping of the four CPT workers, two hundred foreigners had been kidnapped in Iraq. The kidnappers killed thirty-eight of these foreigners.

U.S. and U.K. governments due to the illegal attack on Iraq and the continuing occupation and oppression of its people' (Canadian Broadcasting Corporation, 30 Nov.).

On a number of occasions the kidnappers released footage that suggested that the two Canadians, Harmeet Singh Sooden and James Loney, were receiving better treatment than the other captives, perhaps a reflection of Canada's decision not to join the U.S.-led 'coalition of the willing' in Iraq. The Briton and the American, Norman Kember and Tom Fox, appeared in jumpsuits and shackles, whereas the Canadians had not received similar treatment (at least in the footage released).

Throughout December the kidnappers extended their deadline on several occasions, arguably due to pressure and advocacy from a number of parties. Prime Minister Martin, for instance, indicated that Canada would follow all avenues, formal and informal, to ensure the safety of the Canadians and their fellow CPT members: 'I want you to know that there is no more urgent issue than ensuring the safety of our citizens' (Canadian Broadcasting Corporation, 29 Nov.). The families of the kidnapped CPT workers released public statements pleading for their loved ones' safe return. The Canadian Islamic Congress sent an envoy, Ehab Lotayef, to Baghdad to help secure their release. Muslim scholars and antiwar activists also called for their release; in light of the CPT's past advocacy of human rights and its support for aggrieved Muslim populations, even Hamas and Hezbollah joined the call for the workers to be set free. Similarly, because three of the four CPT members had previously worked in the West Bank in support of Palestinian causes, Palestinian activists demanded their release as well. Nevertheless, in spite of this wide-ranging and somewhat surprising activism, the fate of the four kidnapped CPT workers remained in the hands of the Swords of Righteous Freedom at the year's end.

Challenges in Canada–U.S. trade

Beef

On 29 December 2004, the United States named Canada as a 'minimal-risk region' for bovine spongiform encephalopathy (BSE), or 'mad cow disease.' The United States was again to receive imports of Canadian beef on 7 March, thus terminating restrictions that had cost the Canadian beef industry approximately CDN$5 billion since May 2003. However, another BSE-positive cow was discovered in Canada on 3 January 2005, which was followed in early March by a temporary injunction to prevent reopening of the American border to Canadian live beef. This injunction was put in place at the request of R-CALF, a group of U.S. ranchers concerned that a reopened border would cause significant harm to the U.S. beef industry. To help soften the blow for Canadian ranchers, the federal government initiated a CDN$321-million financial assistance plan on 29 March. The prospects of Canadian beef exporters brightened, however, on 14 July, when the U.S. Ninth Circuit Court of Appeal overturned the injunction. As a result, U.S. agriculture secretary Mike Johanns indicated that the border would open 'immediately' to receive Canadian beef imports (Canadian Broadcasting Corporation, 15 July).

Swine

In 2005 Canada continued its battle with the United States regarding the latter's quest to impose and/or maintain countervailing and anti-dumping duties against Canadian live swine exports. At the heart of this U.S. pressure was the 5 March 2004 decision of the National Pork Producers Council to request U.S. investigation into Canadian swine export policies. On 7 March 2005 the U.S. Department of Commerce (DOC) announced that Canadian swine were indeed not unfairly subsidized. Although this meant that Canada's swine exports were not countervailable, the United States nevertheless kept in place anti-dumping duties that had been set following a preliminary finding made on 15 October 2004. Given that the duties threatened as many as 15,000 Canadian pork producers, international trade minister Jim Peterson made it clear that Canadian policymakers would not rest until Canada was completely cleared of charges relating to unfair trading practices: 'The subsidy decision shows that Canadian live swine are traded fairly.... We will keep working with the Canadian industry to prove there is no injury and to show that the provisional anti-dumping duties should be dropped' (DFAIT News Release 41, 7 March). Relief finally came on 6 April, when the U.S. International Trade Commission reversed the earlier decisions, thus terminating the collection of anti-dumping duties. In light of this relief, predictions were that U.S. imports of hogs and pigs from Canada might increase by 200,000 from 2004 totals.

Wheat

In response to the U.S. imposition of duties in March 2003, Canadian policymakers continued in 2005 to argue that Canada was a fair trader with respect to wheat, and especially in terms of hard red spring wheat. A partial victory came on 11 March 2005, when a NAFTA panel determined that the DOC countervail determination on hard red spring wheat was not in keeping with U.S. law. The DOC had lumped together three separate Canadian government programs under one determination, when each program should have been dealt with individually. The same panel also found, however, that the DOC did have the right to be concerned about government-owned and -leased rail cars used by the wheat industry, despite protestations made by transport minister Jean-C. Lapierre: 'Our position remains that the use of government-owned hopper cars for the movement of grain to the United States does not distort bilateral trade' (DFAIT News Release 43, 11 Mar.).

Despite this setback, further victories for Canadian wheat exporters followed later in the year. On 7 June, a NAFTA panel decided that the U.S. International Trade Commission had not demonstrated that Canadian hard red spring wheat imports were causing damage to U.S. producers. On 9 August the DOC responded to the March 2005 determination by indicating that two of the three Canadian programs were countervailable. Because one program – Canada's lending guarantee – was not, duty rates fell from 5.29 per cent to 2.54 per cent. Finally, on 5 October, the ITC responded to the June decision by confirming that there was indeed no injury. This was excellent news for Andy Mitchell, Canada's agriculture and agri-food minister: 'This is a clear victory for Canadian wheat farmers ... The ITC determination on remand should put to rest the unwarranted allegations of the past decade concerning the Canadian Wheat Board' (DFAIT News Release 176, 5 Oct.). Although the North Dakota Wheat Commission challenged the ITC's finding the week after its release, a NAFTA panel rejected the appeal in mid-December. Canadian wheat exports to the United States were likely to enter duty-free in the new year.

Softwood lumber

Even with a number of legal victories during the course of 2005, Canadian policymakers and softwood lumber producers did not receive the satisfaction they sought: removal of all duties and tariffs and the return of the CDN$5 billion that had accrued in the U.S. Treasury since the dispute's start in 2001. With respect to the World Trade Organization (WTO), a compliance panel decided on 1 August that the U.S. position regarding countervailing duties was inconsistent with WTO obligations, thus supporting previous determinations made by the world body. This decision was reinforced by a WTO appellate body that came to a similar conclusion on 5 December. Canada also requested permission from the WTO to retaliate against the United States at a level of approximately CDN$4.1 billion.

With respect to NAFTA, 2005 saw the NAFTA panel and the DOC go back and forth as NAFTA issued its third, fourth, and fifth reports since the dispute's start, demanding that the DOC determinations be consistent with U.S. law; the DOC responded with determinations that were still not consistent. Moreover, on 10 August, the NAFTA Extraordinary Challenge Committee rejected U.S. claims that Canadian softwood lumber threatened to injure U.S. producers. Such a determination should have led to immediate withdrawal of tariffs and duties and the return of monies collected from Canadian producers.

As the year progressed, positions continued to harden on both sides. To Canadian policymakers, the à la carte free trade seemingly being practised by the United States was unscrupulous. Prime Minister Martin described the U.S. decision not to follow through on its NAFTA obligations as ' ... nonsense. More than that, it's a breach of faith. Countries must live up to their agreements' (Canadian Broadcasting Corporation, 20 Oct.). This line was supported by Minister Peterson: 'It is up to the U.S. to show that the institution of NAFTA means something.... Rules are rules, you can't just pick and choose' (DFAIT News Release 200, 28 Oct.). As for U.S. policymakers, they continued to assert their desire for a negotiated solution rather than one determined by legal tribunals and trade panels. This approach was evident in comments made by Robert Portman, the U.S. trade representative: 'This has been litigated to death ... and it's probably time to sit down in a serious way and determine how we can resolve our differences in a way that is long lasting' (Canadian Broadcasting Corporation, 20 Oct.).

Byrd Amendment

In April 2005, Canada finally acted on its long-running threat of trade retaliation against the United States in regards to the *Continued Dumping and Subsidy Offset Act* of 2000, otherwise known as the Byrd Amendment. This law gave U.S. producers double incentive to hit their foreign competitors with anti-dumping charges and anti-subsidy duties. Not only would these competitors suffer the results of U.S. trade restrictions, the duties collected could be distributed amongst U.S. producers. In 2003 the WTO deemed the law illegal and gave the United States until December 2003 to repeal it. When it failed to do so, Canada, along with seven other WTO members, asked the world body for permission to impose retaliatory measures. When Canada did eventually retaliate, it targeted states whose federal legislators supported the Byrd Amendment. Thus, effective 1 May, 15 per cent duties were levelled against live swine (Kentucky), cigarettes (North Carolina), and certain types of seafood (Pennsylvania and Washington State). These duties, valued at CDN$14 million, were set to expire in April 2006.

By the end of 2005, it appeared that the law's termination was in sight. Both the U.S. House of Representatives and the U.S. Senate passed bills that would end it. All that was left was for the two bills to be reconciled and for President Bush to sign the change into law in the new year. On the one hand, for some Canadians, the decision was not entirely satisfactory because companies could still be eligible to receive 'Byrd money' until 1 October 2007. Moreover, the decision left unaddressed the aforementioned CDN$5 billion in duties on softwood lumber collected by the U.S. Treasury. At that time the amount of money dispersed to U.S. softwood lumber producers had been relatively small: between US$2.5 million and US$9.5 million annually. Therefore, as indicated by Minister Peterson, continued vigilance was required: 'We strongly maintain that the Byrd should be eliminated immediately ... The WTO ruling was clear: Disbursements of money under Byrd are illegal. The world continues to watch' (*Globe and Mail,* 26 Dec.). On the other hand, Senator Robert Byrd of West Virginia was convinced that the lawmakers in Washington had betrayed U.S. workers: 'They stand with foreign trade bureaucrats and not with the working people of this country who suffer from illegal foreign trade' (*Globe and Mail,* 22 Dec.).

Newfoundland and Labrador and the rocket controversy

In April, Premier Danny Williams of Newfoundland and Labrador instigated a spat between the United States and Canada. The U.S. Air Force Space Command had planned to launch a Titan IVB rocket that would put into orbit an intelligence-gathering satellite to be used by the U.S. National Reconnaissance Office. Premier Williams was concerned that one of the rocket's two 10,000-kilogram booster engines might hit the Hibernia, Terra Nova, or White Rose offshore oil platform. Whereas it is common practice to warn shipping not to enter a certain area when there is potential for impact, oil platforms, because of their stationary nature, pose more of a challenge. The Hibernia platform, for instance, was located less than two kilometres from the designated hazard zone. Premier

Williams indicated that unless he could receive a guarantee that a platform would not be hit, he was prepared to evacuate the facilities, a decision that would have cost the provincial economy more than CDN$250 million. In fact, the Canada-Newfoundland Offshore Petroleum Board had already begun plans to evacuate the 325 crew members on board.

The dispute brought about fissures in the positions of both the United States and Canada. Although the launch was delayed on several occasions, the U.S. Air Force indicated that this was for technical reasons unrelated to the controversy. Minister Graham, however, was not so sure: 'I believe our representations had something to do with them putting off the launch' (*Charlottetown Guardian,* 30 Apr.). As for Canada, Minister Graham came to the premier's aid. He expressed his concerns regarding the economic and environmental damage that could be inflicted should an oil platform be damaged: 'We do not want any risk whatsoever, not a scintilla of risk ... Frankly, I think the Americans would be well advised to know that they can't afford to have that happen either' (*Charlottetown Guardian,* 30 Apr.). However, the U.S. Air Force Space Command indicated that the chance of a facility's being hit was one in a trillion. In this vein, a spokesperson for public safety minister Anne McLellan went further, indicating that the risk was one in ten trillion, thus putting her at odds with Minister Graham. Nevertheless, Premier Williams wanted 100 per cent certainty as the bottom line: 'They've said one million to one, a hundred million to one, 10 trillion to one – it's the one that's the important number' (*Halifax Herald,* 11 Apr.).

Eventually the U.S. Air Force launched the rocket from Cape Canaveral on 29 April, but not before Premier Williams had received satisfaction. This came through a letter from Minister McLellan indicating that the U.S. Air Force was prepared to destroy the rocket should it in any way deviate from its intended trajectory. For Premier Williams this was the necessary guarantee to ensure that oil extraction operations would not be interrupted: 'After extensive efforts, I am relieved and satisfied that we have been successful in getting the assurances required to ensure the safety of workers on those vessels' (*Vancouver Sun,* 15 Apr.).

Economic integration

On 23 March, the 'three amigos' – President Bush, Prime Minister Martin, and Mexican President Vicente Fox – met for a one-day summit to discuss continental relations. The meetings were held first at Baylor University in Waco, Texas, and later at President Bush's ranch in nearby Crawford. By the end of the day the three leaders had agreed on a 'Security and Prosperity Partnership for North America.' This partnership, basically a working plan for the future, covered several facets: emergency response, intelligence sharing, energy policy, border protection, air and water quality, protection of food and agricultural systems, movement of people and goods across borders, counter-disease initiatives, organized crime, maritime and aviation safety, and drug smuggling. As part of the partnership, officials in each country were to report back in 90 days on relevant activities, followed by later reports every six months. The rationale for the partnership rested in countering the growing economic giants in other parts of the world through streamlining, common standards, and reduction of red tape. For Prime Minister Martin, the three North American countries had to work together to ensure their continued economic growth and welfare: 'There is no doubt there is a recognition that the changes occurring in the global economy as a result of the rapid growth we're seeing in China, to be followed very quickly, in fact already by India, is going to change the nature of the world's economy ... The desire to make North America as competitive as possible ... is certainly an important force behind this' (*Toronto Star,* 24 Mar.).

Despite its considerable breadth, the partnership was not a step towards further integration in North America along the lines of the European Union. Before the trilateral summit, a U.S.-Canada business panel released a report that called for wide-ranging integration.[6] The partnership, however, did not include elements such as a common currency or customs union for the continent, nor did it embrace the notion of a 'Fortress America.' While Prime Minister Martin wished to stress that continental relations had been advanced considerably, he made it plain that the major qualitative step of deep integration was not in the offing: 'Are we going to move towards an arrangement that is going to give us much greater security ... make our respective economies much stronger ... absolutely. What we're looking for is not a big bang, but big progress' (*Vancouver Sun,* 24 Mar.).

The summit was also seen as an opportunity to put U.S.-Canada relations on a better footing in light of ongoing trade disputes and the Martin government's decision (see below) not to endorse the U.S. Ballistic Missile Defence system. President Bush, for instance, stressed that differences were to be expected but that differences were not to preclude advancement on other files: 'I don't know if you'd characterize them as differences that would then prevent us from finding common ground ... I don't view it that way. I understand why people disagree with certain decisions I have made, but that doesn't prevent us from

6 The head of this panel was John Manley, the former deputy prime minister.

co-operating' (*Vancouver Sun*, 24 Mar.). Prime Minister Martin too went out of his way to downplay divisions that could potentially overshadow the achievement inherent in the partnership: 'On BMD (ballistic missile defence), the file is closed, but our co-operation in terms of defence, in terms of our borders ... is being accentuated ... Our relationships are very, very strong. Are there differences in opinion? There have been throughout our history and there will be in the future' (*Vancouver Sun*, 24 Mar.). Certainly, the mere fact that Prime Minister Martin was invited to the president's ranch was considered a coup.[7] Nevertheless, by the summit's end, irritants such as softwood lumber, Canadian beef exports, and U.S. undermining of NAFTA's dispute-resolution mechanisms remained unresolved.

Global warming

During the course of 2005, Canada's commitment towards global warming arguably wavered. On 16 February, the 1997 Kyoto Protocol, designed to reduce the world's greenhouse gas emissions, came into effect following the necessary number of international ratifications.[8] As part of its Kyoto obligations, Canada had agreed to reduce its greenhouse gas emissions by 6 per cent from 1990 levels by 2008–12. However, although Canada had released a plan for emission targets for different sectors in 2002, by 2005 those targets had been scaled back for large Canadian industrial polluters. While the initial plan called for these polluters to cut back by 55 megatonnes in order to reach the overall national goal of 240 megatonnes, the revised plans called for reductions of only 40–45 megatonnes. The government revised these numbers in face of opposition from Alberta, the province that would have been particularly hard hit because of its reliance upon oil and gas revenues. In fact, Alberta devised a special agreement with Ottawa that would allow it to maintain control over environmental rules that would affect the province. Additionally, because the United States had not signed the Kyoto Protocol, other Canadian industries feared they would face double the detrimental impact of Canada's Kyoto commitments because they would be increasingly uncompetitive vis-à-vis their

---

7 Given the tensions that existed earlier between the United States and Canada, Prime Minister Chrétien had never received such an invitation.
8 The Kyoto Protocol's implementation mechanism was based on meeting a threshold of countries that produced 55 per cent of the world's greenhouse gas emissions ratifying the treaty, which was met upon Russia's ratification.

U.S. counterparts. Moreover, other countries with large and expanding economies, such as China and India, were exempt because of their developing-world status.

Despite this apparent backtracking, Canada remained at the centre of the global endeavour to reduce greenhouse gas emissions, hosting the Montreal Climate Change Conference from 28 November to 9 December. This conference, organized by the United Nations Convention for Climate Change, was meant to look at the necessary steps beyond the Kyoto Protocol once it expired in 2012. While it was heartening to see 190 countries participating in the convention – many more than the 146 countries that had signed the Kyoto Protocol – the delegates were nevertheless unsure as to the next step to take. It was only after late-night negotiations that they devised the so-called 'Montreal Action Plan.' This plan included several features: (1) Countries, such as the United States and Australia, that had not ratified the Kyoto Protocol agreed to participate in the talks that would eventually lead to the protocol's replacement; (2) a call was made for binding commitments beyond 2012; and (3) a seven-year negotiation and ratification period would follow 2012. While there was some criticism that the plan was not as beneficial as it might be, Canada's environment minister, Stéphane Dion, who served as the conference's host, felt that it was an adequate step towards the future: 'I don't think there is any weakness in the wording ... It's what it's supposed to be. It's a dialogue, which will free the imagination' (Canadian Broadcasting Corporation, 10 Dec.). To help implement the Montreal Action Plan, officials were to meet in May 2006 in order to plot the next stages.

China and spying

The year 2005 started on a positive note for Canada-China relations, with a successful trade mission to China led by federal government officials, the prime minister included. During the course of the meetings that took place between 18 and 25 January, representatives from 280 Canadian companies interacted with Chinese government and business officials. By the end of the mission, more than a hundred agreements had been signed. Minister Peterson reflected upon the significance of these arrangements: 'With China redefining global trade, a China business plan is no longer an option for Canadian companies; it's a must' (DFAIT News Release 16, 25 Jan.).

Despite the seemingly good relations inherent in these business ventures, Canada's rapport with China soured somewhat in June, when two

Chinese officials seeking asylum in Australia indicated that a thousand Chinese spies were active in Canada. Chen Yongleen, first secretary of the Chinese consulate in Sydney, and Hao Fengjing, an intelligence officer in the Chinese Public Security Bureau, said that Chinese spies and informants, who ranged from state officials to businesspeople to students, were monitoring members of the outlawed Falun Gong movement and/or conducting industrial and scientific espionage. The allegations suggested that Canada was home base to more Chinese spies than the United States, New Zealand, or Australia.

Responses to these allegations were varied. Chinese officials contended that the assertions were false, made by individuals desperate to receive asylum status. Canadian security officials suggested that the allegations were nothing new. An earlier joint study – Operation Sidewinder – conducted by the RCMP and CSIS in 1997 estimated that 200 Canadian companies had been purchased by buyers with links to Chinese intelligence agencies, criminal elements, and/or Hong Kong–based tycoons. Similar concerns were linked to the ultimately unsuccessful 2004 attempt by China Minmetals Corporation to take over Noranda Inc., a Canadian metals producer. Moreover, the allegations of Chinese spying substantiated reported threats made against people living in Canada. The government too wished to stress its continued diligence. Prime Minister Martin, for instance, indicated that he had raised the issue of spying during his visit to China in January: 'I dealt extensively with Canada's interests. I dealt extensively with Canada's sovereignty and the need to respect state sovereignty between countries' (*Globe and Mail,* 17 June). To reinforce this diligence, in June the government unveiled plans to give it the right to prevent foreign takeovers valued at less than CDN$250 million (regulations at the time allowed for government intervention only above this amount).

Disaster response

Asian tsunami

Following the Asian tsunami that occurred on 26 December 2004, the government received considerable criticism related to its response, or lack thereof. Key government officials, the prime minister included, were away from Ottawa when the disaster occurred and were seemingly disengaged and slow to return to the capital. Canadian embassy officials in the numerous countries devastated by the Asian tsunami were criticized for being either unhelpful or under-resourced. Although the Canadian military's Disaster Area Response Team (DART) was capable of deploying seventy-two hours after an event, no authorization was forthcoming. The resulting accusation was that the DART was simply a paper tiger, since it had been deployed only twice since its creation following the Rwandan genocide.[9]

Nevertheless, as 2005 started, Canadian initiatives to help those affected in the disaster region were in full swing. The government eventually deployed the DART on the basis of a recommendation from the seventeen-member Interdepartmental Reconnaissance Team sent to the region on 30 December 2004. On 2 January, Prime Minister Martin announced that the 200-strong DART would be sent to the Ampara region in Sri Lanka as part of Operation Structure. Although the region's population had certainly suffered the effects of the natural disaster – 10,000 people had died and a further 150,000 were left homeless – concern was raised about the safety of the DART personnel, given that the region had earlier been a location of fighting between Sri Lankan government forces and the Tamil Tigers. Nevertheless, Prime Minister Martin was satisfied, as he had received assurances of the DART's safety. Moreover, he wished to assure Canadians and Sri Lankans alike that despite the turmoil in the country, Canadian assistance would be even-handed: 'We will not accept that Canadian aid is not distributed equitably' (Canadian Broadcasting Corporation, 4 Jan.).

DART personnel began to leave for Sri Lanka shortly thereafter, with the last wave arriving in Ampara on 10 January. During the operation the DART carried out several activities, including medical treatment of more than 7,500 people, production of 3.5 million litres of drinking water, and construction and rebuilding of schools and shelters. The DART's activities were withdrawn slowly, such that by 26 February its main contingent had returned to Canada. For Minister Graham, Operation Structure was a mission well accomplished: 'DART members did outstanding work to help the region recover from this terrible tragedy ... Our professional and caring soldiers have made a difference in the lives of thousands of Sri Lankans. Canadians can be proud of their accomplishments' (DFAIT News Release 26, 7 Feb.).

Canadian activism on a number of other fronts was also forthcoming. The prime minister travelled to countries in the disaster region, a journey

9 Canada sent the DART to Honduras following Hurricane Mitch in 1998 and then to Turkey in 1999 in response to an earthquake.

that included time with the DART in Sri Lanka. Canada sent ten RCMP forensic experts to Thailand to identify the remains of tourists killed by the tsunami, Canadians included. On 3 January the federal cabinet voted to double Canada's aid from CDN$40 million to CDN$80 million. Later, additional funding was forthcoming, so that by February Canadian donations, public and private alike, tallied CDN$425 million, to be dispersed over five years. Finally, during the 18–22 January World Conference on Disaster Reduction in Kobe, Japan, the Canadian delegation announced that CDN$1 million would be given to the United Nations Development Programme for disaster reduction efforts, and that the International Federation of Red Cross and Red Crescent Societies would receive CDN$1 million to develop its disaster-preparedness capabilities.

Hurricane Katrina

In the aftermath of Hurricane Katrina's hitting the U.S. Gulf Coast on 29 August, leaving more than one million people stranded and five million without power, the Canadian response took a variety of forms. Because of the severe damage caused to U.S. oil infrastructure along the coast, the Canadian government agreed to pump 91,000 barrels of crude oil across the border daily in order to compensate for U.S. fuel shortages. On 2 September the Canadian military flew Red Cross and Foreign Affairs officials to the region, and this was followed by an Air Canada flight on 3 September that brought in relief supplies. The Air Canada craft remained in the region to offer evacuation flights to Texas. Additionally, in order to fill in the coverage gap left when U.S. Coast Guard helicopters were sent to the devastated region, Canada sent two military search-and-rescue helicopters to Cape Cod, Massachusetts. The Bell CH-146 Griffons, one from CFB Goose Bay and one from CFB Bagotville, arrived in the United States on 4 September, returning to their home bases on 12 September.

The largest Canadian contribution to the recovery effort was Operation Unison 2005. The first wave of this operation sent to the region consisted of navy diving teams based at CFB Halifax and CFB Esquimalt and army engineer divers from CFB Gagetown. By 5 September the divers were in the affected region; their responsibility was to assist U.S. officials in conducting underwater surveys, removing hazards, and recovering bodies. The operation's largest component was Task Force 306, an ad hoc grouping of four ships: the destroyer HMCS *Athabasca* (the command ship), the frigates HMCS *Ville de Québec* and HMCS *Toronto,* and a buoy-finder from the Canadian Coast Guard, *Sir William*

Alexander.[10] On 6 September the ships, with a complement of approximately 1,000 military and Coast Guard personnel, departed Halifax loaded down with a variety of humanitarian and relief supplies, including fresh water, tents, food, and blankets. Although the task force was put together at very short notice, a navy spokesman was confident about its efforts: 'We had five days and it certainly wasn't easy ... The dockyard's been full of activity ... But the difficult is what we do' (*National Post,* 6 Sept.).

A number of officials, including Prime Minister Martin and U.S. ambassador Wilkins, were pier-side in Halifax to see off the departing task force. In their remarks, both the prime minister and the ambassador were keen to point out the good neighbourliness of the Canadian response. For the prime minister, 'Canada was built by neighbours helping neighbours in times of crisis and that doesn't only apply within our borders' (*Globe and Mail,* 7 Sept.). Ambassador Wilkins wished to stress the parallels between this Canadian response and that which occurred in the wake of the terrorist attacks on 11 September 2001: 'once again Canada is coming to our rescue early and eagerly ... What you are doing today, ladies and gentlemen, is important. You are saving lives' (*Globe and Mail,* 7 Sept.).

On 12 September, the three naval ships arrived in the region after completing the 4,000-kilometre journey, followed by the Coast Guard vessel on 14 September. After dropping off supplies at Pensacola, Florida, the naval ships travelled to the waters off Gulfport, Louisiana, and Biloxi, Mississippi. There they disembarked navy and army engineers and joined the emergency relief flotilla, which was some thirty-five vessels strong, including ships from the U.S. Navy, the U.S. Coast Guard, and commercial firms. On 19 September Canadian officials ordered the three naval ships to return home. The military divers and the Coast Guard vessel remained in the region for a longer period.

Earthquake in Pakistan

On 8 October a massive earthquake, registering 7.6 on the Richter scale, struck South Asia, with its epicentre close to Muzaffarabad, Pakistan. This earthquake resulted in the deaths of approximately 86,000 people in India and Pakistan and left many more in need of assistance. In response to a request from the Pakistani government, on 11 October Canada sent a contingent of Foreign Affairs diplomats, aid officials,

10 The task force also included three Sea King helicopters.

and military personnel to the region to assess how Canada might best assist. The resulting determination led to Canada's launching Operation Plateau on 14 October, which at its heart was a DART mission. The first contingent of the 200-strong team arrived in Pakistan on 16 October, and by 23 October the DART was deemed fully operational. Transferring the DART in such a timely manner required several flights by a chartered Antonov AN-225 Mriya, the world's largest cargo aircraft, which operated out of CFB Trenton.

The DART's main responsibilities were threefold: (1) to offer medical assistance in a static clinic located in Gahri Dupatta (15 kilometres from Muzaffarabad), (2) to operate mobile medical clinics in the surrounding region, and (3) to employ reverse-osmosis water purification units to make drinking water available.[11] During the course of Operation Plateau, the DART delivered roughly 500 tonnes of humanitarian supplies, treated 12,000 people, and purified and distributed four million litres of drinking water. By late November the DART had started to wrap up its operations, with tasks being transferred to the International Committee of the Red Cross, the Pakistan Red Crescent Society, and the international NGO Oxfam. By 9 December all of the DART personnel had returned to Canada.

Defence policy

Afghanistan

Military operations

The Canadian military's presence in Afghanistan continued to evolve in 2005. In the spring the government announced that Canadian Forces Base Julien, located in Kabul, was scheduled to close. In August 2004, as part of Operation Athena, Canada reduced its troop contribution to NATO's International Security Assistance Force (ISAF) to 900 individuals from the August 2003 high of 2,000. By the time control of Camp Julien was transferred to the Afghan government, approximately 6,000 Canadians had been deployed there.

The closure of Camp Julien was part of a larger shift towards operations in the Kandahar region. One reason for this shift was the transfer of a Provincial Reconstruction Team (PRT) in the region under U.S.

---

11 At the same time (28 Oct.), the federal government sent one of the military's water purification units to the Kashechewan Reserve in northern Ontario in order to deal with the deteriorating conditions on the reserve.

control to NATO, and thus to Canada. Canada officially took over on 16 August, with an eighteen-month mandate to extend the control of the Afghan government. The PRT was representative of the 'whole-of-government' approach detailed in the government's international policy statement. The PRT included participation of several organizations: the Canadian military, Foreign Affairs Canada, the Canadian International Development Agency (CIDA), and the RCMP. Minister Graham hailed Canada's leadership and the benefits Canada could bring by having numerous government agencies acting in concert: 'This commitment is consistent with our new international and defence policies, which demonstrate Canada's emphasis on bringing stability and humanitarian relief to fragile states.... With this commitment, Canada is assuming a leadership role in paving the way for a secure, democratic and self-sustaining Afghanistan' (DND News Release 05.035, 16 May). The second reason for the shift was to facilitate an increased buildup of NATO's presence in and around Kandahar. By February 2006 approximately 2,000 Canadian soldiers, as part of Task Force Kandahar, were to be deployed in the region in order to counter any resurgence by the Taliban. Canadian Brigadier-General David Fraser was slated to command the multinational brigade in Regional Command South. The brigade headquarters was to remain in place for nine months and the army task force for twelve months.

As the Canadian military began to increase its presence in southern Afghanistan, tragedy struck when a LAV III, a lightly armoured vehicle, rolled over in a single-vehicle accident on 24 November. At the time the LAV III was on the main highway linking Kabul and Kandahar. Private Braun Scott Woodfield of Eastern Passage, Nova Scotia, died in the accident and four other soldiers were injured. While government and military officials were quick to offer their condolences, media investigations determined that the army had been warned previously about the proclivity of the LAV III to roll over. There had been ten previous rollovers, some involving fatalities. Retired Major-General Lewis MacKenzie, however, was quick to defend the merits of the LAV III: 'They're an outstanding vehicle made in London, Ontario, with a good weapons system on them, so I doubt very much if there was any problem with the vehicle' (CTV.ca, 25 Nov.).

Friendly-fire incident

On 23 May four Canadian soldiers, the first to have been killed in a combat zone since the Korean War, were recognized by the U.S. military in a unique ceremony at Fort Campbell, Kentucky. Corporal

Ainsworth Dyer, Sergeant Marc Leger, Private Richard Green, and Private Nathan Smith died in Afghanistan on 18 April 2002 when a US F-16 accidentally attacked them while they trained in a nighttime exercise.[12] To recognize their sacrifice, a granite memorial was unveiled at Fort Campbell. Moreover, because the Canadians had been operating alongside the U.S. 187th Infantry Regiment, their names were included on the regiment's memorial, which commemorates its war dead dating back to the Second World War. This was the first time non-U.S. soldiers had received such an honour. For the U.S. Army's Colonel Michael Steele, the recognition was apt: 'Even though they wore different uniforms, all were brothers' (Canadian Broadcasting Corporation, 24 May). Lloyd Smith, the father of Nathan Smith, felt that despite the drawn-out controversy that had surrounded the friendly-fire incident, the US military's decision to honour the Canadians was genuine: 'It's not a political gesture. This is coming from the men on the ground. This is coming from the heart' (*Halifax Daily News,* 24 May).

Ballistic missile defence

Discussions initiated by the Chrétien government in the spring of 2003 regarding Canadian participation in the U.S. Ballistic Missile Defence system came to an abrupt end on 24 February 2005, when the Martin government announced that Canada would not take part. On the one hand the decision was a surprise for some, given that Prime Minister Martin, shortly after becoming leader of the federal Liberal Party in November 2003, had indicated support for Canadian involvement: 'It's pretty clear that if you're talking about the defence of North America, Canada has to be at the table' (*Montreal Gazette,* 28 Feb.). Moreover, the prime minister wished to repair damage to Canada-U.S. relations incurred by the previous government, and President Bush had lobbied the prime minister during his visit to Canada in late 2004. As well, Canada's ambassador-designate to the United States, Frank McKenna, had indicated earlier in February that Canada was already a de facto participant, given the August 2004 decision that the North American Aerospace Defence Command (NORAD) would share information important for missile defence: 'There's no question that the Norad [*sic*] amendment has already given a great deal of what the United States

---

12 The pilot, Major Harry Schmidt, had thought he was under attack, unaware that the Canadians were training below. As a result of his actions Major Schmidt was found guilty of dereliction of duty in 2004. The reprimand included loss of pay and his right to fly for the U.S. military.

needs in terms of input on North American defence' (Canadian Broadcasting Corporation, 24 Feb.).

On the other hand, the minority parliament made it difficult for Prime Minister Martin to manoeuvre; the New Democratic Party, the Bloc Québécois, and many members of the Liberal caucus were against Canadian participation. Additionally, pollsters found that support was slipping amongst Canadians generally and had never been strong in Quebec, a situation not likely to change, given that the government had never publicly championed Canadian involvement. Thus, with a showdown looming in an upcoming Liberal policy convention with a resolution opposing Canadian participation in the works, the Martin government acted.

The response to the decision was mixed. The Martin government, for its part, was keen to highlight Canada's commitment to continental defence, as manifest in the February federal budget's emphasis on border security and increased military funding. The decision, however, seemingly undermined the credibility of Ambassador McKenna and was accompanied by an indirect rebuke issued by Minister Graham: 'Norad [sic] evaluates a threat. Making a decision to launch a missile is a whole other story' (Canadian Broadcasting Corporation, 24 Feb.). Critics contended that the decision might disrupt Canadian attempts to resolve the softwood lumber and BSE cases and even put into question the continued existence of NORAD. Although Prime Minister Martin asserted that the United States would have to consult Canada regarding an incoming missile, regardless of Canadian participation, U.S. ambassador Cellucci begged to differ: 'We simply cannot understand why Canada would, in effect, give up its sovereignty – its seat at the table – to decide what to do about a missile that might be coming toward Canada ... We will deploy. We will defend North America' (*Edmonton Journal,* 25 Feb.). Minister Pettigrew muddied the waters further by suggesting that although the missile system was not in accordance with Canadian values, Canadian firms were nevertheless encouraged to seek contracts: 'I do not believe that we should control Canadian business ... I would be very pleased if Canadian business can contribute to the defence system of the United States' (*Kingston Whig-Standard,* 28 Feb.).

Prime Minister Martin also came under fire for the way the decision was announced. Although the prime minister could have directly told President Bush of his government's decision, during the NATO Summit in Brussels on 22 February, Minister Pettigrew was instead tasked to convey the government's decision by telephone to U.S. Secretary of State Condoleezza Rice. Furthermore, when Minister Pettigrew was again tasked to make the announcement, this time to the Canadian people, he did so during a poorly attended speech in the House of Commons regarding the federal budget. Upset was also created by the facts that Canadians were officially informed on 24 February, two days *after* the government's decision had been made plain to the Americans, and that the issue had not been put to a debate in the House, as initially promised by the prime minister.

The Arctic

In mid-July a diplomatic tiff was instigated between Canada and Denmark when, as part of his tour of northern military bases, Minister Graham arrived by helicopter on Hans Island, located between Ellesmere Island and Greenland. A week prior to Minister Graham's arrival, Canadian military personnel had also landed on the island, raised a Canadian flag, and left behind an inukshuk. These actions upset Danish officials because the sovereignty of the 1.3-kilometre island was in dispute. Although Canada and Denmark had agreed back in 1973 on a border through Nares Strait, the status of Hans Island had been left undecided. Thus, on 25 July, Canada's ambassador to Denmark, Fredericka Gregory, was summoned to a meeting with a Danish foreign affairs official, Peter Taksoe-Jensen, to receive a letter reiterating Danish ownership. One particular stress for Taskoe-Jensen was that 'a member of the Canadian government made a visit to what we regard as part of Danish territory without formal notice' (*National Post,* 26 July). While Danish officials had travelled to the island on several earlier occasions, including a visit by Denmark's foreign minister in 1984, they had never sought permission from Canada to do so, as this would have damaged their country's legal standing.

While the island itself was not strategically important for either country, larger issues informed the countries' respective positions. With global warming increasing and the possibility of an ice-free polar passage more likely, concerns regarding management of transportation, exploitation of resources, and development of sound environmental policy were more prominent. The Martin government had emphasized a refocusing of its policy efforts on the north.[13] As for the Danes, lack of interest regarding the fate of the island could serve as fodder for

---

13 For instance, in August HMCS *Fredericton* sailed towards Davis Strait. Also, two coastal defence vessels, HMCS *Glace Bay* and HMCS *Shawinigan,* visited the port of Churchill, the first such military visit in thirty years.

pro-independence activists in Greenland, which was already a semi-autonomous region.

In the end, in September at the United Nations in New York, Minister Pettigrew and his Danish counterpart, Per Stig Moller, initiated work on a joint protocol to manage their bilateral approach towards Hans Island. While each side did not drop its respective claim to sovereignty, the matter of handling the dispute was transferred from the political to the bureaucratic milieu. In their joint statement the two ministers said, 'While we pursue these efforts, we have decided that, without prejudice to our respective legal claims, we will inform each other of activities related to Hans Island. Likewise, all contact by either side with Hans Island will be carried out in a low key and restrained manner' (DFAIT News Release 165, 19 Sept.). Minister Pettigrew indicated that this was the appropriate way to handle the dispute with a longstanding NATO ally: 'Officials will be working together, gathering all of the relative information and trying to find a way forward to do this ... We will settle it, but in a mature way' (*Globe and Mail,* 19 Sept.).

Submarines

Following the electrical fire on 5 October 2004 that struck the submarine HMCS *Chicoutimi* on its maiden voyage under the Canadian flag and left one crew member dead (Lieutenant Chris Saunders), the navy launched a military board of inquiry into the incident. The board was to consider a number of questions:

- What was the chain of events that led to the fire?
- How was the fire handled?
- Did the injured crew members receive adequate medical attention?[14]
- What recommendations might stem from the investigation?

Although the board submitted its answers to these questions on 17 December 2004, the commander of Canada's navy, Vice-Admiral Bruce MacLean, reconvened the board on 1 February 2005 with a mandate to produce a supplementary report by 8 March. Of particular interest were crew decisions related to the repairing of *Chicoutimi*'s upper lid vent, one of the key variables that ultimately allowed

---

14 This was of particular concern because of the initial decision not to request medical assistance from the United Kingdom. Lieutenant Saunders ultimately succumbed to his injuries in the midst of being airlifted to receive medical attention.

2,000 litres of seawater to enter the submarine and thus spark the fire. While the military board of inquiry had considered this issue in its initial investigations, Vice-Admiral MacLean wished 'greater clarity and context' before he made his final assessment (DND News Release 05.008, 1 Feb.). This decision added further controversy to the military's handling of the incident. In other navies it was common practice to temporarily relieve from duty the captain of a vessel so stricken until an inquiry's outcome was known. In this case, however, Commander Luc Pelletier, *Chicoutimi*'s captain at the time of the accident, was left in charge as the submarine was being transported back to Canada for assessment and repair.

When the board of inquiry's 700-page report was finally released to the public on 5 May, no one factor, human or technical, was deemed to be ultimately responsible. For Vice-Admiral MacLean there was simply just an unfortunate series of events: 'It's the view of the board – and I agree – that no one is directly responsible for the fire and death of Lieut. Chris Saunders ... I believe it was a combination of human, technical and operation factors that all eventually led to a fire and a tragic death' (CTV.ca, 5 May). No compensation would be sought from the United Kingdom, which had sold the used submarine to Canada in 1998. Additionally, the board determined that decisions made regarding the medical care of the injured submariners was 'reasonable and prudent' (Globe and Mail, 6 May). No court martial was to be forthcoming for Commander Pelletier. To further underscore its confidence in the submarine's personnel, the military announced on 5 October, the one-year anniversary of the accident, that the crew of *Chicoutimi* would be recognized with a Canadian Forces Unit Commendation.

In its report the military board of inquiry provided a number of recommendations for the navy's consideration. First, splash-proof insulation should be installed on electrical wiring in the submarines. Although *Chicoutimi*'s sister ships, while under British service, had received upgraded insulation and sealants for their electrical connections, *Chicoutimi* had not. This was not detected by Canadian or British officials during the years that the mothballed submarines were again being made seaworthy in the United Kingdom following their sale to Canada. Second, operating procedures should be changed to keep conning-tower hatches closed while a submarine was on the surface. Third, Canada's submarines should have more emergency breathing masks and they should be in more accessible locations.

As for the ailing submarine itself, it arrived in Halifax harbour on 1 February aboard a Norwegian transport vessel, at a cost of CDN$2.7

million. Repairs to the submarine were to occur in three phases. In phase one, the submarine was to be docked and inspected. Phase two was to see further assessment and surveying, in part to facilitate eventual repairs and in part to further 'Canadianize' the vessel. Finally, phase three was to include the actual repairs along with the requisite testing and trials. The first two phases were completed in 2005 under the management of Irving Shipbuilding Incorporated. The third phase would likely be ongoing until the summer of 2007, the submarine's estimated return date to service. Minister Graham suggested that despite the accident, the repairs posed a valuable opportunity for both the navy and Canadian industry: 'This ongoing work continues to offer a significant opportunity for Canadian companies to gain invaluable experience working on a modern weapons system and will facilitate further transition to Canadian in-service support of the submarines' (DND News Release 05.070, 19 Aug.). While official estimates for the repairs ranged between CDN$10 million and CDN$15 million, unofficial estimates placed the costs as high as CDN$100 million.

Although there were still some clouds on the horizon, Canada's submarine program recovered somewhat on 17 May when HMCS *Victoria,* based at CFB Esquimalt, returned to sea. On 13 October 2004, the military had ordered this submarine and its two sister vessels, HMCS *Windsor* and HMCS *Cornerbrook,* to dockside pending the outcome of the military board of inquiry. During this time the submarines were inspected, and improved insulation was installed on their high-voltage power lines; the crews were also trained in new safety and maintenance procedures. Vice-Admiral MacLean was confident that these measures would suffice: 'Having implemented all the immediate recommendations from the *Chicoutimi* board of inquiry, I am satisfied that all our crew and submarine verification work has proven *Victoria* ready and safe for operations' (Canadian Broadcasting Corporation, 17 May). Nevertheless, the vice-admiral warned that the problems posed by the accident onboard HMCS *Chicoutimi* threatened the viability of the larger fleet: 'I cannot overstate that the Chicoutimi incident, coupled with other necessary recovery-repair strategies, has impacted the navy to its very core' (*Halifax Herald,* 6 May). He charged not only that repairs and upgrades on the submarines would divert funds away from the navy's destroyers, frigates, and other vessels, but also that the navy as a whole was underfunded; it was to receive only 62 per cent of the CDN$513 required for repairs and maintenance.

Chemical agents and testing

During 2005 the departments of national defence and veterans affairs hoped to put behind them the troubling issue of military personnel who had been exposed to chemical agents on military bases. In 2004, under legal pressure and facing criticism from the then military ombudsman, André Marin, the government put in place a CDN$50-million compensation program for the 3,700 soldiers who had agreed to be subjects for chemical testing at the Suffield Experimental Station in Alberta and at the Chemical Warfare Laboratories in Ottawa. In order to commemorate these soldiers, who were exposed between 1940 and 1970, military officials unveiled plaques in Ottawa and Suffield on 21 April and 22 August 2005 respectively. Additionally, on 22 May the Department of National Defence announced that the widows of veterans who had participated in the tests but who had not made legal wills were nevertheless still eligible for compensation under the Chemical Warfare Agent Testing Recognition Program.

Concern and criticism did not subside, however, because in June 2005 media investigations found that a variety of cancer-linked defoliants, including Agent Orange and Agent Purple, had been sprayed at CFB Gagetown, New Brunswick. Some of the spraying, from the 1950s onward, had been done to clear sightlines and to reduce the possibility of fires being sparked by artillery training. Other spraying, specifically during 14–16 June 1966 and 21–24 June 1967, was carried out as tests by the U.S. military, which at the time was employing the chemicals in the Vietnam War.

Determining the causes and effects of the spraying was a considerable task because of the passage of time and the number of individuals, military and civilian alike, who might have been directly or indirectly exposed to dioxin-laced herbicides. In New Brunswick during the 1950s and 1960s, similar chemicals were commonly used in aerial forest spraying and in clearing for power lines. It was only in 1985 that Canada banned the use of these chemicals. Nonetheless, on 16 August the government launched a CDN$800-million program to investigate herbicide use at CFB Gagetown. The program consisted of five components:

1. collection of information on who was present at the base during the testing;
2. review of the history of spraying on the base, including a consideration of the environmental impacts;

3. assessment of potential human health risks;
4. study of epidemiological effects to determine the incidence of illness; and
5. public hearings involving New Brunswickers and other possibly affected groups.

To manage the process, the government selected Vaughn Blaney, a former provincial environment minister, to be the fact-finding and outreach coordinator. Blaney was responsible for interacting with concerned populations, overseeing the numerous initiatives, and communicating the findings to the public.[15]

Criticism, however, dogged the government's reaction. The program's estimated reporting time of eighteen months was felt by some to be too long. For one former serviceman, the government's response was little more than a stalling tactic as more veterans died: 'We don't have to take a year to learn what happened. We know what happened ... We're looking for compensation. That's the bottom line' (CTV.ca, 22 Sept.). Indeed, independent of the government's program, the two claims for compensation related to the 1966–67 tests had already been accepted. Other criticisms emphasized the coordinator's limitations; the mandate did not allow for recommendations and the coordinator's independence was questionable given that he had to rely on testing conducted by government departments. Additional distress was caused by Blaney's decision, due to health concerns, to step down as coordinator in November, as this pushed the reporting deadline back further. In his place the government named Dr Dennis Furlong, a former provincial health minister, as the new coordinator on 16 November.

Changes in the forces

Military ombudsman

In 2005 the Department of National Defence replaced André Marin, the military's first ever military ombudsman, who had served in the position since 1998. Marin moved on to become ombudsman for the province of Ontario in March 2005. As a result, in May 2005 Minister Graham announced the proposed appointment of Yves Côté to the post, which he eventually succeeded to in early August. Côté was an experienced gov-

15 As part of the government's desire for due diligence, in November 2005 it also launched a two- to three-year review of other Canadian military bases, though no testing of herbicides elsewhere was on record.

ernment lawyer, having first served in the 1970s as a legal officer with the Office of the Judge Advocate General before leaving the military in 1981. Other positions in his career had included general counsel in the Human Rights Section of Justice Canada, government coordinator for the Commission of Inquiry into the Deployment of Canadian Forces to Somalia, and legal advisor to the Department of National Defence. At the time of his appointment Côté was the counsel to the Clerk of the Privy Council, Alex Himmelfarb. In light of this considerable résumé, Minister Graham was convinced that Côté was the right individual for the job: 'With his wealth of experience, I am confident that under his leadership the Office of the Ombudsman will continue to contribute to significant improvements in the Department' (DND News Release 05.038, 24 May)

During a non-binding review of Côté's appointment by the Standing Committee on National Defence and Veterans Affairs, several opposition members raised concerns about his credentials and experience. One worry was any role he might have played in advising the Chrétien government to shut down the Somalia inquiry in 1997 before further political damage could be done. Another concern was the role Côté might have had in trying to limit the mandate of the military ombudsman; he was a legal advisor to the department at the time of the position's creation. This raised a more general concern about his approach towards his new 'client' – the Canadian military writ large – given his earlier professional responsibilities of working closely with senior officers and defence officials: a de facto linkage might exist. In this regard it is important to note that Marin argued during his tenure as military ombudsman that the position should be an independent officer of Parliament rather than answerable de jure to the Minister of National Defence. Côté, on his part, indicated that he was more than prepared to investigate individual complaints and to deal constructively and assertively in promoting the well-being of all those in uniform: 'My priority is really to make sure that for the members of the Forces, this office assists them in a way that is real, that is concrete and that produces results' (*National Post*, 20 July).

Leadership and structure

In 2005 a change was forthcoming in the position of chief of defence staff (CDS) because of the November 2004 election of General Ray Henault to chairmanship of NATO's Military Committee. General Henault had served as CDS since June 2001, and his election to the three-year NATO post marked only the second time a Canadian had been so honoured (Admiral Robert Falls held the position from 1980 to 1983). As chairman, General Henault had the responsibility of guiding 'the Military Committee to plan, assess, and develop policy and advice to NATO's Secretary General and the North Atlantic Council on all military matters respecting the Alliance' (DND News Release 05.049, 16 June). Upon officially becoming NATO's highest-ranking officer on 16 June, General Henault set his sights on three goals: expansion of the alliance's operations, improvement of its capabilities, and enhancement of cooperation amongst the alliance membership.

On 14 January the government selected Lieutenant-General Rick Hillier as the next CDS, effective 4 February. Other contenders for the position included Vice-Admiral Ron Buck, vice-chief of defence staff, and Vice-Admiral Greg Maddison, deputy chief of defence staff. One of these officers was arguably 'up next,' given the tradition of rotating the position, as the navy was next in line. Nevertheless, the government selected General Hillier, an army candidate, in large part because of his operational and organizational experience. General Hillier, a member of the Canadian military since 1973, had earlier served as a multinational commander in Bosnia and as the ISAF commander in Afghanistan; as head of the army he had been responsible for guiding the transformation of that organization. Minister Graham found General Hillier to be an ideal choice to make a wider impact on the direction of the Canadian military: 'Lt.-Gen. Hillier's leadership and experience will be invaluable as we move forward in this process to transform the Canadian Forces to meet the security challenges Canada faces' (DND News Release 05.004, 14 Jan.).

The new CDS's transformation agenda began in earnest with shifts in the military's command structure that were in line with the government's agenda as outlined in the Defence Policy Statement. Preparations were made to 'stand up' four new commands: Canada Command, the Canadian Expeditionary Forces Command (CEFCOM), the Canadian Special Operations Forces Command (CANSOFCOM), and the Canadian Operational Support Command (CANOSCOM). Canada Command, with its emphasis on treating Canada as a theatre of operations, was to include six regional headquarters: Northern, Pacific, Prairie, Central, East, and Atlantic. With Canada Command the hope was to create a unified chain of command for operations of all sorts with the authority to deploy military assets from all three services. As for CEFCOM, it was to be responsible for setting training and readiness standards that would allow for continuous deployment abroad of 5,000 personnel. To make real this responsibility, CEFCOM was to manage a Standing Contingency Task Force, mission-specific task forces, and the DART. CANSOFCOM was to be charged with special operations and counterterrorism tasks both domestic and international. In this sense, CANSOFCOM might, depending on the situation, support Canada Command and CEFCOM or operate independently of them. Finally, CANOSCOM was to support the three aforementioned commands in a variety of areas: health services, military engineering, logistics, military police, land equipment maintenance, resource management, and communications and information systems. Canada Command in its embryonic form began in June 2005, with plans set for development of the other commands to full strength over the course of 2005 and into 2006.

EMMANUEL BRUNET-JAILLY, SERENA KATAOKA,
AND WARREN MAGNUSSON

Municipal affairs

Municipalities were generally pleased about the fact that the federal government's 'new deal for cities and communities' was at least partially implemented in 2005. The new Ministry of State for Communities and Infrastructure was established. For the first time, the Canadian Federation of Municipalities was formally consulted about federal budget measures, which included provision for a municipal share of gasoline taxes (as well as some other new federal funding); tripartite agreements were worked out between the federal government, the provinces, and municipalities to put the new fiscal measures into effect; and there was at least a vague promise that more was to come if the Liberals remained in power in Ottawa. Meanwhile, in Canada's two largest cities there were ongoing debates about their powers, internal structures, and boundaries, coloured in Montreal's case by the 2004 vote of various municipalities to demerge from the city that had earlier absorbed them at the insistence of the province, and in Toronto's case by a loosely articulated campaign to have it recognized as a government with special powers and responsibilities. The idea that there had to be a new deal for the big cities so they could cope with the challenges of the new economy was very much in the air. On the other hand, there was much resistance from smaller municipalities and rural areas to any measures that would favour the big cities. Concerns about the environmental effects of urban development generated various 'green plans' and initiatives, while questions of social and cultural policy also gained greater prominence. In terms of electoral politics, the most dramatic change was in Vancouver, where Sam Sullivan, a quadriplegic, won the mayoralty at the head of a revived conservative coalition. He was to become a symbol for people with disabilities, especially in the context of Vancouver's preparations for the 2010 Olympics.

Cities in the marketplace

Shifts in thinking at the municipal level are well illustrated by the economic development strategies adopted by Montreal and Hamilton in 2005.

Montreal's strategy, 'success@montreal,' turned on the idea that a new economic paradigm has raised competition to a global scale. The central claim was that knowledge, culture, creativity, know-how, and openness to the world are the keys to economic success. Two core values were also proclaimed: sustainable development and solidarity. Many of the measures anticipated were of a familiar kind, but a few of them stood out, such as efforts to accelerate industrial clusters (in aerospace, life sciences, nanotechnology, etc.), to develop the city as an avant-garde cultural metropolis, and to brand the city internationally. In Hamilton (which might have had a greater need than Montreal for rebranding) the analysis presented in the new strategy was similar but (as perhaps befits a traditional manufacturing centre) the focus on industrial clusters was even stronger. The film and cultural industries, biotechnology, and de-velopment surrounding the airport ('aerotropolis') were singled out as emerging clusters. Thus Steeltown apparently aspired to be another Soft City – or, in the new jargon that had emerged in response to competitive concerns, a creative, smart, and sustainable city.

Concerns about the productivity gap between the United States and Canada informed almost every discussion about economic policy, and this focused attention on deficits in investment in education and tech-nology, deficits that could be larger than the 'infrastructure deficit' about which the municipalities had been talking for years. Industrial clusters of the sort that can develop only in large cities or city regions were supposed to bring science and creativity to bear in a way that facilitated innovation and enterprise. As the Big City Mayors' Caucus of the Federation of Canadian Municipalities noted in its June report, *Cities: Partners in National Prosperity*:

Successful economies in the 21st century are increasingly measured by their capacity to generate wealth through innovation and to attract labour and capital to support the global knowledge economy. These economies are now centred in large cities more than in the traditional nation state. Canadian cities are in-creasingly challenged to compete with cities in Europe, Australia, Japan and especially the United States, making the importance of urban quality of life as an element of competitiveness more apparent. (3)

To highlight quality of life as a central concern with respect to eco-nomic competitiveness represented a shift from the traditional focus on taxes, business regulations, and hard services. *Canadian Business,* in its annual survey about the best places to do business in Canada, used operating costs for business, the cost of living, the crime rate, the level of unemployment, and non-residential building permits as indicators of a place's attractiveness. Using those criteria, St John's, Newfoundland; Saguenay, Quebec; and Saint John, New Brunswick, came out on top, with Vancouver, Montreal, and Toronto all near the bottom. Such an analysis distracted from the reality the big-city mayors were trying to highlight: that business continued to need what the larger centres could offer, despite the higher costs there. Policymakers in the bigger cities were becoming sensitive to analyses offered by people such as Richard Florida, who highlighted the success of American cities such as San Francisco and Boston and connected that success with the attractive cultural, social, and physical environments that those places were able to maintain. Of particular note to Canadian municipal leaders was the fact that many successful American cities had more autonomy and greater fiscal resources than their Canadian counterparts. It was also alleged by many that the pattern was similar in Western Europe.

In Canada, analysts such as Neil Bradford and Thomas Courchene (who produced important reports for the Canadian Policy Research Networks and the Institute for Research on Public Policy in March and June respectively) elaborated on the connections between vigorous local government, quality of life, environmental sustainability, and economic competitiveness. Bradford argued for place-based public policy, rooted in local knowledge and viewed through an urban lens, which would involve collaborative arrangements between the various orders of government, business, and civil society. Courchene focused on the importance of global city regions in the knowledge-based economy and the need to focus on what Florida described as 'technology, talent, and tolerance.' Courchene noted that Canadian cities have generally done well in terms of tolerance but not so well in terms of technology and talent, especially the development of human capital. Both Bradford and Courchene argued that cities, especially the larger centres, needed more autonomy and more resources to deal effectively with challenges associated with the new global order. If the 'new deal for cities' was to work as expected, it would have to go much farther than the federal government had been prepared to go and to offer more to the big cities in particular than to municipalities in general.

Although business was still concerned about high taxes, red tape, and restrictions on entrepreneurial freedom, the new refrain was reflected in reports from the Toronto-Dominion Bank, the Canada West Foundation, and the Conference Board of Canada. Cities had to make themselves more attractive to entrepreneurs by becoming notable for their quality of life, healthy environment, social solidarity, cultural diversity, and high level of education, as well as for fast and efficient transportation and communication; the federal and provincial governments would have to work with the cities, give them more resources and more latitude, and encourage them to develop an entrepreneurial spirit that would bring business, government, and civil society together in a common project to make Canadian cities more competitive internationally. Although the Federation of Canadian Municipalities and its provincial counterparts were supportive of these ideas up to a point, the smaller towns and rural areas still wielded great influence within these organizations, and they pressed for measures that would not disadvantage them. The effects of this pressure were apparent in both provincial and federal policymaking.

The culture of cities

As noted, one of the implications of the new thinking about the economy was that culture could become an economic asset for a city. Thus the demand arose for new cultural amenities modelled on the Guggenheim Museum in Bilbao, Spain – iconic structures that would attract attention, bring in tourists, and lure investors, thanks to the rebranding that would occur. Toronto was at the beginning of a phase of renewal in this regard, with the cranes at work on a spectacular extension to the Royal Ontario Museum and with planning well advanced on a variety of other iconic cultural projects. This was a source of anxiety in Montreal, which was striving to compete. In *Imagining: Building Montréal 2025, a World of Creativity and Opportunities,* the overall plan developed by the city and issued in September, much attention was given to the culture of the metropolis as well as to possibilities for developing its cultural industries. It included claims about the city's creativity, diversity, openness, and effervescence; celebrations of its rich natural, historical, artistic, and architectural heritage; and a marked emphasis on its character as a city of hospitality and immigration with outward-looking attitudes. Similar themes were articulated elsewhere, including Toronto and Vancouver; the latter had begun preparations for the 2010 Olympics, which was meant to be an iconic cultural event that would boost the city economically.

In Montreal and elsewhere, connections were made not only between culture and the economy but also between culture and social well-being. In Montreal's plan there was talk of using the wealth generated from private development to subsidize more than 40,000 units of affordable housing by 2025. Also, in June the city adopted the first municipal charter of rights and responsibilities in the country, which was to come into effect on 1 January 2006. Among its principles were 'a sustained struggle against poverty and all forms of discrimination' and 'the inclusion of and harmonious relations among its communities and persons of all origins,' tempered by recognition that 'Montreal is a French-speaking city that also provides services to its citizens in English, under the law' (Montreal Charter of Rights and Responsibilities, 5). The charter was 'binding on Montreal, its paramunicipal agencies, city-controlled corporations, their employees, civil servants and any other parties doing work on behalf of the city. It is also binding on all Montreal citizens' (ibid., 10). An ombudsman was supposed to receive complaints, investigate them, recommend remedies, and negotiate their implementation, but the 'Charter is not intended to serve as the basis for a legal action nor to be used in a judicial or quasi-judicial form.' It remained to be seen what the practical implications of the charter would be.

In its ongoing national study of quality of life in Canadian cities, the Federation of Canadian Municipalities (FCM) not only noted the need for improved educational opportunities but also talked of support for 'rich social interactions and the inclusion of all residents in community life.'[1] Particular attention was directed towards women, immigrants, and Aboriginal people in this regard. In a study titled *A Very Hostile System in Which to Live': Aboriginal Electoral Participation in Winnipeg's Inner City,* the Canadian Centre for Policy Alternatives found that Aboriginal people 'feel outside of the system, they feel excluded or marginalized from the system, and from the mainstream electoral system in particular, and therefore do not vote in that system' (iv). However, with rising educational levels – and an appropriate response from candidates for office – that could change in future. The FCM's national focus was on a campaign to increase women's engagement in politics and policymaking. Vancouver adopted a gender equality strategy premised on the idea that social sustainability depended on involving women in policymaking. The city's Social Planning Department formed a Women's Advisory Committee, hired a 'sex-worker advocate,' and attempted to coordinate with other levels of government in addressing the specific needs of vulnerable girls.

Immigrant settlement was a particular challenge in both Vancouver and Toronto, but the relevant agencies were hard pressed in many other

---

1 Federation of Canadian Municipalities, *Quality of Life in Canadian Communities: Growth, the Economy and the Urban Environment.* (Ottawa: Federation of Canadian Municipalities, 2005), 40.

communities as well. Immigrants could be viewed as an economic or even a cultural resource – one that economically declining or stagnant communities were increasingly interested in exploiting; for instance, a municipal nominee program was proposed, similar to existing provincial nominee programs, that would enable authorities to pick potential immigrants with the desired skills and expedite them through the system. However, newcomers still posed a difficult challenge to even the most welcoming communities, which had to provide services and support. Many of the tasks involved were assumed by immigrant service agencies that were at one remove from the municipalities and dependent on funding from the federal and/or provincial governments.

Drug addiction and homelessness continued to attract much attention, particularly in the Greater Vancouver region. The Downtown Eastside was as much a concern as ever, but so too was the outlying community of Maple Ridge, where the focus was on the effects of a relatively new drug, crystal meth (methamphetamine). Unusually, the lead actors included a Conservative MP and the local Rotary Club. Action to get people housed, as well as to inform them about the noxious effects of the drug, was at the centre of initiatives launched in a number of British Columbia communities, following the Maple Ridge model. Vancouver already had its own model for dealing with drug addiction; it was backed by the Union of British Columbia Municipalities (UBCM) in its efforts to get support from a dubious provincial government. Nevertheless, controversies were ongoing over the various strategies of engagement suggested, not surprisingly, as they touched on delicate moral issues as well as questions of law enforcement.

Regional governance

Environmental questions inevitably loom large with respect to issues of regional governance. As the FCM noted in its report *Quality of Life in Canadian Communities,* 'The scale and complexity of the challenge of managing growth to achieve sustainable development often places matters beyond the control of any one municipality' (iii). According to the FCM, the ecological footprint of Canadians was nearly eight times the world average; this was connected with the fact that Canadian cities and towns are not only spread out over a large country but are also relatively low in density within their regions. As the federal government's Cities Secretariat discovered, however, Canadians were rather attached to low-density development, so change was not seen as easy to achieve. The most dramatic policy response was in Ontario, where the provincial government established a green belt around Toronto and the other cities at the western end of Lake Ontario. The proclaimed intent was to protect about 1.8 million acres of environmentally sensitive and agricultural land, including 800,000 acres of land within the Niagara Escarpment Plan and the Oak Ridges Moraine Conservation Plan. Critics suggested that these measures were insufficient, and of course there was the predictable opposition from those whose economic ambitions would be compromised.

Throughout the year the Ontario government engaged with municipalities in a complex process designed to enhance their powers in some respects while obliging them to conform more closely to provincial planning guidelines. The focus was on the Greater Toronto area. Complementary to the *Greenbelt Act* was the *Places to Grow Act,* which specified that 40 per cent of new urban growth had to be contained within existing built-up areas by 2015, and that density had to be doubled by 2031 in twenty-five urban centres. According to the new provincial planning guidelines, municipalities had to promote more compact living and build 'complete communities' where people could live their lives without needing cars. Affordable housing goals were also set. The *Respect for Municipal Government Act* reversed some of the measures adopted by the previous Conservative government and gave the municipalities more flexibility with respect to fiscal policy. Revisions to the *Planning Act* and a narrowing of the role of the Ontario Municipal Board (OMB) were intended to make it easier for municipalities to impose conditions on developers and so achieve the planning goals the province was setting out. The OMB had long been criticized for being too attentive to the rights of developers and not attentive enough to broader planning goals. Now the municipalities were being required to adapt to the province's overall planning agenda rather than defer to the market, as the previous provincial government had expected. Perhaps inevitably, the province regarded itself as the regional government for Greater Toronto, and ultimately responsible for larger issues that involved municipalities but were difficult for the municipalities to resolve on their own. The new Greater Toronto Transit Authority, established in October, was in line with such thinking.

The City of Toronto continued its campaign for special recognition from the provincial government. It insisted that it had to deal directly with the province rather than through the Association of Municipalities of Ontario (AMO), the body that the provincial government had recently recognized as the consulting body for dealing with municipal issues. In December the McGuinty government introduced its *Stronger*

City of Toronto for a Stronger Ontario Act, which was to give the city natural-person powers, authorize it to 'provide any service or thing that the City considers necessary or desirable for the public' (section 8), and indicate to the courts that its powers were to be broadly construed. Among the new powers were rights to impose road tolls and to levy taxes on tobacco and liquor, although Mayor Miller indicated that these powers would not be used immediately. The AMO responded to the Act by saying that similar powers should be given to other municipalities.

In Quebec there was considerable outfall from the thirty-one municipal demergers approved in 2004 referenda. Fifteen of the demergers were in Montreal, where all of the suburbs on the island (which is at the core of the metropolitan area but does not encompass all of it) had been amalgamated with the City in 2002. Many of the English-speaking West Island suburbs regained their former municipal status, as did several former municipalities that had been completely surrounded by the City. On the other hand, the 2002 reforms had established borough councils with considerable powers throughout the City. The boroughs restored to municipal status did not regain all their former powers; they were obliged to be part of an 'agglomeration council,' effectively controlled by the City of Montreal, that managed all services not delegated to the boroughs. The reinstated municipalities were given authority over the same services as the boroughs, but no more. The City was also at the centre of the wider Montreal Metropolitan Community, which had powers related to strategic regional planning for waste management and infrastructure. Despite concerns about the effects of the demergers, it seemed that the framework for regional governance in greater Montreal – such as it was – remained largely intact.

Local democracy

Municipal elections were held in British Columbia, Quebec, and Newfoundland and Labrador, and there was disappointment everywhere about declining voter turnout. Across British Columbia there were no electoral surprises; twelve municipalities and two regional districts (RDs) did not have elections because all their members were acclaimed. In the remainder – 145 municipalities and 25 RDs – there were acclamations for 24 per cent of the mayors and 46 per cent of electoral directors of RDs (previously close to 29 and 22 per cent, respectively), as well as 9 per cent of councillors. Newly elected officials counted for about 45 per cent of all local elected officials, and only 32 per cent of the electorate exercised their rights. The problem was not quite so marked in Quebec, but there were concerns about the new arrangement of having all the municipal elections on the same day. Some members of the press complained that this made it difficult to give adequate attention to the contests in smaller municipalities. In St. John's a mail-out ballot was used for the second time, resulting in 49 per cent participation, which was relatively high for the country as a whole. In Newfoundland and Labrador too many communities did not have candidates for local elections. Despite public campaigns to rally participants and explain how to become a local candidate, fifteen municipalities had no candidates at all, and the province was obliged to ask incumbents to remain in their positions.

In Vancouver there was a shift back to the right. The Coalition of Progressive Electors (COPE), which had swept to power in 2002 in the wake of Larry Campbell's successful campaign for the mayoralty, was split almost down the middle between centrist and left-wing factions. In the summer Campbell unexpectedly announced that he would not be seeking another term, and the centrists aligned with him broke away from COPE and formed their own party, Vision Vancouver. Councillor Jim Green, long associated with grass-roots activism on the Downtown Eastside, became the party's candidate to replace Campbell. In response, many of the heavyweights in the Non-Partisan Association (NPA), a right-of-centre party that had long dominated Vancouver politics, promoted the candidacy of Christy Clark, a former provincial cabinet minister. She failed to get the NPA nomination, however. That went to Councillor Sam Sullivan, who had already demonstrated his skill at grass-roots electoral organizing in a referendum about the introduction of a ward system in the city, a measure he strongly (and successfully) opposed. A quadriplegic as a result of an accident in his youth, Sullivan was competent enough in Cantonese to win much support in the Chinese community. An independent candidate named James Green seemed to have drawn enough support from Jim Green to give Sullivan his margin of victory; however, Sullivan might have won anyway, since his party, the NPA, won a majority on council against Vision and COPE. Sullivan promised a more restrained municipal government that would not deal with issues beyond its mandate, and he launched a triple-R review of the roles, responsibilities, and relationships of Vancouver's councillors, staff, and citizens.

In Montreal, incumbent Gérald Tremblay turned back a challenge from his predecessor, Pierre Bourque, who had lost the office when the city was enlarged to encompass the entire island. Tremblay, who had begun his political career in the suburbs, rebranded himself as a progressive downtown mayor and won quite decisively. Bourque positioned himself as the conservative candidate, while Richard Bergeron – who managed to get elected to council while running third in the mayoralty race – attracted some attention with a campaign centred on ecological issues.

In Toronto, Mayor David Miller was involved not in a campaign for re-election but instead in one to enhance his powers in relation to the municipal council. Miller wanted a shift towards a 'strong-mayor' system that would enable him to choose committee chairs and form an executive committee of his own liking. These changes had the support of the Toronto Board of Trade and (more importantly) the provincial government, but of course they were controversial within the council itself. Former mayor David Crombie spoke against them, but an independent advisory panel established at Miller's behest recommended the changes he wanted. The rationale was to ensure greater coherence in public policy, enable long-term strategic planning, and provide for better overall management of what was now one of the country's largest governments, responsible for more constituents than six of the ten provinces. Interestingly, the Board of Trade was sensitive to concerns about centralization and recommended that 'community councils' within the city be given enhanced powers. On the other hand, the provincial government, which was touting its new measures to enhance the powers of municipal governments, made it clear that it would impose a strong-mayor system on Toronto if the municipal council balked at the measure. So much for the idea that local democracy involves the right to decide on the way that local government should be organized.

Cities in the confederation

Canadian municipalities were claiming, nevertheless, that they had a role to play internationally. In *Our Place in the World: Municipal Government and Canada's International Policies and Programs,* the FCM noted four global trends:

The majority of the world's population is now urban-based, putting significant pressure on municipal governments.... Municipalities everywhere are struggling to meet a growing list of responsibilities with inadequate resources.... A new global economy, in which production and labour have become globalized and migrate to the most favourable conditions for economic success, positions municipalities as key economic actors.... International relations [thus] are no longer the exclusive domain of national governments.

The FCM recommended a stronger federal-municipal partnership with respect to development assistance, trade and economic development, and international representation. It said that Canadian municipalities were 'prepared to significantly expand their partnerships with urban and rural municipalities in developing countries, and contribute to the building of democratic institutions and governance processes that reduce poverty, increase the quality of life and establish the basic conditions for peace, order and good government.'

In its February budget, the federal government delivered on its promise to provide the municipalities with a share of gas tax revenues. However, the funding was not unconditional – it was to be directed towards 'environmentally sustainable infrastructure projects' such as public transit, water and waste-water treatment, community energy systems, and handling of solid waste – and most of it was to be delivered at the end of a five-year period, when the municipal share would reach five cents a litre. Moreover, the funding was to go to the municipalities on a per capita basis, not (as the big cities had hoped) on a basis that reflected the greater need for public investment in public transit in the larger centres. Green municipal funds (for infrastructure projects to 'deliver cleaner air, water and soil, and climate protection') were doubled and the government promised to continue with the promised GST rebate to municipalities and accelerate spending under the Municipal Rural Infrastructure Fund. The minister of finance had met with municipal representatives as part of his pre-budget consultations, and he promised to do so in the future as well. The Cities Secretariat was to be replaced by a new Department of Infrastructure and Communities, with a mandate that would encompass the rural areas but more narrowly focused on infrastructure. That department was to be the federal government's primary point of contact with the municipalities.

The so-called New Deal for Canada's Communities was to be implemented by means of tripartite agreements between the federal government, the province concerned, and municipal representatives. Agreements of this sort were completed between April (British Columbia) and November (New Brunswick) 2005. In British Columbia, the UBCM was asked to administer three funds: Community Works ('local priorities that are in alignment with the desired outcomes of greenhouse gas emission reduction, cleaner air and cleaner water'), Strategic Priorities ('strategic investments that are larger in scale or regional in impact'), and Innovations ('projects and initiatives by Eligible Recipients that reflect an innovative approach to achieving the intended outcomes of reduced greenhouse gas emissions, cleaner air and cleaner water').

In Ontario the Association of Municipalities of Ontario was to play a similar role with respect to distribution of the fund, but special arrangements were made for the City of Toronto, which signed the agreement separately.

As the Canada West Foundation observed, the great promise of the New Deal was in the voice it seemed to offer to the municipalities. Although the municipalities were obviously concerned about the money they would get, they also sought to be recognized as a third order of government, worthy of consideration in relation to major policy decisions at all levels. Clearly there was some progress in this respect, but the big cities were disappointed about the way the money had been spread out rather than focused on their needs. As Thomas Courchene put it:

Ottawa failed to step up to the plate. Rather, the recent fiscal initiatives have actually *discriminated against* the GCRs [global city-regions] relative to smaller cities and smaller communities. A more apt headline for recent federal initiatives might be 'A nation of villages awaits Paul Martin's New Deal for Equalization and Regional Development' (*Citistates and the State of Cities,* 23).

Under NDP pressure the federal Liberals amended their budget to improve terms for the big cities, for instance, by adjusting the allocations to municipalities in accordance with public transit ridership. The cities and other municipalities continued to lobby for more in the context of renewed budget discussions at the end of the year, but of course by that time the fate of the government in Ottawa looked extremely uncertain, to say the least.

KRISTIN BURNETT

First Nations

Federal developments

*The budgets of 2004: government spending
on First Nations issues*

On 23 February Liberal finance minister Ralph Goodale presented
the eighth consecutive balanced federal budget to the House of Commons. The proposed budget contained no new funding for First Nations housing or other priorities such as health and education (*Globe
and Mail,* 22 Dec.). Phil Fontaine, the national chief of the Assembly
of First Nations (AFN), registered his disgust at the contradiction apparent in the federal government's growing fiscal commitment to address world poverty abroad while ignoring similar conditions at home:
'this budget will condemn our people to last place for a lot longer.
The prime minister's commitment to transformative change must be
backed up by real investments and a real effort to work together to fix
a broken system that's holding us back' (*Windspeaker,* Mar.). Instead,
First Nations health systems would see a $27-million cut that would
decrease access to non-insured health benefits and gradual phasing
out of $36 million in investments in First Nations health information
systems (ibid.). The federal budget passed with some minor changes
on 23 June.

A poll conducted by the Centre for Research and Information on
Canada in January found that most Canadians did not consider improving the quality of life of Aboriginal people to be a high priority for the
federal government (*Windspeaker,* Jan.). Lorena Fontaine, a professor
of indigenous studies at the First Nations University of Canada in Regina, said she was not surprised by these findings, because 'unless the
issues are definitely affecting the public, why would they place it high
in terms of their considerations?' (ibid.).

Bill C-20

Bill C-20, otherwise known as the *First Nations Fiscal and Statistical Management Act,* received royal assent on 23 March (*Windspeaker,* Apr.). This legislation created four institutions: the First Nations Finance Authority, First Nations Tax Commission, First Nations Financial Management Board, and First Nations Statistical Institute (ibid.). The act was designed to provide First Nations with property taxation powers. C.T. (Manny) Jules, who had pushed for development of the act, said that 'the formal adoption of Bill C-20 is a triumph for First Nations and Canada. This bill was conceived by First Nations and is about building infrastructure, attracting investment, and creating jobs on reserves' (ibid.).

Support for this legislation within the Aboriginal community was divided. While National Chief Phil Fontaine supported Bill C-20, the AFN did not. The AFN had passed a resolution against Bill C-20 during a meeting in Ottawa early in December 2004 (*Windspeaker,* Jan.). In particular, opponents voiced concern about elements of the bill that dealt with the gathering of statistics (ibid.). Harold Calla, a band councillor for the Squamish Nation, explained: 'First Nation people believe they've been studied to death, too often the data gathered in those studies is not used to the benefit of First Nations people ... One Elder said to me, "We realized that if we actually registered our [children], six years later they came and took them"' (*Windspeaker,* May).

Alternate dispute resolution process

The alternate dispute resolution (ADR) process instituted by the federal government as an out-of-court method for survivors of residential schools to resolve claims of sexual and physical abuse once again came under fire. In February the AFN released its report on the efficacy of the ADR process, with the following findings:

- While 87,000 former students were still alive, only twenty-seven claims had been settled.
- Four survivors died every week but at the current rate it would take fifty-three years to resolve all of the cases.
- The current system would cost $5.5 billion over thirty years, with only 29 per cent of that money being paid to former students.
- The current system required survivors to recount their stories to strangers repeatedly in order to convince them of their suffering.

(*Globe and Mail,* 23 Feb.)

The AFN passed a resolution suggesting an alternative plan that would reduce costs and ensure that all survivors received compensation. The AFN solution would cost at least $4.3 billion over two years, with 93 per cent of the money going to former students (ibid.). Phil Fontaine presented the AFN's plan to resolve Indian residential school claims to the Standing Committee on Aboriginal Affairs on 22 February. Fontaine began by saying he was 'saddened to be here yet again, finding myself pleading with the Canadian government to fulfill its legal and moral obligations to First Nation people' (*Windspeaker*, Mar.). Fontaine outlined the failures of the ADR process: since 1991 20,000 survivors had died without justice and reconciliation, and the current system did not take into account loss of language and culture or family life. He offered an alternative, streamlined solution to resolve claims outside of court. Survivors would be paid lump sums upon verification of school attendance, and in the case of sexual, physical, or serious emotional abuse, further compensation would be negotiated and offered quickly (ibid.). Fontaine also argued that the plan would actually save the federal government money. Under the new plan, the Office of Indian Residential School Resolution of Canada (OIRSRC) would pay each survivor a lump sum of $10,000, with an additional $3,000 for every year spent in school, whether they claimed abuse or not (ibid.). In late May, Deputy Prime Minister Anne McLellan, representing the federal government's position, spoke before the Standing Committee on Aboriginal Affairs; she stated that compensation for loss of culture was not 'a recognized legal cause of action in Canada' (*Globe and Mail*, 31 May).

After many months of negotiations among the AFN, church organizations, former students, more than seventy lawyers, and the federal government, an agreement in principal was signed on 20 November, pending Cabinet and court approval. The compensation package for residential school survivors was announced in Ottawa three days later. The package offered common experience payments of $10,000 per student, with an additional $3,000 for every year spent in school (*Windspeaker*, Dec.). The average payment would be $24,000. The package also provided money to the Aboriginal Healing Foundation and sets aside funds to establish a truth and reconciliation commission. In the AFN's words, 'by opening a door on Canadian history our proposal pursues justice and promotes mutual healing through a truth sharing and reconciliation process' (*Windspeaker*, Mar.).

Responses in the Aboriginal community were mixed. Nellie Carlson, an elder from Edmonton, Alberta, stated that she would not respect herself if she agreed to receive money for what had happened to her: 'This is nothing for replacement in terms of what we had to suffer. It's just a drop in the bucket' (*Windspeaker,* Dec.). Beatrice Gladue, executive director of the Tansi Friendship Centre Society, said the compensation was too little, too late for many, including her seventy-two-year-old father, who still needed to work to support himself: 'no amount of money will make up for the physical and sexual abuse he suffered' (ibid.).

Nor did this agreement include all residential school survivors. A group of Métis survivors who were excluded from the federal settlement launched a class action lawsuit. Tony Merchant, the lawyer for Métis students who attended Île-à-la-Crosse Indian Residential School, commented on the omission: 'the exclusion affects the Metis people who were not given a place in the recent settlement negotiations. Their voice was unheard' (*National Post,* 10 Dec.).

Residential schools: joint responsibility

On 21 October the Supreme Court of Canada ruled that the churches that had run residential schools shared responsibility for the abuse that took place in them (*Globe and Mail,* 22 Oct.). This decision overturned that of British Columbia's Court of Appeal, which had said that only the federal government was responsible for the actions of boys' ward supervisors at the Alberni Indian Residential School in the 1960s (ibid.). The United Church was required to pay 25 per cent of the $165,000 awarded to Frederick Leroy Barney (ibid.). The ruling confirmed the federal government's position that the churches had to shoulder some of the financial burden of compensating survivors. The federal government had already reached joint responsibility agreements with the Anglican Church of Canada and the Presbyterian Church, with both agreeing to pay 30 per cent of the costs (ibid.).

Barney was dissatisfied with the court's decision because it did not increase the financial settlement he had been awarded. The Supreme Court considered only the sexual abuse Barney suffered and refused to take into account his claim for the physical and mental abuse he endured while attending Alberni Indian Residential School. Fiona Sampson, counsel for the Legal Education and Action Foundation, said, 'It's this big invisible web of violence and what the court has done is try and clean it up, to say he can be compensated for anal rape but not for any of the physical or emotional abuse' (*Globe and Mail,* 22 Oct.). After Barney was raped he had tried to commit suicide; when the attempt failed, as punishment the school authorities stripped him naked, stood him in front of the other boys, and beat him (ibid.). Sampson noted that 'if Barney hadn't been raped he would have gotten nothing' (ibid.).

First Ministers' Summit on Aboriginal Issues

On 23 November the First Ministers' Summit on Aboriginal Issues commenced in Kelowna, British Columbia. This meeting was the first of its kind in Canada. At the summit the prime minister, the provinces, and First Nations leaders pledged themselves to a ten-year, multi-billion-dollar program designed to eliminate the gap between Aboriginal and non-Aboriginal people in health care, education, and housing (*Globe and Mail*, 25 Nov.).

This announcement came at the same time as Indian and Northern Affairs Canada (INAC) was slashing core programs, including ending key land-claim negotiations (*Globe and Mail*, 24 Nov.). Internal memos showed that INAC continued to face budgetary problems because of a decade-old policy that capped the growth of program spending at 2 per cent annually, well below the annual rate of inflation (ibid.). On the United Nations Human Development Index, the average Canadian ranked eighth while First Nations people were sixty-third (*Globe and Mail*, 28 June).

Appointments

On 21 September Sandra Lovelace Nicholas was appointed to the Senate. Lovelace was the second Aboriginal women to be appointed (*Globe and Mail*, 22 Sept.). The first indigenous woman in the Senate was Thelma Chalifoux, in 1997.

Assembly of First Nations

Two years before, the AFN had established a Renewal Commission because of growing criticism over the body's failure to effectively represent all of Canada's First Nations (*Globe and Mail*, 19 Oct.). The commission's report, released in October, recommended key changes (ibid.):

- doing away with the existing system of electing the national chief (by the 633 chiefs sitting in the Assembly) and instead holding national elections in which all First Nations people would vote;
- creating the position of an independent auditor who would be empowered to monitor the AFN's spending;

- requiring all elected officials to swear an oath of office and adhere to a code of conduct; and
- creating conflict-of-interest rules by which national and regional AFN leaders would be required to abide.

Over the year the AFN faced increasing criticism and internal dissent. The Assembly met in early November to develop a united front before attending the First Ministers' Summit on Aboriginal Issues (*Globe and Mail,* 3 Nov.). Chiefs representing the eleven numbered treaties and the Quebec chiefs declared they would not allow the AFN to represent them in Kelowna (ibid.). The dissenting chiefs rejected the Assembly's position and maintained that the summit should focus on the rights outlined in post-Confederation treaties. The chiefs of the numbered treaties argued that by dealing with provincial governments the AFN was undermining their relationship with the federal government. Chief Norman Bone of the Keeseekoowenin First Nation in Manitoba withdrew his community permanently from the Assembly, presenting Phil Fontaine with tobacco before announcing his decision. In Bone's words, 'the deal is going to smother or do away with the treaties and we cannot support that' (ibid.).

Provincial and territorial developments

British Columbia

Growing protests over national resource extraction. At the end of January, Tahltan elders occupied band council offices in an effort to speak to Chief Jerry Asp about their concerns over resource development in the area (*Globe and Mail,* 26 Feb.). After thirty-nine days they were still waiting. On 25 February the elders declared a moratorium on resource development in their traditional lands by NovaGold Resources and called for Asp's removal as chief (ibid.). Elder Pat Edzerza said, 'I am concerned about accountability, transparency, and responsibility. We're organized here. We're elders with e-mail. We know what's happening in the outside world. And we know that it's not right for development like this to take place without consultation' (ibid.). Asp resigned and was replaced by his close associate and friend Curtis Tattray (*Globe and Mail,* 15 Nov.).

NovaGold Resources Incorporated, a Vancouver-based mining company, was surprised by this turn of events. The company had held extensive talks with the Tahltan and believed they had good working relations with the nation. In mid-September NovaGold was awarded a two-month injunction against the protestors (*Globe and Mail,* 17 Sept.). Subsequently fifteen of the protestors were arrested for contempt of court, but the charges were later dropped (*Globe and Mail,* 17 Sept. and 1 Nov.). When NovaGold sought to renew the injunction for one year, the motion was denied by British Columbia's Supreme Court (*Globe and Mail,* 24 Sept.).

Over the weekend of 19 February, thirty members of the Tsawataineuk First Nation stopped road-building efforts by International Forest Products Ltd, also known as Interfor (*Globe and Mail,* 21 Feb.). The area under dispute was the Holden Creek Valley, which is at the head of Kingcome Inlet on British Columbia's central coast, a region rich in both old-growth cedar and history. Kingcome Inlet is opposite Port Hardy and accessible only by boat or float plane. The valley is a sacred place for the Tsawataineuk First Nation and contains a 6,000-year-old village site (ibid.). Archaeological evidence confirmed elders' stories that identified Holden Creek – Wasa'lis to the Tswataineuk – as the place where the nation met and renewed alliances (ibid.). According to Chief Joseph, 'Interfor did an archeological assessment too. But I would say our findings are at odds with theirs. We're finding a lot more things than they are. There is the village site; there are lots of CMTs [culturally modified trees] and rock shelters. Not caves, but concave places where people found shelter when they were hunting. The archeologists are looking there and finding evidence of fires from long ago' (*National Post,* 21 Feb.).

Aboriginal rights and land claims. On 4 April a framework agreement was signed by the federal government, the government of British Columbia, and the Musqueam First Nation (*Globe and Mail,* 5 Apr.). This was the third step in a five-stage process and represented significant progress in a series of complex negotiations among the three levels of government. The Musqueam live along a narrow strip of land on the north side of the Fraser River, between the residential districts of Kerrisdale and Southland and the University of British Columbia. The urban location of the nation and the fact that the disputed traditional lands had been developed made for difficult negotiations. Since only Crown land is subject to land claims, the remaining urban Crown land was being hotly contested (ibid.).

On 11 March Justice Carol Ross of the Supreme Court of British Columbia ruled that the sale of 70,000 hectares of land from one forestry company to another would adversely affect the rights and title of the Hupacasath First Nation of Vancouver Island (*Windspeaker,* May).

Further, Ross found that the Hupacasath Nation would suffer irreparable harm if jurisdiction over the land was transferred from the *Forest Act* to the *Private Forest Lands Management Act* (ibid.). However, the court did not rule against the land sale itself, citing the 'balance of convenience test' (*Windspeaker,* May). Will Horter, an environmental lawyer and executive director of the Dogwood Initiative, criticized the unfairness of the convenience test, saying that 'it's basically comparing apples and oranges. How do you put a dollar value on a constitutional right as opposed to something that's worth $1.2 billion' (ibid.).

The Supreme Court's 2004 Haida decision required governments to consult with First Nations people before proceeding with resource development on their lands. However, 2005 witnessed local and provincial governments avoiding this responsibility by selling land to development companies without consultation (ibid.).

United Native Nations Society. In April the *Globe and Mail* (5 Apr.) reported that the B.C. Ministry of Finance was auditing the United Native Nations Society (UNN). A non-profit organization, the UNN represented about 90,000 status and non-status indigenous people in British Columbia and delivered housing and social programs for the provincial and federal governments. Allegations of financial and professional misconduct were levied against the president and vice-president, who were subsequently fired (ibid.). Later a government audit revealed that the former executives and certain board members owed the UNN $234,000 for unsupported or unapproved expenses (*Globe and Mail,* 6 Apr.).

The UNN held elections in August. Lillian George was elected president and David Dennis vice-president (*Globe and Mail,* 1 Aug.). Dennis was elected just weeks after being the target of a take-down operation by the RCMP's Integrated National Security Enforcement Team on the Burrard Street Bridge in Vancouver (*Vancouver Sun,* 29 June). When asked how he thought his arrest and release would affect his job at the UNN, Dennis responded by saying, 'In Indian country, it seems, people do not assume you are guilty of anything just because you have been busted' (*Globe and Mail,* 1 Aug.).

Transferring services. In 2002, under the Kith and Kin Program, nineteen-month-old Sherry Charlie was placed with her uncle, Ryan George. At the time George was on probation for spousal abuse (*Globe and Mail,* 13 Aug.). Tragically, only weeks after her placement with the George family, Charlie was killed by her uncle. Nuu-chah-nulth Tribal

Council USMA Family and Child Services on Vancouver Island was responsible for the placement.

The Kith and Kin Program had been introduced by the Ministry of Children and Family Development in 2002, eight weeks before Charlie's death, to place Aboriginal foster children with Aboriginal families. The ministry performed an internal review of the incident and released its findings in 2005, concluding that the following mistakes had been made by both the ministry and the Nuu-chah-nulth agency: the government failed to disclose information about the family to the agency, especially George's domestic abuse; the ministry did not provide the Nuu-chah-nulth with adequate training or guidelines for the Kith and Kin Program; and the Nuu-chah-nulth agency failed to perform a criminal background check before they placed Charlie in the home (*Globe and Mail*, 22 Sept.).

The Prairies

Housing. The Dakota Plains First Nation (southwest of Portage la Prairie, Manitoba) filed suit against the federal government for failing to rectify black mould problems in their homes (*Windspeaker*, Feb.). The National Aboriginal Health Organization had recently undertaken a study that found that 43.6 per cent of homes on the reserve were infected with mould (Ibid.). Black mould is toxic and causes chronic respiratory problems, nosebleeds, and allergies. Chief Orville Smoke stated that the problem was rooted in the location of the reserve – on a bog – making it a perfect breeding ground for black mould. In addition, the shifting groundwater created further hazardous living conditions by corroding electrical wiring and breaking the pipes in septic systems, causing septic gas leaks into people's homes (ibid.). Smoke said that the only way to rectify the problem would be to relocate the reserve to drier ground. Concern over the housing crisis at Dakota Plains had first been raised in April 2003 by Sheila Fraser, the federal auditor general (ibid.).

Court decisions. The Manitoba Court of Appeals released a ruling on 14 February that affected the manner in which bands would handle their finances in the future. The court ruled that sections 89 and 90 of the *Indian Act,* intended to protect communally owned reserve property from seizure, only applied to assets physically on reserves (*Windspeaker*, Apr.). The decision allowed the Winnipeg-based firm McDiarmid Lumber to garnish the God's Lake First Nation's bank account, located at a branch of Peace Hills Trust in Winnipeg (ibid.).

Court of Queen's Bench Justice Marsha Erb overruled the conviction of five members of the Whitefish Lake First Nation, located near St. Paul in northeastern Alberta. The five were convicted 1 July 2000 for possessing undersized northern pike and walleye in contravention of federal and provincial laws aimed at preserving depleted fish stocks (*National Post*, 29 Mar.). Ben Houle, one of the defendants, said that it was 'a huge victory for treaty Indians' because the decision recognized the constitutional rights of First Nations to fish for subsistence, and he maintained that although fish populations are threatened by overfishing, band members were not to blame (ibid.).

On 24 November the Supreme Court of Canada criticized the federal government for failing to consult with the Mikisew Cree First Nation in northern Alberta six years before, when Ottawa approved the creation of a winter road through Canada's largest national park, which straddles the boundary of Alberta and the Northwest Territories. The purpose of the road was to connect Fort Smith with the south (*Globe and Mail*, 25 Nov.). Aboriginal trappers and hunters believed that the creation of the winter road would harm their livelihoods (ibid.).

Economic development. Manitoba's Roseau River Band sought to purchase twenty acres of land in an industrial suburb of Winnipeg, creating the city's first urban reserve (*Globe and Mail*, 21 Sept.). The band wanted to use the land to develop various business projects to fund development on the reserve. Residents of the suburb were against the proposed development because they felt it would bring more crime to the area (ibid.). A similar project was undertaken in Saskatchewan by the Muskeg Lake First Nation. That band bought land in Saskatoon and opened a business park with forty on-site companies owned by indigenous and non-indigenous people. This project created jobs and prosperity for the band.

The Saskatchewan Treaty Land Entitlement Framework Agreement was signed in 1992, and in 1997 Manitoba reached a similar agreement with the federal government and First Nations groups (*Globe and Mail*, 23 Nov.). At the time the Department of Indian Affairs (DIA) supported such agreements and agreed to draft a plan to follow through on written pledges to expand the size of reserves in order to build strong local economies. Under the deal, bands could expand their reserves using Crown land or receive money to buy land in urban areas. Critically, in the latter case the urban satellites would enjoy reserve status (ibid.). In November the auditor general, Sheila Fraser, criticized federal and provincial governments for failing to fulfil these promises, thereby preventing bands from creating strong economies (ibid.).

Adoption. The Saskatchewan government's policy on Aboriginal adoptions, which required the consent of adoptees' bands before any adoptions could proceed, was declared unconstitutional on 10 December by Madam Justice Jacelyn Ann Ryan-Froslie of Saskatchewan's Court of Queen's Bench (*Globe and Mail,* 1 Jan.). The case in question involved five siblings who had spent most of their lives in temporary foster homes. For example, one of the children, an eight-year-old girl, had lived in twenty different homes over the previous five years (ibid.). Government spokesperson Dorothea Warren said that in light of the ruling, the province had set aside the policy and would immediately begin discussions with Aboriginal child welfare authorities (ibid.).

The lawyer representing the children, Greg Walen, said, 'First Nation bands refused to allow their children to be adopted. As a consequence, these children, who have been apprehended by the department, languish in foster care for years, moving from foster home to foster home to foster home' (ibid.). This policy had been instituted in response to an enormous outcry in the Aboriginal community over children being removed from their homes and alienated from their communities and culture. Of the 3,000 children in foster care in Saskatchewan, 70 per cent were indigenous (*Globe and Mail,* 4 Jan.).

Stolen Sisters and Project Kare. Since 1983, twenty-three prostitutes, most of whom were indigenous women, were murdered in Edmonton and the surrounding area (*Globe and Mail,* 17 June). As of 2005, only five of these crimes had been solved. There were so many unsolved murders of prostitutes in Edmonton that a local tabloid newspaper called the areas outside the city where many of the bodies had been found the 'killing fields' (ibid.). An RCMP-led task force called Project Kare was investigating the murders. Alberta's justice minister called on Ottawa to create a national DNA database of johns convicted of soliciting. Irwin Cotler, Minister of Justice, said that 'the feds recently passed substantial changes to that law by making the collection of DNA samples mandatory for those convicted of the very worst and most violent offences.' Cotler urged the federal government to include convicted johns in their DNA collection because, 'unlike other murderers, people who pick up prostitutes have a level of anonymity' (ibid.).

Elections. The chief and band council of the Red Pheasant First Nation, located south of North Battleford, Saskatchewan, were removed from office after an investigation by the federal government revealed electoral misconduct in the previous spring's election (*National Post,* 15 Dec.). According to the *Indian Act,* the minister of Indian affairs and northern development could – and did – remove Chief Charles Meechance and eight band councillors for buying votes (ibid.).

In April Tammy Cook-Searson became the first woman to be elected chief of Lac La Ronge, Saskatchewan's largest First Nations community (*Globe and Mail,* 17 Sept.). Her victory reflected the growing formal involvement of Aboriginal women in band politics, a trend that some people claimed was changing the style and substance of indigenous politics (ibid.). According to John Lagimodiere, Aboriginal women had

markedly different priorities and leadership style[s]. They are more diplomatic and inclusive because they are often 'closer to home' and more concerned with social issues that face modern bands, such as health care and child welfare. An old boys' club is still running things in Saskatchewan, but the growing number of women shows change is coming. It's creeping, but it's coming. ... (ibid.)

In 1951 the *Indian Act* was amended to make it legal for women to be elected as chiefs or to band council positions. According to Beverly Jacobs, president of the Native Women's Association of Canada (NWAC), 'They want their traditional roles back. Far too long, male Aboriginal leaders have focused on "colonization issues" such as treaty negotiations and self-government, while social and cultural concerns are ignored or minimized' (ibid.). At the time, only 15 per cent of bands recognized by the federal government had elected women to executive positions (ibid.). The AFN had never been led by a woman; in fact, only two women had ever run for the position, and they never came close. Local chiefs voted for the leader of the AFN, and 85 per cent of chiefs were men (ibid.).

First Nations University of Canada. The Saskatchewan government released a report in early April to the board of the First Nations University of Canada (FNUC) that raised grave concerns over institutional practices around academic freedom, governance, and political interference (*Globe and Mail,* 30 July). FNUC had been mired in controversy over firings and suspensions of university administrators. In February, amid allegations of financial mismanagement, three university administrators were suspended and later fired (*Globe and Mail,* 28 Nov.). Morley

Watson, vice-chief of the Federation of Saskatchewan Indian Nations (FSIN), alleged that there was financial wrongdoing. By the end of the year no charges had been laid. The executive director of the Canadian Association of University Teachers, James Turk, described the events as a political coup orchestrated by the leaders of the FSIN (ibid.). An interim report questioned the large size of the board, recommended governance reform, and expressed unease over the number of people who had been hired outside of the formal recruitment process (ibid.).

Powley decision. The Manitoba Métis Federation (MMF) rescinded its recent decision to award Manitoba's Premier, Gary Doer, the Manitoba Order of the Sash (*Globe and Mail,* 12 Sept.). The about-face came as a result of disputes between the province and the Métis Federation over hunting rights. Under the Powley ruling of 2003, the Supreme Court had recognized Métis people as a distinct Aboriginal group with protected constitutional rights, upholding their rights to hunt, fish, and trap without a provincial licence in areas where they had historically hunted (ibid.). Unlike other provinces, Manitoba had not acknowledged the Supreme Court's ruling, because of the government's concern for wildlife conservation and because it was unclear who held Métis status in the province (ibid.). Annually the province issued 176,000 hunting licences and the Métis Federation handed out 800. Since 2003 over a dozen Métis people in Manitoba had been charged with illegal hunting or had their firearms or game seized by provincial wardens (ibid.).

Ontario

Residential schools. In a class action suit filed by former students of the Mohawk Institute Residential School in Brantford, the defendants – Canada, the Anglican Church of Canada, and the New England Company – tried to introduce new evidence during the appeal showing that the alternate dispute resolution (ADR) process was preferable to the courts (*Windspeaker,* 22 Jan.). On 3 December Justice Goudge ruled against the defendants, stating,

It is a system unilaterally created by one of the [defendants] in this action and could be unilaterally dismantled without the consent of the [former students]. It deals only with physical and sexual abuse. It caps the amount of possible recovery and, most importantly in these circumstances, compared to the class action it shares the access to justice deficiencies of individual actions. ... (ibid.)

This ruling set the stage for survivors to file class action suits across the country.

Ipperwash inquiry. In June tape recordings made on 6 September 1996 of conversations between OPP officers, hours before Dudley George was shot by Acting Sergeant Kenneth Deane (later convicted of criminal negligence causing death), were released (*Windspeaker,* 23 June). The recordings showed that at least one officer believed that Mike Harris, then premier of Ontario, was advocating police violence to remove the First Nations protestors from Ipperwash Provincial Park. The recording was of a phone conversation between Inspector Ron Fox, the OPP liaison officer for the Ontario legislature, and Ipperwash incident commander Inspector John Carson. During the conversation Fox related his interpretation of Harris's perspective on the occupation of the park, saying, '[Harris] views it as a simple trespass on property ... He's not getting the right advice. Or if he is getting the right advice he sure is not listening to it in any way, shape or form ... We're dealing with a redneck government. They are fuckin' barrel suckers, they are just in love with guns ... they couldn't care give a shit less about Indians' (*Globe and Mail,* 19 May). In particular, Fox expressed concern over the opinions voiced by Deb Hutton, Harris's top aide (*Globe and Mail,* 15 July).

During the investigation, Charles Harnick, former attorney general of Ontario, testified that in a meeting held in the premier's dining room he had overheard Harris say "he wanted the fucking Indians out of Ipperwash Park" (*Globe and Mail,* 29 Nov.). Larry Taman, the deputy attorney general, supported Fox's statement when he testified that he had been passed instructions by Harnick reversing the Ministry of Justice's strategy on the standoff, from a 'wait and see' approach to a more forceful one (*Globe and Mail,* 16 Nov.). When OPP chief superintendent Christopher Coles appeared before the inquiry in September, he testified that the situation at Ipperwash Park was not urgent on the day that George was slain and two other activists were wounded by police gunfire (*Globe and Mail,* 19 May).

The primary question before the commission investigating the death of Dudley George was what had prompted the OPP's actions. In particular, had the OPP taken action as a result of political pressure? (*Globe and Mail,* 14 July) During the occupation of Ipperwash Park, the premier had formed an ad hoc group drawn from various ministries, called the 'blockades committee,' to deal with the situation. However, the OPP and other police forces are supposed to operate at arm's length from government. To some observers the evidence suggested that this principle had been violated by the Harris government in its handling of the Ipperwash crisis (*Globe and Mail,* 15 July).

Kashechewan. The remote community of Kashechewan, a reserve 200 ki-lometres north of Timmins on the shore of James Bay, had been under a boil-water advisory for two years. In early October the situation de-teriorated when *E. coli* bacteria was discovered in the drinking water (*Globe and Mail,* 25 Oct.). Kashechewan's drinking-water problems stemmed from its water treatment system, which was about 135 me-tres downstream from the release point of the community's raw sewage (*Globe and Mail,* 20 Oct.). Chief Leo Friday was seeking money from the federal government to evacuate the community.

Federal-provincial jurisdictional confusion postponed help to Kashechewan. David Ramsay, Ontario's minister of natural resources, called on Ottawa to address the problem, saying that although he was prepared to act, his hands were tied because responsibility for First Nations people fell under federal authority (*Globe and Mail,* 25 Oct.). Ontario's premier, Dalton McGuinty, echoed Ramsay when he said that, although the conditions at Katshechewan were deplorable, it was up to the federal government to deal with the crisis (*Globe and Mail,* 26 Oct.). Ottawa's immediate response was to send bottled water and government officials to the reserve, which is not accessible by road or train (*Globe and Mail,* 20 Oct.).

In a dramatic shift, the Ontario government declared a state of emer-gency at Kashechewan in late October, and all members of the commu-nity in need of medical attention were evacuated from the reserve. This announcement was made after a copy of the Emergency Preparedness Agreement, signed in 1992 by Ottawa and Ontario, was 'discovered' (*Globe and Mail,* 26 Oct.). The agreement stated that the province was responsible for providing emergency assistance when requested by the DIA or a First Nations community; the federal government would cover costs incurred by the province (ibid.). Health officials estimated that as many as 60 per cent of the reserve's 1,900 residents required medical attention (ibid.). After two months of living in Ottawa, almost every-one from Kashechewan was home by the end of December (*Globe and Mail,* 24 Dec.). The water treatment system had been repaired but the necessary upgrade had not been performed because a contractor had not been hired (ibid.). As a result, the boil-water advisory remained in effect.

While the federal government agreed to build a new community for the residents of Kashechewan, critics observed that this would not resolve the long-term problem of access to safe water faced by many remote indigenous communities. A similar situation existed, for instance, in the community of Keewaywin, near Sioux Lookout (*Globe and Mail,* 28 Oct.), where the reserve's water supply was contaminated with uranium. Keewaywin was one of thirty-nine communities in Ontario whose drinking water contained dirt, uranium, or fuel oil (ibid.).

Andrew Orkin, a human rights lawyer who represented First Nations groups struggling to improve drinking water in their communities, commented that 'they live with the ongoing trauma of being terrified of what they have to drink. That trauma grinds on for years and years and years. It splits families and it drives people away from their communities' (ibid.). Orkin maintained that the failure of the federal and provincial governments to provide clean drinking water in First Nations communities was part of a deliberate national policy (ibid.). Howard Hampton, the Ontario NDP leader, criticized the provincial government for not allocating to reserves any of the $90 million earmarked in the provincial budget for water quality projects in rural communities (*Globe and Mail,* 1 Nov.). McGuinty retorted that reserves were the responsibility of the federal government.

Harvesting natural resources. In 2004 MPP Gilles Bisson introduced a private member's bill, the First Nations Resource Revenue Sharing Act, which was designed to redistribute profits harvested from natural resources on traditional territories (*Globe and Mail,* 23 Sept.). Bill 97 was designed to guarantee indigenous people a share of the proceeds from the extraction of resources on their lands. The bill underwent its first and second readings before being sent to the Standing Committee on Finance and Economic Affairs, where it was stalled at year's end.

Quebec

Kanesatake. Former Grand Chief James Gabriel, along with three other chiefs, made a decision during the fall of 2004 to replace Kanesatake's current acting police chief, Terry Cross, and bring in an outside police force drawn from the RCMP, the Sûreté du Québec, and Aboriginal constables from more than twenty reserves (*Windspeaker,* Mar. 2004). Members of the band council opposed this decision. When the new police force arrived, a crowd of protestors surrounded the police station and Gabriel's house and car were set on fire (ibid.). Gabriel and his family fled the community. The twenty-four-hour standoff ended after the Sûreté du Québec signed an agreement with the protestors, allowing the interim police force to leave the station (ibid.).

On 31 October 2005 seven Mohawk men were found guilty of rioting and forcible confinement for their involvement in the events at Kanesatake in 2004. Five others were charged with unlawful assembly (*National Post*, 14 Dec.). The people charged included a former Kanesatake police officer and a civilian police commissioner. Gabriel expressed his happiness over the verdict: 'I'm very satisfied with the key figures in the riot have been found guilty – we always knew they were' (ibid.).

This incident led to Gabriel's defeat in elections held in June. Gabriel, who had been grand chief since 1996, was defeated by Steven Bonspille (*Globe and Mail*, 27 June). The major issue of the campaign was privately owned cigarette shacks that were selling tobacco at discounted prices (ibid.). Trees from the Pines were being cut down to make room for the shacks; this area had been at the centre of the dispute that triggered the Oka crisis in July 1990. Gabriel opposed expansion of the shacks into the Pines, while Bonspille believed the shacks did not pose a threat (ibid.).

Natural resource development. The Innu Council of Pessamit, led by Chief Raphael Picard, renewed its struggle with the province for control over natural resource development on René-Levasseur Island after the Quebec Court of Appeal lifted a temporary injunction against the forestry company Kruger Inc. (*Globe and Mail*, 27 June). The council asked the Supreme Court to stop all logging on the island, which is in Quebec's vast North Shore region. On 18 July the council placed more than fifty forest companies on notice, stating that they would be asking the Supreme Court to bar logging on more than 250,000 square kilometres of ancestral land, a territory the size of Great Britain (*Globe and Mail*, 19 July). Picard wanted the provincial government to participate in 'nation-to-nation' negotiations around natural resource development: 'we don't want to stop economic development. We want Quebec to listen to what we have to say. We want to develop natural resources in a civilized way that takes into account our rights as well as environmental concerns' (ibid.).

Removal and resettlement. During the 1950s the Washaw Sibi Cree were relocated by the federal government from their traditional hunting and trapping territories near James Bay to the Algonquin Pikogan Reserve (*Globe and Mail*, 9 Aug.). As a result of their relocation, the Cree were excluded from the ground-breaking James Bay and Northern

Quebec Agreement signed in 1975. In protest of their relocation, the Washaw Sibi Cree journeyed in August to La Sarre, a traditional summer gathering place (ibid). In September they set up a tent city at the former Joulac campground on the Abitibiwinni First Nation Reserve; they were determined to remain there until the federal government addressed their grievances (*Eeyou Eenou Nation,* Winter).

Atlantic Canada

Treaty rights. On 20 July the Supreme Court handed down its decision regarding the Marshall and Bernard cases. The Marshall case involved thirty-five Mi'kmaq loggers who had been charged with cutting timber on Crown land in Nova Scotia (*Windspeaker,* Sept.). In New Brunswick, Joshua Bernard had been charged with unlawful possession of logs harvested from Crown land and transporting them to a sawmill (ibid.). The cases were combined because the plaintiffs offered the same defence: their treaty rights and Aboriginal title, which they maintained had never been extinguished, meant they did not have to acquire permission from the province for logging activities. The Supreme Court restored the trial judge's decision, which ruled that modern-day logging activities were not a 'logical evolution of traditional Mi'kmaq trading activity' (ibid.). This ruling had wide-ranging implications for other First Nations groups, especially in British Columbia, where many outstanding indigenous land claims were based on the legal arguments made in the Marshall and Bernard cases (*Globe and Mail,* 21 July).

The North

Mackenzie Valley pipeline. Work on the Mackenzie Valley pipeline was halted on 28 April because of concerns over rising costs (*Globe and Mail,* 29 Apr.). The five-member consortium backing the project said they were stopping construction on the $7-billion megaproject until they could resolve concerns around federal regulations and negotiations with indigenous groups (ibid.). Michael Yeager, senior vice-president of Imperial Oil, said that 'proposals from the Aboriginal groups far exceed the amount and scope of what the companies deem to be related to the pipeline, [and] the requests would cost hundreds of millions to meet' (ibid.).

Stephen Kakfwi, former premier of the Northwest Territories and negotiator for the Sahtu (one of the four principal First Nations groups on the pipeline route), said that 'there's no way we're going to remain the poorest people in Canada when there's a $7 billion dollar project going on here' (*Globe and Mail,* 12 May). First Nations communities along the pipeline were determined to negotiate recurring payments directly from Imperial Oil rather than having the money funnelled through the Ottawa and Yellowknife governments (ibid.). Imperial Oil rejected this position and remained determined to pay taxes and royalties only to recognized governments. The Deh Cho, led by Grand Chief Herb Norwegian, were equally determined to force the consortium to deal with them as a nation (*Globe and Mail,* 3 May). However, this position was softened when the federal government settled a two-year lawsuit by agreeing to give the Deh Cho $31.5 million: $15 million for economic development, $6 million so the Deh Cho could participate in the pipeline review, and $10.5 million so the Deh Cho could prepare for negotiation with Ottawa on broader land claims and self-government settlement (*Globe and Mail,* 12 July).

The stalemate between the consortium and the federal government broke in late November, when the federal government agreed to fiscal concessions. Ottawa promised to address social and economic issues among northern First Nations people (*Globe and Mail,* 24 Nov.). Land access agreements with individual groups remain unresolved, but Imperial Oil expected to have those in place by the end of the year (ibid.). By year's end, however, it was clear the project would continue to face challenges from First Nations groups. In early December the Supreme Court agreed to hear a case filed by the Dene Tha' First Nation, a group of seven reserves in northwestern Alberta and northeastern British Columbia. The Dene Tha' filed an injunction to halt the pipeline, as they had been excluded from negotiations (*Globe and Mail,* 10 Dec.). Robert Freedman, the lawyer for the Dene Tha' who filed the suit in May, said 'they were never told about the process' (*Globe and Mail,* 18 May). The pipeline would potentially cross about 100 kilometres of Dene Tha' traditional territory (ibid.).

Nunavut. Thomas Berger was brought in to restart talks, stalled since 2003, to renew the 1993 Nunavut Land Claims Agreement (*Globe and Mail,* 12 July). Berger issued his report on 31 August, reserving his harshest criticism for tactics employed by the Crown, especially concerning article 38 of the agreement (*Windspeaker,* Oct.). Article 38 created the Nunavut Arbitration Board (NAB), which had been designed to resolve disputes arising around interpretation, application, and implementation of the agreement (*Globe and Mail,* 23 Oct.). However, Canada had refused in every case to agree to arbitration, on the grounds that it would interfere with Parliament's exclusive authority over the appropriation of money (*Windspeaker,* Oct.). Berger's report censured the federal government for using technicalities to impose its will and for refusing to abide by all elements of the agreement (*Globe and Mail,* 14 Oct.). He questioned 'the pass[age] of legislation which creates a new territory and settles the land claims of the Inuit of the eastern Arctic while placing all rules governing funding and authorities in a separate, nonlegislated contract. The legislation has the full protection of the Canadian constitution; the separate contract does not' (*Windspeaker,* Oct.).

Education. On 21 June, the Akitsiraq Law School graduated its first class, increasing the number of Inuit lawyers in Nunavut from one to twelve (*Globe and Mail,* 11 June). The school was part of a broader effort to develop a body of professionals in the region who could participate in the development of policy grounded in Inuit values (ibid.). Professor Shelley Wright, a supporter of the law school, said, '[The Inuit] need to do these things rather than bringing people up from the south all the time who don't know the culture' (*Globe and Mail,* 11 June).

CAREY HILL[1]

British Columbia

2005 was an incredibly eventful year in politics in British Columbia. The year began on a positive economic note: December 2004 had seen growth in British Columbia's employment, with half of all new jobs created in Canada and a drop in unemployment to its lowest rate since June 1981 (*Alberni Valley Times,* 10 Jan.). While the year's economic news was upbeat overall, NDP leader Carole James noted that although part-time employment had grown, the lack of jobs in places such as Prince Rupert continued to be of concern (*Nanaimo Daily News,* 8 Jan.).

The year was marked by elections and strikes. The provincial election occurred in May, as expected in accordance with provincial legislation. In addition to election of the province's members of the Legislative Assembly, it involved a referendum on a new electoral system for British Columbia, the single transferable vote. Municipal elections took place in November, delivering a new mayor for Vancouver, and December saw the start of a federal election in which B.C. was considered a 'wild card.'

Among striking workers in B.C. in 2005 were teachers, truckers, and Telus workers. The Campbell Liberals' battle with public sector unions continued, this time with prosecutors and teachers. Perhaps the bigger labour story, however, was the private sector strikes that occurred in B.C., first by independent truckers and then between Telus and the Telecommunications Workers Union.

The biggest story was the performance of the B.C. economy – it was 'hot.' Mid-year, Statistics Canada announced that it was the top-performing economy in the country. By year's end it would finish up second in growth only to Alberta.

1 The author wishes to thank Karen Ward for research assistance.

Two throne speeches

There were two throne speeches, one in February and one in September. Both focused on the Liberals' 'Golden Decade' goals.

The February speech, read by Iona Campagnolo, outlined several goals for British Columbia to accomplish over the next ten years, recognizing that the Olympics were on the horizon and the province would attract worldwide attention. The Golden Decade goals included the following:

- Make British Columbia the best-educated, most literate jurisdiction on the continent.
- Lead the way in North America in healthy living and physical fitness.
- Build the best system of support in Canada for persons with disabilities, those with special needs, children at risk, and seniors.
- Lead the world in sustainable environmental management, with the best air and water quality and the best fisheries management, bar none.
- Create more jobs per capita than anywhere else in Canada.

The September speech reiterated these goals. Interestingly, among other measures, it also extended question period from fifteen to thirty minutes.

Provincial budget

The economy performed well throughout the year. In February Campbell's Liberals introduced the provincial budget, with finance minister Colin Hansen boasting, 'British Columbia is once again the economic leader in all of Canada. The province is running on all cylinders' (*Globe and Mail,* 16 Feb.). He also announced that the Liberals had overcome the 'economic mess' they inherited from the NDP in 2001. He predicted a $400-million surplus during 2005–06 and suggested that B.C. would become a 'have' province. Furthermore, he explained that the zero-zero wage mandate for labour negotiations would expire in the spring of 2006, but noted, 'We do not believe British Columbia should be a wage leader in all of Canada' (*Vancouver Sun,* 16 Feb.).

A major aspect of the budget speech was tax cuts, including reduction or elimination of provincial income taxes for about 730,000 people and reduction or elimination of Medical Services Plan premiums for about 215,000 people (*Summerland Review,* 20 Feb.). There was also significant funding for health care, including capital grants to regional health authorities. Some funds were designated for upgrades to interior and rural roads (*Vernon Morning Star,* 25 Feb.). The speech set the tone for the provincial election campaign, which began in April.

In response to the budget speech, NDP leader Carole James said that the Campbell Liberals had balanced the budget by ignoring seniors and breaking its campaign promise to build 5,000 long-term-care beds by 2006 (*Burnaby Now,* 19 Feb.). In early February health minister Shirley Bond admitted that only 100 beds had been added (*The News – Abbotsford,* 12 Feb.).

Provincial election

The provincial election date was fixed, in accordance with provincial legislation that had been introduced by the Campbell Liberals, and it took place on 17 May 2005. This was an historic election in three major ways: (1) it was the first fixed election date in provincial history, (2) there was a referendum on a new electoral system for B.C., and (3) the outcome saw the first re-election of a B.C. premier since Bill Bennett. In addition to its historic nature, the election represented a comeback for the NDP.

There are 79 seats in the provincial legislature. In the previous election, in 2001, 77 were taken by Liberals, with just two held by the NDP. When all the votes were counted in the 2005 election, 46 Liberals formed the government, with 33 NDP in opposition. Among the NDP seats was one for its leader, Carole James, who had lost a close race to the Liberals in the 2001 election in her riding of Victoria-Beaconhill. Tom Morino, leader of the Democratic Reform Party, did not get elected, nor did any of the four members of his party, including incumbent Elayne Brezinger.

Even though only two parties ended up with representation in the legislature (something electoral reformers would point to in a critique of the system), forty-three political parties were registered in B.C. in addition to the Liberals and NDP. Some notable examples included the Sex Party and the Annexation Party of B.C., which aimed to make British Columbia the fifty-first state in the American union (*National Post,* 2 May).

There were some exciting races in the election. In the Fort Langley–Aldergrove constituency, B.C.'s 'Prince of Pot,' Marc Emery, was pitted against the province's solicitor general, Rich Coleman. Emery used the election as an opportunity to raise issues around the legalization of marijuana, explaining, 'Even though the public wants to reform our marijuana laws, the Solicitor General is pushing for draconian U.S.-style drug war tactics that don't work in the U.S. and won't work for Canadians' (*Aldergrove Star,* 24 Feb.).

The tightest race in the election was between incumbent Liberal Lorne Mayencourt and NDP Tim Stevenson in the riding of Vancouver-Burrard. Elections B.C. announced that Mayencourt had won the riding by eighteen votes after all the absentee ballots were counted. At the end of the election evening, prior to counting the absentee ballots, Tim Stevenson had been in the lead. Both were well-known in their west-end community and both were openly gay politicians. Stevenson, a former United Church minister, could be expected to continue to be very active in local politics, building on his more than ten years of work in Vancouver's Downtown Eastside. Mayencourt, a small-business owner, was known for his work as founder and former executive director of the Vancouver Friends for Life Society, supporting people living with AIDS, cancer, and other life-threatening diseases. During his first term as MLA, he introduced the controversial *Safe Streets Act* and *Trespass to Property Act*, which criminalized aggressive panhandling and squatting.

The Liberals campaigned on their record, emphasizing the positive economic news and their vision of a 'Golden Decade' for the province. Their campaign slogan was 'B.C. is back.' This contrasted with the NDP, which fought the campaign by focusing primarily on health care and education, using the slogan 'Everyone matters.' The campaign was not viewed as one of ideas. It was described by UBC political scientist Allan Tupper as one of opponents attacking one another (*Nanaimo Daily News,* 11 May). One issue that did receive some attention, however, was education. John Dyck, a political scientist at Trinity Western University, noted the importance of the Liberals' connecting the NDP to teachers' strikes, referring to this as a 'hot button issue' and explaining that this advantage gave the 'Liberals a body blow' (*Nanaimo Daily News,* 14 May).

The issue of the labour negotiations between the provincial government and the province's teachers garnered attention when the NDP said it would reinstate the teachers' right to strike if it was elected. In addition, Gordon Campbell argued that the British Columbia Teachers' Federation (BCTF) had a hidden agenda; rumours suggested that the BCTF would hold a strike vote two days after the election (*Prince George Citizen,* 13 May). Post-secondary education policy was also on the radar during the campaign, as the NDP stated it would freeze tuition fees if elected. The Liberal plan was to institute a tuition cap, pegging fees to the rate of inflation. Connecting the NDP to big labour was a Liberal strategy throughout the campaign, as evidenced by the arguments around the BCTF and also by comments made by Bill Bennett, MLA for East Kootenay. He suggested that a rally held in support of the NDP proved that 'big labour and the NDP are synonymous' ('Daily Bulletin,' 12 May).

The first poll, conducted by Ipsos-Reid in late April, showed the Liberals in the lead. It also suggested that four in ten NDP supporters did not think the NDP could win the election. In addition, according to the poll, the new electoral system under consideration on the ballot – BC-STV – was not well understood by the public: 39 per cent said they knew very little about it, 25 per cent said they knew nothing at all, and only 4 per cent felt they knew a great deal about it (*Vancouver Sun,* 30 Apr.).

The first debate took place in early May and included Gordon Campbell, Carole James, and Adriane Carr, leader of the Green Party. Commentators in the *Vancouver Sun* emphasized the decorum and respect shown throughout the debate (5 May). Even though Campbell's Liberals would emerge victorious in the election, analysts called James the winner of the first debate (*Nanaimo Daily News,* 11 May).

Single transferable vote

This historic election included a referendum on replacing the existing first-past-the-post electoral system with the single transferable vote (STV), as recommended by the Citizens' Assembly on Electoral Reform. The Citizens' Assembly had completed its work on 10 December 2004. It overwhelmingly endorsed the STV (149–7), which is a way of ranking candidates on a ballot in order of preference (*Tri-City News,* 26 Feb.). In the proposed BC-STV system there would still be seventy-nine candidates, but riding boundaries would be expanded to elect multiple members. For example, two members might be elected in some rural ridings, whereas cities might elect up to seven representatives. Parties could run as many candidates as they chose (*Tri-City News,* 23 Feb.). The referendum question was 'Should British Columbia change to the BC-STV electoral system as recommended by the Citizens' Assembly on Electoral Reform?' Proponents of the STV argued that the preferential ballot ensured that no votes would be wasted and gave smaller parties a chance to elect members (*Prince Rupert Daily News,* 9 May). By contrast, opponents noted that a different form of STV had been tried in B.C. in 1952 and 1953 but then abandoned as 'unwieldy' and 'unfair' (*Times-Colonist,* 8 May).

The referendum required a double threshold of 60 per cent of the popular vote and majority support in 60 per cent of the constituencies. The result on 17 May 2005 saw BC-STV miss narrowly: it received 57.69 per cent of voter support and vastly surpassed the second threshold as 97 per cent of constituencies voted in favour of adopting the new system, according to Elections B.C. In light of this close result, on 12 September 2005 the Speech from the Throne indicated the government's intent to hold another referendum on electoral reform to decide the future of BC-STV.

Labour issues: strikes and legislation

The Campbell Liberals' battle with labour continued in 2005, this time focusing on prosecutors and teachers. The bigger labour story was private sector strikes during the year, first among independent truckers and then between Telus and the Telecommunications Workers Union.

On the first day of March, Campbell's Liberals introduced legislation to settle a contract with the province's four hundred Crown prosecutors (*Alberni Valley Times,* 1 Mar.). The legislation took away the prosecutors' right to strike, removed the government's obligation to accept formerly binding arbitration, and imposed a four-year wage decision, with no increase for the first three years and 13 per cent in the final year (*National Post,* 14 May). The prosecutors accused Campbell of breaking the law. The arbitrator's ruling that came down in February upheld a January 2004 panel finding that called for wage hikes. In response, following Campbell's re-election, the provincial prosecutors issued a lawsuit claiming $30 million in back pay, arguing that the Liberals had acted in bad faith and abused their office. The prosecutors stated that they were underpaid compared with other, similar workers across the country (*National Post,* 14 May).

Telus 'strike'

The most protracted labour dispute of the year was between Telus and its main employees' union, the Telecommunications Workers Union (TWU). The dispute was already four years old when the year began, as TWU's previous contract had expired in December 2000. On 22 April Telus CEO Darren Entwistle set a deadline for unionized employees to respond to the company's contract offer. The offer would have set Telus back $200 million in additional costs. Entwistle called the offer 'affordable' to shareholders and 'generous' to bargaining-unit employees

(*Vancouver Sun,* 22 Apr.). In July Telus said it would bring in an offer without a vote by the union, which the union took as provocation (*Toronto Star,* 13 July). The company had modestly increased its offer, though most of the increases were not guaranteed and would be based on Telus's performance. On 22 July the TWU said that its more than 13,000 workers were locked out, and they began picketing Telus buildings in B.C. and Alberta. Telus claimed the workers were on strike. On 23 July Telus imposed a new contract offer but the picket lines remained in place. The company suggested that 3,000 TWU workers – half the Alberta bargaining unit – had crossed picket lines to perform work, but this was disputed by the TWU (*Edmonton Journal,* 23 July).

A big issue in the labour dispute, according to the B.C. Federation of Labour, was Telus's desire for a collective agreement that would give them the option of exporting work to the Philippines or India or other places than B.C. (*The Province,* 27 July). Another sticking point was that the contract that expired in 1999 had been with BC Tel, and TWU employees believed they should start negotiating based on that contract. Meanwhile Telus management argued that they needed a new start because the BC Tel contract had been written when there was a monopoly in the industry that no longer existed.

After months of being locked out, the TWU reached a deal with Telus in October. It offered some flexibility for Telus while giving some job security to B.C. Telus workers (*Alberni Valley Times,* 11 Oct.). However, the October settlement was rejected by a 53-vote margin by the 13,700 TWU workers. In November a second vote was held; 64 per cent of workers were in favour of the settlement, resulting in acceptance of the deal. The new agreement extended to 2010 and included a lump-sum payment in lieu of raises that had not been paid since the contract expired. The ratified agreement offered TWU workers base pay increases of 2 per cent and 2.5 per cent in 2005 and 2006 and 2 per cent in 2007 and beyond, plus cost-of-living adjustments in 2009 and 2010. During the strike/lockout, Telus had moved work to a call centre in the Philippines; it said it would return that work to British Columbia as part of the settlement.

Independent truckers' 'strike'

In another private sector strike, on 27 June about 1,200 independent container haulers walked off the job in a dispute with the fifty trucking companies that employed them. Their work stoppage affected most of the traffic at the Port of Vancouver. Truck hauling was considered to account for 40 per cent of the business at the port (*Today's Trucking.com*, 4 July). The dispute concerned pay, costs of fuel, and long waits at the port for which the independent operators did not get compensated. When the strike was ten days old, B.C. labour minister Mike de Jong appointed Vince Ready as mediator. The owner-operators, represented primarily by the Vancouver Container Truck Association (VCTA) led by spokesman and owner-operator Paul Uppal, demanded that they receive a fuel surcharge because of rising diesel prices, as well as a 15 per cent general rate increase. The drivers explained that it cost about $350 a day to operate a truck and they were being paid between $300 and $400. The British Columbia Trucking Association refused to get involved, stating that labour negotiations were not part of its mandate (*Today's Trucking*.com, 4 July).

Some Vancouver business people demanded that the federal government step in to end the strike. The government argued, however, that it could not use the *Canada Transportation Act* to force the drivers, who were small-business owners, back to work; they had the right to refuse to work. The Vancouver Board of Trade estimated that the strike cost the provincial economy $75 million a day in transportation costs alone (CBC, 26 July).

The strike lasted six and a half weeks, ending on 9 August 2005. In early August the VCTA was asked to vote on Vince Ready's recommendations, which included increases to container rate schedules, fuel surcharges when the price of diesel rose about $1.05 per litre in any quarter, and a way of enforcing the agreement (*Tyee,* 30 July). The VCTA's lawyer noted that there would be no deal until all eleven lawsuits faced by the association were dropped (*Tyee,* 30 July).

Teachers' strike

As September ended, the British Columbia Teachers' Federation (BCTF) held a strike vote, and 88.4 per cent of teachers voted in favour (*Lake Windermere Valley Echo,* 28 Sept.). The BCTF had been without a contract since 2004. The teachers were not legally allowed to strike, and the Labour Relations Board told them not to authorize a strike and not to picket and to immediately resume their duties. Despite the illegality of the strike, B.C. Federation of Labour president Jim Sinclair explained, 'I would expect that all the workers who work in the public-school system will, in that great tradition of British Columbia, respect those picket lines, including over 25,000 CUPE members, BCGEU members, operating engineers, carpenters and others' (*The Province,* 7 Oct.).

The B.C. government tried to stave off the strike by passing legislation extending the teachers' contract to the following spring (*Whitehorse Star,* 11 Oct.). On 14 October Justice Brenda Brown of the B.C. Supreme Court handed down her ruling, confirming that the BCTF was in contempt of court for authorizing an illegal strike (*National Post,* 14 Oct.). She ordered the federation not to use any of its resources to support the strike, meaning especially no strike pay, which had previously been provided to the teachers at $50 a day. The BCTF also faced fines of $150,000 a day for continuing the strike. The teachers argued that their salaries were below those of Alberta and Ontario (*Prince George Citizen,* 12 Oct.) and wanted class sizes to be addressed.

On 15 October the president of the B.C. Federation of Labour, Jim Sinclair, was joined by fourteen labour leaders, including George Heyman of the British Columbia Government Employees Union (BCGEU) and Barry O'Neill of the Canadian Union of Public Employees (CUPE). The leaders agreed to support teachers by taking job action and rallying in support on the following Monday. On 18 October union members across the province walked off the job and joined members of the BCTF in defiance of the Supreme Court ruling, demanding improved wages and better working and learning conditions in B.C.'s schools. Vince Ready was appointed as mediator to end the dispute, and by 22 October BCTF executives were determining whether or not to encourage their members to support his recommendations. Jinny Sims, leader of the BCTF, demanded that the provincial government agree to address class sizes by June as the price of her members' returning to work (*Edmonton Journal,* 22 Oct.). The illegal strike ended on 26 October.

Other labour disputes

Another protracted private sector strike also began in July and ended in October. Teck Cominco workers at the company's lead and zinc smelting operations in Trail went on strike, demanding pay increases and pension improvements. They aimed to share in the company's profits, which had doubled in the first six months of the year to more than $450 million (*The Province,* 27 July). The workers, members of the United Steelworkers of America, included 1,140 production and maintenance workers and 170 technical and office workers. The strike lasted seventy-nine days, ending on 3 October with a new collective agreement to 2008 (*Teck Cominco Annual Report,* 2005).

Softwood lumber dispute

Labour was not the only policy area in which disputes were protracted in 2005. In softwood lumber the year opened with an exchange of threats between Canada and the United States. The Liberals suggested that wine imports from the United States might not be accepted, that regulatory approvals of the Alaska pipeline might be delayed, and that cattle being shipped from Hawaii through Vancouver's port would not be permitted. For their part, U.S. politicians threatened that although the lumber duties had been ruled illegal by NAFTA, $4 billion might never be returned (*National Post,* 5 Mar.).

The dispute continued throughout the year, with several events of note. In July a U.S. proposal put a ceiling on lumber imports from B.C. amid fears that their domestic market would be flooded with large amounts of wood from the province's pine beetle–infested interior (*Sault Star,* 20 July). In August a NAFTA panel rejected a U.S. Department of Commerce appeal on a decision that Canada did not subsidize lumber producers. As a result of the ruling, Canada expected that the United States would stop collecting duties and would refund the duties it had already collected (*Kingston Whig-Standard,* 11 Aug.).

As the year closed, the United States announced that it would appeal a November NAFTA ruling that removed some U.S. duties on Canadian lumber. The duties were imposed, the Americans argued, because Canada's four major lumber-producing provinces (British Columbia, Ontario, Alberta, and Quebec) were subsidizing timber rights to get a third of the U.S. market (*National Post,* 21 Dec.).

Mining

Some of the positive growth in the B.C. economy in 2005 could be attributed to growth in the mining sector. A mining report released by the Fraser Institute placed British Columbia forty-fourth out of sixty-four jurisdictions, which surprised some in the industry. The B.C. Yukon Chamber of Mines argued that this ignored the province's successes in mining in recent years. The previous year had seen mining exploration double to $130 million, with 12 per cent of all Canadian exploration taking place in British Columbia (*Prince Rupert Daily News,* 8 Mar.). B.C.'s mining boom was also noted by PricewaterhouseCoopers (*National Post,* 12 May). In particular, the coal industry saw demand for coal pushing prices to more than US$50 per tonne in 2004. The B.C. Liberals were viewed as contributing to this mining success; since 2001 they had encouraged investment in new mines and removed some bureaucratic barriers, as demanded by the mining industry (*National Post,* 12 May).

New relationship with Aboriginal peoples

Besides weathering strikes and emerging victorious in the provincial election, the B.C. Liberals could also claim some credit for improving the province's relationship with Aboriginal peoples in 2005. The government announced a 'new relationship' with Aboriginal peoples in June, and British Columbia's First Nations endorsed the agreement. The agreement was with the First Nations Leadership Council, which included representative chiefs from the Assembly of First Nations B.C. Region, the Union of British Columbia Indian Chiefs, and the First Nations Summit. The First Nations Summit had existed since 1990 and the Assembly of First Nations B.C. Region was the regional arm of the AFN, which represented on-reserve First Nations. The Union of British Columbia Indian Chiefs had been referred to as 'radical' and 'historically hostile to the Campbell government' (*The Province,* 21 June). For their part, the chiefs of the three organizations agreed to work together, signing the 'Leadership Accord' on 17 March 2005. This new relationship marked a significant turn for the Campbell Liberals, who in opposition had opposed the Nisga'a agreement.

Kelowna Accord

Perhaps in part to demonstrate its commitment to the new relationship, the B.C. Liberals welcomed representatives from across the country and from national Aboriginal organizations to Kelowna. The Kelowna Accord was an historic moment wherein the provinces, the federal government, and national Aboriginal leaders together agreed that the gap in health status, including life expectancy, between Aboriginal peoples and the average Canadian needed to be narrowed. The Accord was concluded on 25 November 2005. It included $5.1 billion in spending over five years, including $1.8 billion for education, to create school systems, train more Aboriginal teachers, and identify children with special needs; $1.6 billion for housing, with $400 million to address the need for clean water in remote communities; $200 million for economic development; and $1.3 billion for health services. This agreement stipulated funding for both on- and off-reserve First Nations, Métis, and Inuit. The national Aboriginal organizations that participated in the Accord included the Assembly of First Nations, the Métis National Council, the Inuit Tapiriit Kanatami, the Native Women's Association of Canada, and the Congress of Aboriginal Peoples.

Vancouver municipal election

The year included three elections, the provincial election in May, the municipal elections in November, and commencement of the federal election in December. In July Larry Campbell, mayor of Vancouver and famous as the coroner who inspired CBC television's *Da Vinci's Inquest,* announced that he would not seek re-election. He explained, 'Quite simply put, I am not a politician' (*Ottawa Citizen,* 1 July). In June there had been rumours that Prime Minister Paul Martin would appoint him to the Senate; this took place in August. Larry Campbell had brought the Coalition of Progressive Electors (COPE) to power in Vancouver. His party held most of the seats on city council but was split between the hard-line left and the more centrist Campbell and his supporters. This split led to the creation of Vision Vancouver, a new municipal political party.

The Coalition of Progressive Electors, after holding town halls to consider the issue, decided not to run a candidate for mayor so their members could support Vision Vancouver`s choice, Jim Green. Green, well-known for his work on housing projects on the Downtown Eastside, had been a COPE councillor and an ally of Larry Campbell. Campbell and Green had left COPE to start Vision Vancouver. When asked about the split, Green explained,

... for two years, I spent eight hours a week inside caucus, and we could never come to agreements. Some of those people don't believe in voting, so the discussions go on forever and go nowhere. They have good hearts and good ideas, but they don't know how to get things done. The process was draining and we had nothing to show for it. (*Tyee,* 17 Nov.)

Campbell, a very popular Vancouver mayor, not surprisingly endorsed his friend and ally.

In September Christy Clark, a former B.C. Liberal cabinet minister, announced her intention to run for leadership of the Non-Partisan Association (NPA), a right-leaning, pro-business Vancouver political party. In order to signal her commitment, she even moved her family from their Port Moody home into the city. Her opponent for the leadership was Sam Sullivan, a Cantonese-speaking quadriplegic city councillor who was elected to the COPE-dominated city council in 2002. Sullivan defeated Clark in a narrow race to become the NPA's 2005 mayoralty candidate.

The election took place on Saturday, 19 November, and 130,011 Vancouverites voted. NPA's Sullivan won the election with 61,543 votes, defeating Vision Vancouver's Green, who garnered 57,796 votes. An independent candidate named James Green also ran for mayor; he received 4,273 votes, enough to have put the more widely known Jim Green over the top; at least, that was the view of some of his supporters. Only one COPE candidate, David Cadman, was successful in the race. The ten-member city council was rounded out by five NPA councillors and four Vision Vancouver councillors.

Federal election

As the year closed the federal Liberals were defeated in the House of Commons, precipitating an election in the new year. For British Columbia, a riding to watch was Vancouver Centre, where the NDP's Svend Robinson attempted his comeback in a fight with Conservative Tony Fogarassy and Liberal Hedy Fry. British Columbia's thirty-six seats were considered to be in play in several ridings. Commentators referred to B.C. as a battleground, as an Ipsos-Reid poll found that B.C. support was split almost evenly among Liberals, Conservatives, and the NDP (*Edmonton Journal,* 10 Dec.).

Economy

Since 2005 was a year of election struggles and labour strife, the good news about B.C.'s economy was especially welcome. In April Statistics Canada reported that British Columbia's was the top-performing economy in the country for the preceding month (*Prince Rupert Daily News,* 28 April). It consistently outpaced other provinces, and in July it was predicted that B.C. might rival Alberta for top spot (*Kimberley Daily Bulletin,* 6 July). In July BMO chief economist Rick Egelton predicted that Alberta would lead all the other provinces with growth of 4 per cent, followed by British Columbia, which would grow 3.5 per cent (*Calgary Herald,* 12 July).

Early in the year, B.C.'s debt rating was boosted from AA (low) to AA by the Dominion Bond Rating Service, underscoring improvements in the province's tax competitiveness, debt burden, and cost controls (*Globe and Mail,* 16 Mar.). Moody's, a leading international credit-rating agency, increased British Columbia's credit rating from Aa2 to Aa1 with a stable outlook.

Reports in 2005 noted that while bankruptcies were on the increase in Atlantic Canada, they were on the decline in the West, with British Columbia's personal bankruptcies falling by 10.1 per cent and business bankruptcies down by 10.5 per cent (*Cranbrook Daily Townsman,* 11 Mar.). The positive economic news continued as Statistics Canada reported that in the first quarter of 2005 the province saw a net increase of 1,073 people, compared to a net decrease of 250 in the first quarter of 2004 (*Williams Lake Tribune,* 12 July). First quarters tend to be slow for growth, and 2004 turned out to be a very positive year for interprovincial migration to British Columbia; therefore, these numbers suggested an extremely positive outlook.

Despite all the positive economic news, some critics of the economy explained that its positive effects were uneven. They referred to 'the two British Columbias': the B.C. of the lower mainland and economic hotspots such as the Okanagan, Kamloops, and southern Vancouver Island, and the B.C. of Lilloet and the Kootenays, which people were leaving (*Vancouver Sun,* 18 Mar.).

HAROLD JANSEN

Alberta

2005 was a year of optimism in Alberta. Record high prices for oil and natural gas led to an economic boom reminiscent of the late 1970s and early 1980s. The province grew as people flocked to Alberta from across Canada, seeking employment and a better future. The provincial government was in an enviable position, with the accumulated provincial debt paid off and massive surpluses. Indeed, the big problem in the province seemed to be what to do with these new-found riches. On top of it all, Alberta was celebrating its hundredth year as a province of Canada. It was clearly a year to party.

Oil leads the way to an economic boom

One of the perennial concerns in Alberta's economy has been the extent to which it has been diversified to reduce the province's traditional reliance on oil and gas. Considerable effort and provincial government policy had gone into trying to encourage and develop other sources of economic activity for the province (and revenue for the provincial government). Although some progress had been made towards that goal over the years, the province's tremendous economic growth in 2005 showed how much oil and gas continued to dominate its economy. In 2005 economic growth in the province was around 4.3 per cent, the highest in the country. In fact, Statistics Canada reported that Alberta was in the midst of the biggest boom ever recorded for any province in Canada (*The Daily,* 14 Sept. 2006). Driving the growth was a spike in the price of oil, which rose above $70 a barrel in the peak demand months; over the year, oil averaged around $60 a barrel. Natural gas also had a good year, partly because of the disruption of production in the Gulf of Mexico caused by Hurricane Katrina and other tropical storms. At its peak the price of natural gas topped $15 a gigajoule (GJ); over the year it averaged more than $8 per GJ. The North American economy's insatiable demand for all kinds of energy extended even to coal, which also saw a price spike – good news for those who were developing Alberta's abundant reserves.

The price of oil had a direct effect on the province's economy, with a significant increase in exploration and drilling to develop conventional reserves. The biggest impact, however, was felt in unconventional energy development, particularly northern Alberta's oil sands. Extracting oil from the oil sands is expensive and resource-intensive; the higher price of oil made more development commercially feasible. Various companies announced almost $10 billion in investments in oil sands development, either in new projects or in expansion of existing activity. This movement was more than 50 per cent higher than investments announced in 2004. As more analysts advanced the 'peak oil' thesis – that oil production had reached its maximum and was in decline – the large reserves in the oil sands became of increasing interest to both domestic and international investors. The rising profile of the oil sands was best seen in a planned visit by U.S. vice-president Dick Cheney in September, a trip that ultimately had to be postponed because of Hurricane Katrina. Combined with the ongoing decline in Alberta's natural gas reserves, the province's energy industry was continuing its transformation to dependence on non-conventional sources.

The booming oil sector had significant spin-off effects for the rest of the economy. Unemployment averaged below 4 per cent for the year and was around 3 per cent in some regions, particularly Athabasca and Fort McMurray, which housed the bulk of the oil sands production in the province. Help-wanted signs were in store windows across the province and businesses reported difficulty in recruiting and employing skilled workers. The burgeoning oil patch did little to increase Alberta's high-school completion rates. Lured by high-paying jobs that required little, if any, formal education, increasing numbers of high-school students were opting not to complete their diplomas. In rural Alberta, nearly 25 per cent of students were choosing not to complete high school. As economic theory would predict, the combination of high demand for labour and short supply of skilled workers led to large wage increases. In 2005 Alberta surpassed Ontario as the province with the highest hourly wages. Pay increases averaged 7 per cent and were more than 10 per cent in Calgary (Statistics Canada, *The Daily*, 14 Sept. 2006).

The rosy economic conditions led to growth in Alberta's population, both naturally, through childbirth, and also through interprovincial migration, as workers flocked to Alberta to take advantage of the demand for labour. The population increase, general prosperity, and low mortgage rates led to a steady escalation in the price of houses, particularly in Calgary. By December the price of houses had increased by 18 per cent over December 2004. Surprisingly, the province's inflation rate averaged only 2.1 per cent during the year. Strong domestic pressure on prices was offset by the high Canadian dollar, which made imported goods and food much cheaper. Still, as the year went on, the inflation rate was creeping upwards.

As the owner of the province's oil and gas reserves, the provincial government was one of the primary beneficiaries of the boom. In its spring budget the government forecast a $1.5 billion surplus, based on an oil price of $42 a barrel. As oil blew past that point, it quickly became clear that the government was going to have more money than it knew what to do with. During the fiscal year that ended on 31 March 2005, the provincial government paid off its debt. It had always used the need to pay down the accumulated debt as a tool to defer demands for spending. As the province looked at the prospect of a nearly $10-billion surplus for the 2005–06 fiscal year, the government faced the thorny political question of what to do with the money. There was no shortage of ideas. Some called for investment in social programs, education, and health care. Many called for increased spending on the province's infrastructure needs, arguing that the tremendous growth in the province had strained resources, particularly in the major cities. Others called for tax cuts, arguing that lower taxes would give Alberta a comparative advantage in attracting other forms of business to the province. Finally there was a call for saving, by increasing provincial government contributions to the Alberta Heritage and Savings Trust Fund or some other investment vehicle. Pointing to jurisdictions such as Alaska and Norway, advocates of increased saving argued that it would prevent the government from becoming overly reliant on resource revenues to fund day-to-day operations and would also represent an intergenerational transfer of wealth.

Premier Ralph Klein had yet another idea. In September he announced that every man, woman, and child in Alberta living in the province as of 1 September would receive a $400 prosperity bonus, to be paid out in 2006. The plan would cost the province an estimated $1.4 billion, to be taken out of the unbudgeted surplus. Not surprisingly, the plan generated significant criticism from all parts of the political spectrum. Those on the right argued that tax cuts would generate a more enduring advantage for Alberta, while those on the left pointed to the many unfulfilled social needs in the province. Still others pointed out the difficulties in fairly administering the payments. Ever the populist, Klein shrugged off the criticism and stuck to his plan, which quickly became known as 'Ralph bucks.'

Alberta's unparalleled prosperity began to be noticed outside the province and to generate some resentment among residents and governments of other, less prosperous parts of the country. Some of the other provinces were running deficit budgets and were seeing their economies stall, while Alberta's government was literally giving money away. To be sure, some of the concern about how Alberta's wealth would be perceived by the rest of Canada was a product of Albertans' imaginations. For many older residents of the province, memories of the federal government's National Energy Program, during the height of the early 1980s oil boom, were still fresh. When Ontario premier Dalton McGuinty commented to reporters that the growing economic disparity between Alberta and the other provinces was the 'elephant in the room' in Canadian federalism (*Globe and Mail,* 24 Aug.), it reawakened those fears. Despite Prime Minister Paul Martin's assurances that the federal government had no intention of going after Alberta's oil revenue, Ralph Klein still implored the rest of the country to 'keep your hands off' Alberta's riches (*Globe and Mail,* 26 Aug.). Despite all the posturing, there were no signs of movement in the direction of another National Energy Program, leaving Alberta's concerns a vague fear at best.

Centennial celebrations

Its booming economy was not the only cause for celebration in Alberta. The year 2005 also marked its hundredth year as a province. It was a time to reflect on the province's history and achievements. Throughout the year many government policies and actions were packaged as centennial programs. For example, in Klein's February television address to the province, he announced a freeze on tuition and fees for post-secondary students as a centennial gift. His government also funded a number of arts initiatives as part of the centennial, including an expansion of the provincial museum.

The centrepiece of the centennial celebration was a visit by Queen Elizabeth in May. After leaving Regina, where she had taken part in Saskatchewan's centennial celebrations, she travelled to Jasper to spend a quiet private weekend with Prince Philip. She then journeyed to Edmonton for a celebration at Commonwealth Stadium. Sadly, cool and rainy weather marred that event and kept people away. To commemorate the Queen's visit, Premier Klein announced that the highway linking Edmonton and Calgary – in many ways the economic backbone of the province – would be renamed the Queen Elizabeth II Highway, or

'QE2,' as it quickly became known. While in Edmonton, the Queen also addressed the provincial legislature and renamed the Provincial Museum of Alberta the Royal Alberta Museum. After a lengthy walkabout in downtown Edmonton, she flew to Calgary for several events, including a large celebration at the Saddledome.

The main centennial celebration was held on 1 September. Events across the province commemorated Alberta's history and its place in Canada. The official launch for the day of celebration was in Edmonton, where Premier Klein was joined by Prime Minister Martin, Governor General Adrienne Clarkson, and Lieutenant-Governor Norman Kwong to get things started. Albertans gathered at parties in Edmonton and Calgary, as well as eight other cities across Alberta. The day ended with large simultaneous fireworks displays in all ten cities.

Tragedy in Mayerthorpe

Although it was generally a year of celebration and optimism, not everything that happened in 2005 was a happy event. One of the saddest events occurred in early March, when four constables with the Royal Canadian Mounted Police (RCMP) were killed in the line of duty in Mayerthorpe, a small town northeast of Edmonton. The incident started with a search warrant for stolen auto parts at a farm near Mayerthorpe owned by James Roszko. While there, the officers found marijuana plants and thought they might have discovered a grow op. Two of the officers guarded the site overnight, and at 9:00 a.m. two other officers joined them. It was not entirely clear what happened after that. It appeared that Roszko was either hidden on the farm or had snuck back onto the property overnight. When two more officers came to the scene at about 9:15, they heard shots coming from the property's Quonset hut. Roszko had apparently ambushed the four officers. When he came out of the Quonset hut, he fired on the two officers who had arrived later, and they returned fire. Later that afternoon they entered the hut and found the four officers and Roszko dead. It appeared that Roszko had taken his own life after being wounded in the shootout.

The deaths of the four officers – twenty-eight-year-old Constable Anthony Gordon, twenty-nine-year-old Constable Brock Myrol, thirty-two-year-old Constable Leo Johnston, and twenty-five-year-old Peter Schiemann – made this the worst day for the RCMP in more than a century. Not since the Northwest Rebellion in 1885 had more officers been killed in the line of duty on a single day than in the skirmish at Mayerthorpe. The incident rocked the small Alberta community, where the local RCMP officers were important figures. As 2005 drew to a close, it became clear that the RCMP's investigation would continue. Analysis of Roszko's mobile phone records indicated that he had been communicating with people in the area before the showdown in the Quonset. The RCMP were exploring the possibility that people in the community might have assisted Roszko and thus contributed to the deaths of the officers.

The incident raised questions about RCMP procedure when it was revealed that Roszko had a long history of violent behaviour, including convictions for sexual assault, and was known for his hatred of the RCMP. After the incident, reports surfaced that Roszko would stalk the families of officers in the Mayerthorpe detachment. Given his history, many wanted to know why four relatively young and inexperienced officers had been dispatched to deal with a potentially serious situation. Constable Myrol had served only seventeen days with the force when he was killed. Other questions centred on why Roszko was free despite his history of violent behaviour. Those questions only intensified in the fall, when the province released a report on Roszko's past, revealing that he had faced forty-four charges and had been convicted of fourteen. Only one of the charges, however, had led to jail time, and then for only two and a half years, while several charges had been stayed or withdrawn. It appeared that Roszko had fallen through the cracks of the criminal justice system, with deadly consequences for the four officers and their families.

Finally, the incident at Mayerthorpe had an impact on debates over gun control and the decriminalization of marijuana. Roszko apparently had an illegal, unregistered assault rifle. For opponents of the gun registry, the incident showed the futility of gun registration, as it seemed to be no deterrent for criminals intent on acquiring weapons. Proponents of gun control seized on the Mayerthorpe incident as evidence that Canada needed even more stringent limitations on firearm ownership. The fact that Roszko appeared to be involved in growing marijuana certainly did not do much to advance the argument that marijuana was a relatively harmless vice, worthy of decriminalization.

In the end, though, such debates were of little comfort to the families of the four men, whose funerals and memorial services were national news. In May the families of the four men had a private meeting with the Queen and Prince Philip in Regina. As the year drew to a close, the province was planning construction of a memorial to the officers in Mayerthorpe.

Wind and water: environmental issues

In water-starved southern Alberta, rain is usually seen as a blessing. That was not the case in June, as record rainfalls swelled rivers and caused flooding in several communities. It was the worst flooding to hit the province since 1995, when a flood caused $100 million in damage to southern Alberta. The town of High River was hit particularly hard as the Highwood River overflowed in the first week of June, forcing 150 residents of neighbourhoods near the river to evacuate their homes. Several communities in the foothills west of Calgary faced boil-water advisories as water treatment plants were unable to keep up with the muddy inflows. Calgary was hit when the Glenbow Dam on the Elbow River overflowed for the first time in its history, despite having its spillway gates wide open. This led to the evacuation of about twenty homes in a couple of neighbourhoods. Just as people were returning home and starting the task of cleaning up, southern Alberta got hit by another spate of heavy rain in the middle of the month, which led to more evacuations in Calgary. There was some good news: communities that had faced a lot of damage in 1995 – Pincher Creek, Lethbridge, and Medicine Hat – fared much better this time, either because the flooding was not as bad or because the anti-flood measures instituted after 1995 had worked well.

The provincial government stepped in with assistance to cover some uninsured losses due to the flooding. Prime Minister Martin came to High River at the end of the month. Although he faced some criticism for taking so long to check out the damage for himself, he did come with promises of considerable federal government assistance to those affected by the flooding. There was some criticism of the publicly funded compensation plan, as it would benefit primarily wealthy homeowners who had chosen to build their homes near rivers because they were either oblivious to or wilfully ignorant of the potential for flood damage.

Although abundant water is not something for which southern Alberta is usually known, strong winds are a regular feature of the prairie landscape. With the spike in energy prices and worry about supply shortfalls, there was increasing interest in developing wind power in the south. As concern over climate change and the environmental costs of oil and gas production in the province mounted, wind power became an increasingly attractive option, particularly in a province heavily reliant on relatively dirty coal-fired power plants for much of its electrical supply. Several projects were announced, including a $100-million wind farm northeast of Pincher Creek. No proposed wind development raised more concern than a plan to put a wind farm in the picturesque Cypress Hills area near Medicine Hat. Ironically, it was environmental groups who were opposed to the project, arguing that it would harm the aesthetics of the area by obscuring the view and creating noise. The debate ended up pitting environmentalists against one another as some argued that wind power provided a sustainable, clean, and renewable form of energy.

Canadian National Railways got into trouble in August when one of its trains derailed just outside Edmonton and spilled oil into Lake Wabamun. The oil formed an eight-kilometre slick on the popular recreational lake. The sight of oil-soaked ducks was certainly not good public relations for the rail company, and accusations of poor communications by CN did little to bolster its image. It turned out that at least one of the cars contained oil used to treat poles – oil that contained carcinogens. Although CN apparently knew about this fairly early on, the company did not immediately pass on the fact to people who lived around the lake. Frustrated by the lack of communication, local residents blockaded the rail line, which also happened to be CN's main line to British Columbia. Alberta Environment imposed tight deadlines to prevent the oil from spreading. Although the company paid the cost of bringing in clean drinking water and offered to buy any homes damaged by the derailment, it was clear that its reputation had been stained by the incident.

Where's the beef?: The cattle industry

BSE crisis

In 2003 Canada's cattle industry had been rocked by the discovery of a case of bovine spongiform encephalopathy (BSE), or 'mad cow disease,' on a farm in Alberta. This had caused the closure of the American border to all Canadian beef products. Part of the ban had been lifted but live cattle were still not crossing freely. Given the close links between the two countries' industries, this was devastating for Canada's beef producers. It was particularly brutal for Alberta, home to most of the country's cattle and beef industry. Although some of the pain of the border closure had been dealt with through an increase in slaughtering and packing capacity in Canada, ranchers were still counting on the border's reopening. In late 2004 the U.S. Department of Agriculture (USDA) announced that live cattle imports from Canada would resume in March 2005. When the American government remained committed to that policy, despite the January confirmation of another case of BSE in Alberta (in a dairy cow discovered in December 2004), ranchers were finally allowing themselves a bit of hope.

These hopes were dashed by an American federal judge in Billings, Montana, who granted an injunction to R-CALF, an American protectionist cattle lobby, just five days before the border was to reopen. The news was heartbreaking for Canadian producers, who had been gearing up to resume full production. Provincial officials and cattle producers feared that years of legal wrangling could delay the border reopening. The USDA appealed the temporary injunction, and on 13 July an appeals court overturned it, opening the doors for cattle to move across the border again. A three-judge appeals court panel ruled further that the Montana judge had been in error and that the risk of BSE from Canadian cattle imports was minimal. R-CALF tried to overturn this decision but was denied leave to appeal. This appeared to put an end to the legal wrangling. As cattle began to move across the border and food safety officials in countries such as Japan and South Korea began to reconsider their bans on Canadian beef products, it appeared that Alberta's beef producers would be able to return to some degree of normality.

Lakeside Packers strike

The other issue in the cattle industry involved Lakeside Packers in Brooks, one of Canada's largest meat processing plants. In a vote in 2004, a slim majority of workers at the plant had recently signed up with United Food and Commercial Workers (UFCW), and the union was trying to negotiate the plant's first ever union contract. Besides the typical issues of wages and benefits, the union had expressed concern over working conditions and safety at the plant. The plant's workforce was distinctive because it largely comprised immigrant workers, from thirty-six different countries. There was fear that a labour disruption could quickly take on racial overtones. The two sides were unable to reach an agreement and the workers went on strike in July. The strike was short-lived, however, as the provincial government ordered the two sides to submit to a mediation process for sixty days; during that period the workers were forbidden to strike and management was forbidden to lock out the employees.

When the mediator's report came out in September, UFCW was happy with it and the employees endorsed it. Tyson Foods, the American owner of Lakeside Packers, rejected the proposal, however, which put the whole process back to where it had been in July. About one thousand workers went on strike in mid-October. There were considerable fears of violence on or around the picket line; both the RCMP and UFCW urged that protests be kept calm and peaceful. Despite those efforts, there were some violent incidents on the picket line over the course of the twenty-six-day strike. A bus carrying supervisors to work had its windows smashed as it tried to enter the plant. To try to cool things down, the Alberta Labour Relations Board limited the number of picketers to fifty and banned the union leader from the picket line. Police charged the leader with property damage and a weapons offence; later they charged four people with ties to the plant's management for dangerous driving, after a car crash sent the union president to the hospital with injuries.

Although the plant was able to resume limited production using management staff and workers willing to cross the picket line, federal food inspectors were not willing to cross the picket line, arguing that it was too dangerous. This prevented Lakeside Packers from shipping its meat and infuriated the plant's owners. Eventually the inspectors did return to work, allowing the plant to resume limited production. In early November the two sides came back to the negotiating table and hammered out a four-year contract that would raise wages by $1.90 over its lifespan; 56 per cent of the workers ratified the deal and they returned to work. Although things remained tense at the plant and in Brooks when full production resumed, there were no reports of additional violence.

Calgary's Ward 10 election scandal

Besides the BSE crisis, the other major story that carried over from 2004 was the scandal over the municipal election results in Calgary's Ward 10. In the 2004 municipal election, Margot Aftergood was elected as alderman for Ward 10. Soon her campaign faced accusations of campaign misconduct, including requesting mail-in ballots on behalf of voters in the ward. The city ultimately reached a settlement with Aftergood in which she agreed to resign in return for payment of some of her legal bills. Although the settlement dealt with the question of Aftergood's status, it left many Calgarians wondering how such a scandal had happened in the first place.

The provincial government had appointed former ethics commissioner Bob Clark to inspect the results of the disputed election. He began by gathering information and then held public hearings. Clark, however, abruptly terminated the hearings, saying that the inspection was limited to matters not being investigated by the police. This meant that the only thing approaching a public inquiry would not hear most of the concerns over the conduct of the election. Clark's report did little to answer questions or satisfy critics of either Calgary's election practices or the way the provincial government had dealt with them. Ultimately Calgary's citizens were going to have to wait until February 2006 for answers, which was when Aftergood's husband, David, and other campaign volunteers would be tried on charges related to their part in the scandal. The only clear answer was to the question of who would represent Ward 10 on Calgary's city council. In a by-election at the end of February 2005, Andre Chabot was elected to represent the eastern Calgary district, upsetting Diane Danielson, who had been the incumbent before losing to Aftergood in the controversial election.

Provincial legislature

The 2004 election marked the end of a legislature, so the opening of the session in March marked the first time the twenty-sixth legislature would meet. The first order of business was the election of the Speaker, a process that went quite quickly as incumbent Ken Kowalski ran unopposed for re-election. More interesting was the changed opposition in the legislature. Not only was it larger overall than in the twenty-fifth legislature, but the New Democratic Party had doubled its seat totals from two to four. Furthermore, the Liberals had established a small beachhead in Calgary and were eager to increase the profile of their MLAs from that city. Finally, the Conservatives had to face questions from a party situated to their ideological right, as Alberta Alliance MLA Paul Hinman was representing Cardston-Taber-Warner. The Liberals hit the Conservatives hard, focusing many of their attacks on problems in the Alberta Securities Commission, which was facing questions over its office and personnel management as well as accusations that it favoured companies with ties to the Conservative government. Another tactic used by the Liberals over the course of the sittings was to target potential successors to Ralph Klein in Question Period. The NDP were frustrated by a ruling by Speaker Kowalski at the beginning of the session that limited them to only two questions, the same number as in the previous legislature, even though the party had doubled its seat totals. Hinman's presence was felt, particularly on gay marriage, an issue that was central to his party but which also divided the Conservatives internally.

The central theme of the legislative session in 2005 was advanced education. In his annual television address that preceded the opening of the legislature, Klein promised that the province would create 60,000 new post-secondary spaces over the next fifteen years, along with a commitment to freeze tuition and raise the minimum wage. That theme carried through to the Throne Speech, in which the government promised a $4.5-billion investment in three endowment funds. The interest from these funds would pay for scholarships, grants, and research. The commitment to advanced education flowed partly from a desire to invest in the future in recognition of Alberta's centennial, but it was hard not to see a bit of political motivation as well. In the 2004 provincial election, the seats the Conservatives lost in Calgary were heavily populated by students. The government appeared to have concluded that it had a problem in this policy area and were starting to pay a political price for it.

The desire of the government to focus on post-secondary education went up in smoke – literally. Everything else in the legislature was overshadowed by a debate over how to regulate smoking. At issue was Calgary MLA David Rodney's *Smoke Free Places Act,* a private member's bill that would ban smoking in public. This issue deeply divided the Conservative caucus internally, with some MLAs seeing it as too intrusive into the private sector and others wanting to exempt places such as bars and casinos. Ultimately the bill was amended to allow smoking in bars, casinos, and any restaurants where minors were not allowed. Hotels would also be allowed to designate certain rooms as smoking rooms.

When the budget came out, however, advanced education was back in the spotlight, with a 30 per cent increase over three years. Administrators at the province's post-secondary institutions were ecstatic, although there was some grumbling over the lack of any infrastructure money to construct new buildings on campuses. There was also a big spending bump ($707 million) for health care and increased spending on seniors and new police officers. In addition, the budget increased funding for the Assured Income for the Severely Handicapped (AISH) program, an issue that had become prominent in the 2004 election. The net result was a 6 per cent increase in spending, a projected $1.5-billion surplus, and the province's first debt-free budget in more than fifty years.

Of course, as the province's coffers overflowed with money from oil and gas royalties, it became clear that the budgeted $1.5-billion surplus was essentially meaningless. The provincial government had far more money than that. As the premier announced spending plan after spending plan – 'Ralph bucks,' money to finance a movie about Canada's battle at Paaschendale, funding for the Calgary Zoo – the media and opposition leaders began to ask questions about the legislature's role in overseeing and approving this unanticipated surplus spending. In the fall sitting of the legislature, both Liberal leader Kevin Taft and NDP leader Brian Mason argued that Klein was dodging any pretence of fiscal accountability and legislative oversight (*Calgary Herald,* 16 Nov. 2005).

Leadership politics

The concern over spending was also a factor in the race to replace Ralph Klein as party leader. In the 2004 election campaign, Klein had indicated that it would be his last. In February he gave the green light to his potential successors to begin organizing their campaigns. A number of figures emerged as possible replacements. The minister of advanced education, Dave Hancock, benefited from the high profile given to his portfolio in 2005; he began to stake out his position as the Edmonton candidate. Transportation minister Lyle Oberg was also organizing a bid for the leadership, as was intergovernmental affairs minister Ed Stelmach. Both represented rural constituencies, in the province's south and north, respectively. Outside the Cabinet, rookie MLA Ted Morton, a University of Calgary political scientist, was staking out his place as a strong defender of Alberta's position in the federal system and as a defender of the traditional family. Former Edmonton MLA Mark Norris, who had been defeated in 2004, was also rumoured to be preparing a leadership campaign. The frontrunner, however, was former provincial treasurer Jim Dinning, who had been quietly organizing and campaigning for quite some time. He received a major boost in September, when Klein's chief of staff, Rod Love, quit his position to manage Dinning's campaign. Love had been widely credited with masterminding Klein's ascension to the leadership in 1992. Dinning was already a credible candidate; the addition of Love to his campaign strengthened his position as heir apparent.

The big question lurking over the leadership campaign was timing. During the 2004 campaign, Klein had indicated that he would leave in 2008. Over the summer he changed that to the fall of 2007. There was, however, no firm date, and it was difficult to see how the party could sustain a two-year leadership contest without ripping itself apart. Furthermore, the large spending increases in the second half of the year did not sit well with many members who had been attracted to the party because of its vision of fiscal austerity. Klein's penchant for policy adlibbing – the 'Ralph bucks' being a prime example – over the concerns of his caucus also raised some questions about whether he could effectively stay on as leader.

The other political party that went through a leadership change was the Alberta Alliance. Party leader Randy Thorsteinson resigned his position in the spring after failing to win a seat in the 2004 election. In a convention in Red Deer, the party chose its only sitting MLA, Paul Hinman, as its leader.

Other events

The RCMP publicly admitted that they believed a serial killer was working in the Edmonton area, preying on the city's sex-trade workers. This admission came shortly after the discovery of two more bodies in the fields surrounding the provincial capital. Charlene Gauld's and Ellie Meyer's bodies were found within three weeks of each other in the spring, bringing to twelve the number of the city's sex workers who had been found murdered since 1988. The RCMP expanded the size of the task force investigating the murders and released a profile of the suspected killer, but as of the end of 2005, no one had been charged.

In other sad news, Lieutenant-Governor Lois Hole died on 7 January after a lengthy battle with cancer. The death of the 'Queen of Hugs' was mourned by the entire province. So many people logged on to sign an online condolence book that it crashed the provincial government's website. Hole was an outspoken advocate for the arts and education, a tendency that occasionally put her at odds with Premier Klein. Nevertheless, Klein had requested that her term be extended so she could preside over the province's centennial celebrations. Unhappily, Hole died before that could happen. Prime Minister Martin appointed former CFL football star Norman ('Normie') Kwong to replace her.

JOSEPH GARCEA

Saskatchewan

The year 2005 marked the centennial anniversary of Saskatchewan as a province. As part of the celebration the provincial government sponsored a contest for a centennial song. The winning submission was titled 'Saskatchewan, We Love This Place.' Saskatchewanians celebrated the centennial year province-wide, with more than four thousand official events (*StarPhoenix*, 7 Sept. and 27 Dec.). These included fireworks in the fifteen largest communities that were watched by more than 300,000 people. Some of the celebrations included Queen Elizabeth II and Prince Philip, whose royal visit added the requisite regal aura to the centenary. A notable part of the celebrations was the hosting of the Canada Summer Games, an initiative designed to ensure that many Canadians would become more aware of the province for at least two weeks. The celebrations provided all with an opportunity to reflect on the trajectories of the province's history, including its demographic, political, policy, and economic legacies with their cyclical swings of boom and bust. In 2005, as in 1905, Saskatchewan was on an economic upswing verging on a boom. The eternal optimists from 'next-year country' felt vindicated in their steadfast belief that good days would be here again. Others marvelled at what was happening and hoped that what they were experiencing would be substantial and sustainable rather than just another bubble that would soon burst.

Elections

In 2005 there were no federal or provincial general elections or by-elections. The only notable event on the electoral front was that a committee consisting of members of all three parties and the chief electoral officer reached an agreement on several major amendments to the provincial election act. These included:

- a permanent electronic voters list;
- simplification of absentee voting;

- increases in compensation rates for candidates and parties for election spending to match federal standards of compensation;
- simplification and shortening of the approval process for advertisements;
- expanding prisoner voting rights; and
- lowering the threshold for official party status from ten members to two.

Some of the amendments were not well received by all. Former chief electoral officer Myron Kuziak argued that some of the changes were unnecessary and excessive while other, glaring deficiencies had been ignored. For example, Kuziak indicated that compensation regulations in Saskatchewan lagged behind the rest of Canada, as this was the only jurisdiction that allowed payment for campaign work to be donated back to the party (*StarPhoenix*, 11 and 21 May).

Political parties

This was a relatively quiet year for the New Democratic Party. Premier Lorne Calvert continued to serve as party leader. At the NDP's annual convention, Ken Rauch was elected party president and Doug Still, former mayor of Humboldt, was elected party secretary to replace outgoing president and former cabinet minister Ed Tchorzewski. The annual convention was followed by a massive gala in honour of the province's centennial that was attended by Allan Blakeney and Roy Romanow, both former party leaders and premiers, and Lorne Calvert, the current leader and premier. At the same time as they were celebrating the province's history and their party's contribution to it, NDP members attending the gala continued to ponder the results of the previous election and the timing and outcome of the next one. The prevailing question was whether the NDP could reinvigorate itself and strengthen its electoral support while in power, or whether bleaker prospects awaited (*The Commonwealth* 60, no. 5).

For the Saskatchewan Party, this was a year devoted to expanding and consolidating confidence in its new leader and the party itself, and developing a policy platform that would place it on firmer footing for the next election. Following his election as leader of the Saskatchewan Party in 2004, Brad Wall had focused on two goals: revamping and re-energizing the party and charting a slightly different policy platform. His efforts at modifying the platform included a change regarding the competition that provincial government departments, Crown corporations, and other agencies posed for private sector firms. In an attempt to allay fears that the party would privatize what the public considered valuable Crown corporations and other business ventures by the provincial government, they modified the party's previous policy. Whereas the previous policy had been to terminate any competition that government enterprises offered private sector enterprises, the new policy was merely to review the nature, extent, and implication of such competition. In publicizing their new policy, both Wall and the Saskatchewan Party's house leader Dan D'Autremont indicated that the major utilities would likely remain; however, some of their particular business ventures, such as SaskTel's involvement in providing security alarms and internet access services, would be reviewed more carefully because their importance as core functions was open to question.

A second major plank in that party's platform was the endorsement of Wall's call for the creation of Enterprise Saskatchewan, a partnership between the government, the private sector, and other stakeholders to set an economic development policy. Its goal would be to direct government investment in the economy and make recommendations on tax regimes.

A third major plank consisted of a series of policy directions in the justice, social, health, Aboriginal, and gaming sectors. These included:

- creating a youth justice board to provide advice on best sentencing practices rather than a policy for harsher sentences and boot camps;
- increasing the food allowance for people on social assistance;
- increasing support for people with permanent disabilities;
- implementing a dedicated strategy against crystal methamphetamine;
- making instruction in the history and content of First Nations treaties part of the core school curriculum;
- consulting with First Nations before passing any legislation that affected their jurisdiction; and
- dedicating part of liquor and gaming revenues to addiction programs and facilities.

This platform was developed to eliminate the problems that the Saskatchewan Party had faced in the previous election campaign, in which the NDP was successful in raising questions and fears in the minds of voters regarding hidden agendas and potentially problematical policies of the Saskatchewan Party. In effect, the latter was trying to fireproof itself against the efforts of the other parties to demonize it (*StarPhoenix*, 7 Feb.).

For the Liberal Party of Saskatchewan, 2005 was a relatively un-eventful year. At the beginning of the year, the party leader, David Kar-wacki, found himself drawn into lobbying the federal government over an energy accord that had implications for federal equalization pay-ments to the province. The premier and the leader of the official Oppo-sition challenged him to use the influence he claimed to have with the prime minister, Paul Martin, and the Liberal government of Canada to convince them to give Saskatchewan the same agreement that had been given to Newfoundland and Nova Scotia for calculating revenues from the energy sector in relation to the equalization formula. By the end of the year no progress had been made on giving Saskatchewan what the three political parties considered a fair equalization deal that did not penalize the province for its increased good fortune in the energy sector. Apart from some media coverage on this particular issue and the issue of proposed increases to the gas rates charged by SaskEnergy, the Liberal leader and his party had a relatively uneventful year. Their focus was on preparing a policy platform and strategy for the next provincial election, the outcome of which likely would be of crucial importance for both the leader and the party.

In 2005 the New Green Alliance Party changed its name to the Green Party of Saskatchewan and produced a more detailed constitutional framework for its operations. It outlined the functions of various party officials and some processes for increasing democracy within the party. It also passed a resolution that sanctioned creation of a special commit-tee to review the operations of the party in the province and to consider its relationship with the Green Party of Canada (Green Party of Saskatch-ewan, *Party Policy,* http://www.greenpartysask.ca/policy/party_policy).

The legislature and government

This was the first year of the new legislative schedule. One consequence of the new schedule was that there was no Throne Speech for the spring sitting of the legislature; since the legislature had not been prorogued, the one delivered at the start of the session in the fall of 2 004 was still in force. In commenting on the legislative agenda for the spring sit-ting, the government house leader, Harry Van Mulligen, frankly stated that the government would not be introducing any controversial legis-lation, because it would likely be subjected to partisan machinations in light of the prospect of an election in the near future (*StarPhoenix,* 12 Mar.). Despite the absence of contentious legislation, there was no absence of theatrics, acrimony, and unparliamentary language on both

sides of the legislature. The high degree of partisanship and the pau-
city of significant policy proposals that were evident from the start led
one columnist to call it the 'lost session' (*StarPhoenix*, 20 Apr.). At
the end of the session one analyst asserted that it had been one of the
most unproductive in years, and described the behaviour of the legislators as mean-spirited, highly personalized, sanctimonious, and self-
serving (*StarPhoenix*, 27 May). Nevertheless, some progress was made:
the budget was passed, basic social assistance was raised, $48 million
was directed to implementing the recommendations of the Commission on First Nations and Métis People and Justice Reform, the labour
laws were reformed to protect various types of workers, and legislation
was passed to protect communities from organized crime and gang activity and to increase the amount of protected land in the Great Sand
Hills (*StarPhoenix*, 27 May). As well, during that session the provincial
government launched the Green Team employment program for young
people, recycling programs for paint and electronic equipment waste,
some changes to the health-care system, and a program to provide early
learning and child care for Saskatchewan families (Saskatchewan, news
release, 27 May, http://www.gov.sk.ca/news?newsId=91a9d547-5017-
472a-8431-944c3d6de396).

In the fall of 2005 a new session of the legislature began with a Throne
Speech that outlined the government's long- and short-term plans for
Saskatchewan. A main focus was once again finding the balance between a prosperous and an environmentally sustainable economy. The
major highlights included:

- dealing with the recommendations of the Business Tax Review Committee, expected in fall 2005;
- doubling the value of manufacturing shipments from the province
  over the next ten years;
- fully funding the province's 2005 share of the Canadian Agriculture
  Income Stabilization (CAIS) program;
- a multi-year northern road building strategy, including an all-weather
  road to the Far North;
- twinning the highway between Saskatoon and Prince Albert;
- welcoming five thousand new immigrants per year by 2008;
- funding and regulating midwifery in the province;
- developing a strategy for training and retention of health-care professionals;
- developing a task force on missing persons;

- developing and implementing a climate change strategy and a series of energy initiatives, including transformation of 10 per cent of arable land to tree farms over the next twenty years; and
- a goal of ensuring that by 2030 one-third of energy needs would be met by renewable resources (*StarPhoenix,* 7 Nov.).

The fall sitting of the legislature, like the spring sitting, was marked by excessive acrimony, insults, and pettiness. The tenor of the session was set during the debate on the Throne Speech. Following his critique of that speech and of the government's performance, the leader of the official Opposition, Brad Wall, introduced a motion of non-confidence against the government for its lack of vision, poor financial management, failure to deliver needed services, and failure to provide incentives for people to stay in Saskatchewan (Saskatchewan, *Hansard,* 8 Nov.). During the ensuing debate, MLAs continued to criticize each other. One notable critique was directed at NDP MLA Eldon Lautermilch upon his being reappointed to Cabinet as minister of highways. While he was the minister responsible for Spudco, the failed public/private venture into the potato industry, Lautermilch had to apologize publicly for misleading information that had been provided regarding that company's contracts. This occurred after the legal aspects of the venture had been resolved in the courts in 2004. The fiasco, which cost the provincial government $34.4 million, was given a 'Teddy Award' by the Canadian Taxpayers Federation (CTF) as part of its campaign to raise awareness about government waste and mismanagement in Canada (*StarPhoenix,* 2 Mar.).

Despite the barrage of criticism from the official Opposition during the fall sitting, positive economic developments during that time helped the government deal with some issues. The government was able to announce that as a result of financial windfalls from oil and gas royalties, it would be able to spend even more than had been anticipated in its budget the previous spring. With approximately $900 million extra in revenues, finance minister Harry Van Mulligen announced that as well as fully funding the Canadian Agricultural Stabilization (CAIS) program, the government would provide funding for two hundred additional police officers, $59 million for northern roads, $76 million for long-term debt reduction, and $100 million for the planned Academic Health Sciences Centre at the University of Saskatchewan (*StarPhoenix,* 17 Nov.).

The fall sitting of the legislature was also interesting in that the parties began to broach the issue of uranium enrichment and the production of nuclear energy within the province. Politically, this had been a taboo subject for approximately two decades. The political parties had been relatively silent on it because neither the energy sector nor the public were advocating it. That started to change in 2005, as SaskPower, the province's Crown energy corporation, and the municipal sector began to ask whether it was an option for the province. Towards that end, the two major municipal associations (Saskatchewan Urban Municipalities and the Saskatchewan Association of Rural Municipalities) partnered with the University of Regina to hold a conference on the topic in January of the following year. Efforts by Brad Wall to constrain the government to articulate a policy on the matter generated a pragmatic and politically expedient response: nuclear energy if necessary, but not necessarily nuclear energy. Although he was pressing the government on the matter, the leader of the official Opposition was not himself articulating a position, saying only that the risks and benefits of the nuclear energy option should and would be examined by various stakeholders (Saskatchewan, *Hansard,* 16 and 30 Nov.).

In 2005 there was only a minor change to the Cabinet; in October two new ministers were added. As noted above, Eldon Lautermilch was appointed as minister for highways and the Saskatchewan Transportation Company. Graham Addley was appointed minister for healthy living services, a newly created portfolio to oversee addictions, mental health services, health promotion, and a smoking-reduction campaign *(Star-Phoenix,* 15 Oct.).

Some cabinet ministers found 2005 quite difficult, as they had to deal with financial mismanagement problems involving officials in their departments. One of these was the minister of the environment, David Forbes, who confirmed that $375,000 was missing from his department (*StarPhoenix,* 2 Feb.). Later that year a former executive assistant in the resource stewardship branch of that department was charged with break and enter, for allegedly entering Saskatchewan Environment buildings illegally, and for fraud over $5,000, for embezzling government funds by creating false invoices and having the resulting cheques delivered to her. The same employee had been charged in 1986 with defrauding a retail store in Regina (*StarPhoenix,* 12 Aug.).

In the fall of 2005 the minister responsible for the public service reported that in January of that year his department had been informed that more than a million dollars had gone missing from the Department of Community Resources and Employment over a ten-year period. An employee was fired in connection with the loss, but as of 31 December no charges had been laid. The most surprising revelation was that the accused had been charged previously with defrauding a Newfoundland bank of more than $600,000 while working as a loans officer in Corner Brook in the 1980s. Evidently she had been pardoned for that particular crime and was later hired by the Saskatchewan government (*StarPhoenix*, 25 Jan. and 22 Nov.).

These cases generated extensive criticism of the lax procedures for criminal checks of public employees, eventually forcing the government to modify its regulations and procedures. Whereas previous regulations had applied only to new employees in positions of trust with vulnerable clients or involved with law enforcement, security, or the administration of justice, the reforms made criminal-record checks also mandatory for employees who would be responsible for public money, able to modify information technology systems, or working with third parties (e.g., the federal government) that require such checks. All employees in the designated categories would also be required to submit to mandatory criminal-record checks within five years of their initial appointment and every five years thereafter. Under the new rules, the number of employees subject to the required criminal-record checks rose from 4,000 to 6,000 (*StarPhoenix*, 8 Sept.).

The budget

Harry Van Mulligen gave the centennial budget speech and spoke proudly about Saskatchewan's accomplishments. This was Saskatchewan's twelfth balanced budget in a row. The main goals were to 'make Saskatchewan an affordable place to live and raise a family; build a green and prosperous economy; provide the best health care in Canada; and build a future for our young people here in the province.' The greatest problem for the government was an unexpected reduction in revenues created by a reduction in equalization payments for the province from $582 million in 2004 to $82 million in 2005.

The 2005 budget did not include any increases in taxes and it allocated a substantial amount of money to various programs, including a record $2.9 billion for health care; $357 million for capital projects; $1.2 billion for education, for an array of purposes including tuition relief, additional training spaces, and technical institutions; $125 million for roads and highways; $481 million for agricultural assistance, including $98.8 million to fully fund CAIS; and $137 million for research and development. The budget was based on a projected GDP growth of 3.0 per cent, a 28 per cent debt-to-GDP forecast (compared to a high of 69 per cent debt-to-GDP ratio in 1993), and $179.3 million in permanent debt reduction, which brought the debt down to its lowest point in fourteen years (Saskatchewan, Budget Speech, 2005).

The economy

The Saskatchewan economy was on a relatively positive trajectory. A report produced by Statistics Canada in July indicated that the number of people working in the province since July 2004 had increased by 5,800 and that the unemployment rate was a mere 4.8 per cent, compared to the Canadian average of 6.7 per cent (*StarPhoenix,* 9 July). The provincial government was anxious to build on those positive developments in the economy by launching some important strategies. One such strategy was to minimize losses on some investments and to establish a more attractive investment framework for the private sector. In its efforts to minimize investment, it authorized the buyout of the unpaid debt of the Meadow Lake Pulp Limited Partnership to ensure that Investment Saskatchewan became the sole creditor of the partnership. The buyout was intended to make the resale of its plant easier (*StarPhoenix,* 3 May and 13 Sept.). However, the potential sale of the plant generated considerable consternation in the forestry sector, especially in the Meadow Lake region. This concern was rooted in the fact that the pulp industry was facing barriers such as a rising Canadian dollar and falling prices. By the end of 2005 the future of the pulp mill was still unknown.

Another strategy was to stabilize and stimulate the economy by launching some important initiatives in the mining sector. Towards that end the government focused on the potash industry. In an effort to establish a more attractive investment framework for the private sector, it announced a package that included a ten-year royalty break and capital investment incentives for Saskatchewan potash miners. The package was designed to increase employment by increasing both the number of people working at the mines and the number of people working in developing the infrastructure for that very profitable mining sector. The package helped increase mining activity to meet the rising demand for potash worldwide and to establish Saskatchewan as a major global player in this sector (*StarPhoenix,* 13 Apr.). The announcement prompted the uranium industry to seek a similar deal. However, given the NDP's reluctance to embrace nuclear energy, no deal was reached in 2005 *(StarPhoenix,* 31 May).

As part of its effort to foster a 'green economy' and to increase the level of environmentally friendly energy generation in the province, in 2005 SaskPower began construction of a 150-megawatt wind farm worth $250 million in southwest Saskatchewan, designed to provide energy for 60,000 homes. The project involved two major private sector companies: Hitachi, which was to construct the steel towers, and Vestas, which provided wind power components and expertise (*StarPhoenix*, 29 Jan.).

Despite the economic upturn generated by revenue sources, Saskatchewan still faced the problem, albeit a relatively minor one, of a net loss of population, largely due to outmigration. In July 2005 the population was down to 994,100 from 994,300 in July 2003. The problem was not so much the magnitude of the loss but the fact that, even with the economic upturn, the province was not attracting the number of migrants and immigrants needed to fill jobs in an expanding economy (*StarPhoenix*, 7 Nov.). This challenge motivated the provincial government to continue to expand the financial and human resources that it had started devoting to attracting and retaining immigrants, through the Saskatchewan Immigrant Nominee Program, in previous years. In 2005 the new bilateral Canada-Saskatchewan Immigration Agreement came into force. Pursuant to that agreement, the provincial government was planning to increase the annual intake of immigrants to approximately five thousand; to facilitate their attraction and retention it planned to increase the number of provincial employees for the immigration program.

By the end of 2005, after thirteen consecutive months of growth, the government and Saskatchewanians began to realize that the provincial economy was going through an expansion that it had not experienced for some time, and that it was imperative to capitalize on the upturn as much as possible. This was an opportunity they had been waiting on for decades and one that could not be wasted. For the provincial government, effective management of this economic boom had a political imperative attached to it: the electorate's judgment of its competence in economic management could mean the difference between winning and losing the next election.

The judiciary

The judiciary performed an important role in clarifying whistle-blower legislation related to a protracted case in Saskatchewan. In 2001 an employee of the Ironworkers Union reported to the president that some union officials were engaging in irregular and unlawful financial practices. When the president did not correct the situation, the employee reported the case to the police. Shortly thereafter she was fired and took her case for wrongful dismissal to court. Initially the court sided with her, but subsequently the Court of Appeal acquitted the union because the law stated ambiguously that whistle-blowers should report cases to a 'lawful authority' (*StarPhoenix*, 11 Feb.). According to that court, by going to the union president before going to the police, the employee had not followed proper procedure. The matter was referred to the Supreme Court of Canada for clarification.

The Supreme Court decision, supported by six of the seven judges on the panel, stated that the process the employee had used did not contravene either the letter or the spirit of the whistle-blower legislation. In its decision the court argued that, if the Saskatchewan legislature had 'intended "lawful authority" to be limited to a "public authority" such as the police, it would have said so in its whistleblower law' (*StarPhoenix*, 25 Nov.). Consequently the Supreme Court sent the case back to the Saskatchewan court for sentencing. To eliminate the ambiguity in the legislation, the provincial government had already taken remedial action approximately one year before the Supreme Court rendered its decision, amending its whistle-blower legislation to expand the definition of 'lawful authority' to include explicitly 'direct and indirect supervisors' (*StarPhoenix*, 1 Dec.).

In 2005 the judicial inquiry into the wrongful conviction of David Milgaard, which had resulted in two decades' imprisonment for him, began its work to determine how the police and the judicial system had failed in this case and who was responsible for that failure. The lawyer for the Saskatoon Police Department made it clear from the start that the work of the police officers and detectives in the case should not be judged by contemporary standards of forensic investigation (*StarPhoenix*, 18 Jan.).

Intergovernmental relations

Intergovernmental relations were as intriguing in 2005 as they had been in previous years, involving some very important negotiations and in some cases agreements related to major financial issues. The federal government formally announced its new deal with municipalities in 2005. The deal would provide more than $147 million to Saskatchewan municipalities over five years, through federal gas tax funding to be used for environmentally sustainable municipal infrastructure (public transit, waste-water management, roads and bridges, etc.) and to fund increased municipal planning capacity. The funding would increase annually from $17.7 million in Year 1 to $59.1 million in Year 5 and would remain at that level thereafter (*StarPhoenix*, 24 Aug.).

The Saskatchewan government was not as successful in its negotiations with the federal government for a Saskatchewan energy accord related to equalization funding. The provincial government wanted an agreement comparable to the ones that the federal government had negotiated with Newfoundland and Nova Scotia. Its goal was to eliminate or at least minimize the extent to which the level of equalization payments would be tied to provincial revenues generated from natural resources. The reason for this was that, given the boom the province was experiencing in the natural resources sector, the Saskatchewan government would not receive any equalization funding for the following year. By contrast, the two provinces that had managed to negotiate such an agreement would receive several hundred million dollars ($687 million for Newfoundland and $1.379 billion for Nova Scotia). In the Throne Speech presented in the fall of 2005, the provincial government had committed itself to pursue this matter until it was resolved to its satisfaction (Saskatchewan, *Hansard,* 8 Nov.).

With the federal new deal in hand, the municipal associations hoped they could also develop a new financial arrangement with the provincial government. The government relations minister, Len Taylor, said that his department would continue to examine options for a new provincial–municipal revenue-sharing deal (*StarPhoenix,* 17 Aug.). The provincial government recognized that it would have to find ways to share its steadily increasing revenue streams, but it had not quite decided the best way to do it. Municipal governments and other local authorities and interest groups watched carefully and focused on strengthening their cases that they were entitled to some of those provincial revenues.

Aboriginal affairs

As with other years in the recent past, 2005 included a combination of positive and negative developments in both the First Nations and Métis dimensions of the Aboriginal sector. It was an historic year for the recognition of another category of Aboriginal rights that benefited both First Nations and Métis governments and communities. The Supreme Court of Canada ruled that the federal and provincial governments had a duty to consult when development projects such as logging, mining, forestry, and road building potentially affected Aboriginal rights. Notwithstanding the court's ruling, however, it was left to the governments to figure out how to do so. Initial meetings between the provincial cabinet and the executive of the Federation of Saskatchewan Indian Nations

(FSIN) revealed that considerable efforts and time would be needed to resolve this matter to their mutual satisfaction.

Another positive development was that the Aboriginal and provincial government leaders decided to proclaim 2005 the Year of First Nations and Métis Women. This was done pursuant to a resolution passed in the fall of 2004 by the chiefs-in-assembly to make 2005 the Year of First Nations Women, as well as a consensus among federal, provincial, and territorial ministers responsible for the status of women to focus on issues faced by First Nations and Métis women. As part of this commemorative celebratory event, the provincial government committed itself to review and enhance initiatives, activities, and events of its departments that would contribute to the well-being of First Nations and Métis women and their families in living more secure and healthy lives (Saskatchewan, news release, 22 Feb., http://www.gov. sk.ca/news?newsId=b51e1172-eff5-4f12-ab83-c4bbb78ad5b8).

The negative issue for First Nations in 2005 was the continuing controversy surrounding the governance and management of the First Nations University of Canada (FNUC). Allegations and complaints persisted that politics and personal agendas continued to trump effective management. In February a FSIN resolution was passed granting sweeping powers to FNUC board chair Morley Watson. Shortly thereafter Watson began to exercise his power unilaterally, informing the province, the federal government, faculty, and other universities that they would now have only 'observer status' in the FNUC. Numerous staff members, including the former dean, Dawn Tato, were fired without reason. University employees agreed almost unanimously that the board and Watson were purposefully preventing FNUC from acting as an independent academic institution. As a result of the board's actions, the FSIN passed a resolution that permitted creation of a task force to oversee investigations into mismanagement and political manoeuvring in the FNUC. Key recommendations of the task force included the following: the FNUC board should be reduced from thirty-two to thirteen members; the board should be depoliticized and focus on academic issues; and the board should develop its own accreditation system rather than depending on the University of Regina to grant degrees (*StarPhoenix,* 5 and 13 Aug., 1 Dec.). The problems surrounding FNUC as well as other problems led some to criticize the FSIN leadership. At least one columnist decried what he described as the insolence and isolation of leaders who thought that their decisions and actions should not be subjected to public scrutiny and that they could act with impunity and without full accountability (*StarPhoenix,* 4 Mar.).

The year 2005 proved to be a good one for Métis rights activists, who had been working hard to consolidate fishing and hunting rights. The Provincial Court of Saskatchewan ruled that Métis people had constitutionally protected harvesting rights that must be recognized and respected by governments. In that ruling the judge stated that section 13(1) of the Fisheries Regulations of Saskatchewan, prohibiting fishing during the closed season, did not apply to a Métis citizen regardless of how far that citizen was from any Métis community either inside or outside the Northern Administration District (NAD), which comprised the northern half of the province. This ruling rejected the provincial government's position that Métis harvesting rights were exercisable only around traditional Métis communities in the NAD, by Métis citizens who were ancestrally connected to those communities. The judge did not accept the government's narrow interpretation because it failed to acknowledge that Métis tend to be 'highly mobile people' within and beyond the NAD. The judge added that the fact that the individual had lived and worked outside the province did not negate those rights, and that his reliance on fishing and hunting was enough to meet the cultural identity and engagement criteria laid out in the historic Powley case (Métis National Council, news release, http://www.metisnation.ca/press/05-july18.html).

For the Métis in Saskatchewan, 2005 was a critical year for the future of their governance institutions. The legitimacy of their electoral and governance systems was perceived to be at a very low level. Some wondered whether it would be possible to save and sustain those systems. In June 2005 the Métis Electoral Panel submitted its report to the provincial government. The panel had been established by the minister responsible for First Nations and Métis relations in December 2004, to consult with Métis people on electoral and democratic reform. It did so after it accepted the findings of an independent report by Keith Lampard regarding extensive irregularities and possibly illegal activities related to elections held by Métis Nation–Saskatchewan (MNS) in May 2004, which had compromised their level of democracy and fairness. In producing the report the panel held hearings in twenty-four communities and heard from more than a thousand people. The panel concluded that the majority of those who had participated in the process felt that another election should be held and that it should be organized and conducted by an independent election panel. Throughout 2005 the federal and provincial governments withheld funding transfers to the existing MNS executive until proper and fair elections overseen by independent election officials could be held. During the latter part of 2005 the police laid nine charges of forgery and obstruction of justice against persons who allegedly had been responsible for some of the irregularities and illegalities (Saskatchewan, news release, 6 July, http://www.gov.sk.ca/news?newsId=91cb376c-eea2-4ae2-943f-581e2532d47e; *StarPhoenix,* 7 July and 26 Aug.).

In the fall of 2005 the provincial government outlined its proposal for a new, fair and democratic election for the leadership of the MNS, to be held the following year. Its plan, echoing the recommendations of the Métis Electoral Panel, stated that the proposed election process would be funded by the provincial and federal governments, subject the MNS's agreeing to the following:

- holding a Métis Nation legislative assembly to call the election;
- accepting appointment by the provincial government of a Métis Elections Advisory Committee and a chief electoral officer, who would be responsible for planning the election and developing a valid voters list;
- abiding by the recommendations of that committee and officer during the elections process; and
- holding a general assembly of Métis people to ratify the election (Saskatchewan, news release, 4 Nov., http://www.gov.sk.ca/news?newsId=c1ef2ecf-1e05-46b4-9ba7-183e8f9930e4).

As 2005 drew to a close, Saskatchewanians began to sense that the centennial year had marked the end of an interesting century in the history of the province and the beginning of a new one that would likely result in varying degrees of continuity and discontinuity from both the positive and the negative legacies of the past.

GEOFFREY LAMBERT

Manitoba

The NDP government of Gary Doer proceeded through 2005 as if it did not have a care in the world. The economy was in good condition, the government was generally unobtrusive (and therefore offended few people), and there were no major scandals that might wreck the NDP's re-election chances in 2007 or 2008. Moreover, the two opposition parties in the legislature appeared weak. Indeed, Stuart Murray, the Progressive Conservative leader, announced his resignation at a party conference in November.

But to widespread surprise, an opinion poll appeared in the *Winnipeg Free Press* late in the year showing the government and the Tories tied, with the Liberals holding the position they had usually held since the late 1960s: dead last. The NDP had led comfortably in every poll published since the 1999 election, so if this one was accurate, something was transpiring that was not readily explicable. Some put the change down to Murray's resignation, as if it had awoken sleeping Tories everywhere. Or perhaps the misfortunes besetting the Crocus Fund (see below) had had a deeper impact than previously realized. Whatever the case, there was little doubt that under new leadership the opposition would be relentless in pursuing the the government in 2006.

The legislative session

The legislature reconvened on 7 April and sat until 13 July. It resumed on 27 October, when it heard a new Throne Speech and sat for a few weeks before adjourning for Christmas.

The budget was brought down by Greg Selinger, the finance minister, on 8 April. Naturally he took credit for the government's handling of the economy, which was doing well by Manitobans. The budget was an unadventurous one, accompanied by a healthy surplus ($114 million) that would allow the government to continue to court the constituencies it had cultivated in previous years, including such groups as young couples and Aboriginals. Selinger was also able to increase program expenditures by somewhat more than the rate of inflation, pay off some debt, put a little money into the provincial rainy-day fund, and still implement some previously announced tax cuts – not a bad situation to be in. But the opposition also appeared to be on solid ground in asking why the NDP, which had enjoyed such surpluses every year, did not simply cut taxes.

Government revenues in 2005–06 were estimated at $8.178 billion, of which $4.537 billion was to come from taxes, $849 million from other fees and services, and $2.796 billion in transfers from the central government. Of this last figure, $1.871 billion was to come in the form of equalization payments, themselves a hot topic. Expenditures were to go up, with all major activities enjoying an increase somewhat ahead of inflation; estimated program spending was projected at just over $8 billion.

The session was a busy one. A comparatively heavy volume of bills was introduced, though few were epochal. However, there was a wholesome, workmanlike quality about some of them that fit right in with the pragmatic Manitoban outlook on life. For example, major bills included revisions to the *Workers' Compensation Act* and the *Administration of the Courts Act,* as well as passage of the *Health Freedom Act.*

The House took a summer break in July and came back on 27 October to hear the Throne Speech, read by Lieutenant-Governor John Harvard. The theme was basically one of consolidation and expansion of existing programs, although there were a few new initiatives in the environmental area. This focus reflected the government's no doubt genuine concern for the quality of the air and the sustainability of the economy, as well as its belief that Manitoba had a promising future on account of the high volume of cheap, renewable hydroelectricity that it was likely to be able to produce.

The issue of the Devil's Lake diversion confronted the government all year long. The state of North Dakota, acting unilaterally, planned to divert the floodwaters of Devil's Lake into the Red River system. Manitoba's position (supported by the state of Minnesota) was that the project, if implemented, would cause considerable damage to the fish in the river, and to the waters of the Red. Manitoba demanded action by the federal government, the International Joint Commission, and the U.S. State Department. Nothing significant happened for some time. Finally, in August North Dakota promised to install a filter so that 'nuisance species' of American weeds and fish would not be able to contaminate the Canadian section of the Red River system; it then opened up the diversion. But the issue was not dead, and interested parties were to carry their concerns into the following year.

Much of the Throne Speech reflected the government's pride in what it had accomplished in its six years in office. Certainly the NDP had fulfilled its admittedly thin set of pledges. The government was conspicuously committed to the advancement of First Nations and to the sensible development of the province's resources. And it had handled provincial taxation issues quite well. But on the big issues of health and education, the NDP's performance had not kept pace with its rhetoric.

In the area of health care, the government was spending more (41 per cent of the total budget program expenditure) relative to its predecessors and to most other provincial governments. It had successfully reduced waiting times ('wait times,' in the new parlance) for a number of diagnostic and surgical procedures. However, it had been unable, despite occasional claims to the contrary, to make 'hallway medicine' a thing of the past. Anyone taking a stroll through the emergency ward of any Winnipeg hospital at most times of day would see the hallways as packed as ever with people left to cope in sadly undignified situations. Perhaps there was a better way, but the New Democrats, normally so pragmatic, refused to consider alternative methods of delivering health care. They believed that the solution to the health-care crisis lay in investing more money in the public system, and thus refused to consider private delivery of health services. More than once in 2005, NDP members seemed to become excessively alarmed at the prospect of private clinics opening their doors or serving patients.

The Doer government doubtless had mixed feelings about one health-related issue about which most Manitobans undoubtedly felt a little quiet pride: the success of the mail-order pharmacies, which had originated in Manitoba and had been founded by some young entrepreneurs. These were businesses that filled the prescriptions of elderly Americans at much lower prices than those offered in the United States. To say they were a success would be a considerable understatement. Although completely reliable figures are not available, to describe the volume of business as being 'in the billions' would probably not be far off the mark.

These homegrown Manitoba businesses had many powerful enemies, of course, which perhaps explains why they made the provincial government a little uneasy. The big drug companies, for example, threatened to restrict supplies. Some suggested that the drugs would be tainted in some fashion. Closer to home, some questioned the ethics of local doctors who countersigned prescriptions for people they had never seen. Others worried about the impact on the pharmaceutical research business in Canada, since it was heavily supported by American companies.

Fortunately, the industry also had many American supporters quite apart from the satisfied customers. The governments of some states (such as Massachusetts), some local governments (in Illinois, for example), and school boards signed agreements with their employees that allowed for the purchase of 'offshore' drugs. The governor of Minnesota, Thomas Pawlenty, made a personal trip to the Keystone Province to see for himself. Pawlenty, a Republican, commented that he did not see many Canadians dying in the streets because of bad drugs. Still, it remained to be seen how long the business could continue without the imposition of restrictions or regulations.

As for education, criticism about underfunding was far more prevalent than praise among administrators, especially in the post-secondary sector. For many years, colleges and universities had been able to increase tuition fees as circumstances dictated. Thus, in the 1990s there was a rather substantial increase in student tuition as universities and colleges diverted a higher share of the cost of education to its beneficiaries. Students were predictably horrified, and there were complaints that poorer people were being excluded from higher education. In Manitoba the New Democrats promised, if elected, to freeze tuition rates. This they duly did, and, noting the increased enrolment that followed, suggested there was a causal link between the two. Experts suggested that the relationship between the decision to go to university and the level of fees was rather nebulous. Also, other provinces, including those that had imposed the heaviest increases, had also enjoyed substantial increases in student registration. Only Manitoba had imposed a freeze and, although pressed from various directions, refused to abandon it.

Additionally, the government saw no reason to compensate colleges and universities for the revenue they would have received from increased student tuition. The post-secondary sector protested, arguing that the money was needed for faculty renewal, technological upgrades, and so forth. The government was prepared to go so far as to turn a blind eye to some of the incidental fees the colleges and universities dreamt up to deal with the shortfall. But on the major issue – taking tuition fees out of the freezer – post-secondary institutions might as well have saved their breath.

Politics and political developments

The NDP seemed secure. An oddity of government in an age of mass media, in which people tire of the same old faces and want a 'change' so readily, the party continued to be led by someone who been a fixture in provincial politics since 1986, when he was first elected to the legislature, and who had been party leader since 1988. Put in comparative terms, Gary Doer had led the Manitoba New Democrats since the days of Ronald Reagan, Brian Mulroney, and Margaret Thatcher. There was, moreover, no serious challenge to his leadership in the works. Indeed, a national poll suggested that he was the most popular provincial premier in the land.

Doer seemed to have a knack for anticipating public opinion and avoiding controversy. His gift for one-liners stood him in good stead, and the hint of pragmatic populism he displayed served him well in a province often said to have a blue-collar outlook. But people had said much the same about his Progressive Conservative predecessor, Gary Filmon, when he had been in power. Filmon had been rejected after eleven years in office in large part because of a loss of trust, brought about by a scandal that did not seem overly serious or threatening at the time it received its public airing. Perhaps the Crocus Fund scandal (see below) had the same potential. The government kept its distance, however, and the opposition failed to exploit the situation. Indeed, Stuart Murray, the PC leader, admitted he had been warned off by some important businesspeople who were, presumably, donors to the Conservatives. But perhaps after Murray's departure from leadership (to take place in April 2006), whoever succeeded him would be more aggressive on the issue.

Stuart Murray had been elected leader of his party in 2000, succeeding the long-serving Gary Filmon. Although he had done better than expected in the 2003 election, he failed to inspire the electorate or the party membership. He seemed to lack the instinct to go for the jugular and, worse, to deal effectively with the media. Leading the party when the incumbent NDP seemed so entrenched cannot have been easy. Indeed, the caucus eventually became restive; Murray indicated his intention to resign after the party conference in November voted only 52 per cent against conducting a leadership review. It was ironic that, only a few weeks after his announcement, a poll was published showing the two parties tied, and the Tories in a stronger position than they had been since their ouster from government in 1999. Murray was quick to claim credit. Others put it down to the fact that he was stepping down, and some suggested that the Crocus Fund issue might be hurting the government after all.

There was no apparent front-runner for the Tory succession in late 2005, although a long list of possibilities emerged. One of the most poignant aspects of the situation was that John Loewen, MLA for the expensive Winnipeg suburb of Fort Whyte, would not be among the aspirants. He had crossed swords with his party leader over how to deal with the Crocus Fund issue, effectively being told to shut up and abandon the aggressive posture he had adopted. Loewen, who would have enjoyed considerable support had he sought the leadership, had already signalled his resignation from the legislature in order to run as a Liberal in the upcoming federal election, slated for January 2006. He was to contest the seat won in 2004 by Stephen Fletcher, a Conservative, and the first ever quadriplegic member of Parliament.

The two-person provincial Liberal caucus (although, under House rules, they did not constitute a recognized political party) tried gamely to attract attention but garnered little interest. Both members, Dr Jon Gerrard and Kevin Lamoureux, possessed political skills and considerable experience, but they seemed to lack a political identity that might distinguish them from their rivals. And 2005 was also a year in which their federal counterparts were struggling with issues of corruption, something that doubtless hurt the Manitoba Grits.

The economy

The Manitoba economy performed well in 2005. The economy grew (by about 3 per cent), investment was steady, and consumer demand continued to be strong. The sale of houses was brisk, with prices reaching what were for Winnipeg unprecedented levels.

The population continued to grow as newborns and people arriving from other countries outnumbered the deceased and those departing for other provinces. The provincial population stood at about 1.28 million, with just under 700,000 living in the provincial capital. Work (even if it was uninspiring) was relatively easy to get, and the provincial unemployment rate, at 4.8 per cent, was the second lowest in the country, behind only Alberta. Likewise, unemployment among youth (defined as eighteen-to-twenty-four-year-olds) was, at 9.7 per cent, also second lowest in the nation.

Incomes rose by 3.5 per cent on average, and the consumer price index for Winnipeg was 2.7 per cent. The primary contributor to the increase in the cost of living was higher prices for petroleum products. Like Canadians elsewhere, Manitobans had to accustom themselves to much higher prices at the pump than they had previously experienced.

It is conventional wisdom that the broad and varied nature of the Manitoba economy buffers it against traumatic downturns. This continued to be true. The agricultural sector was badly hit, both by the residual effects of the mad-cow crisis and by wetter than usual weather in the spring, which delayed seeding. However, the sale of hogs continued at a high rate, becoming an even more important component of the farm industry than it had been previously. Indeed, there was a push to use some abandoned wasteland in St Boniface to build a slaughterhouse for pigs.

On the other side of the ledger, manufacturing shipments increased by 6.9 per cent, led by electrical and construction equipment. Moreover, exports to the United States took an even larger share of trade. Hydroelectricity sales outside the province (held up by the incumbent government as the key to Manitoba's future prosperity) increased by an astounding 69 per cent. Thus the conventional wisdom still applied: Manitoba participated fully in the national boom and the mix of elements in its economy served the province well.

The investment community in the province, however, viewed the revelations about the Crocus Fund with dismay. The fund was a labour-backed venture capital scheme with interests in a number of Manitoba businesses. In late 2004 it had ceased trading, as it appeared that its prices were inflated and that unconventional accounting methods had concealed many of its losses. Moreover, some board members seemed to be behind the obfuscation, and a number of them resigned in 2005. The provincial auditor, John Singleton, hammered the fund, citing, *inter alia,* abuse of expense account privileges. By the middle of 2005 the fund had ceased to operate in all but name. The government seemed oddly quiescent, and the opposition originally (under pressure, it appears, from the private business sector) shrugged the matter off. But this afforded no relief to those stuck with investments in the fund, some in the $60,000 range. Hence, by the turn of 2005–06, investors were beginning to exert themselves through legal processes.

The search continued for a formula that would generate interesting, exciting work of the kind that would keep young people in the province. There were construction projects, the Red River Floodway – 'Duff's Ditch,' as it is frequently called, after former premier Duff Roblin, who dreamt up the project – was to be expanded, and construction would soon begin on a new terminal at the Winnipeg International Airport. The new Manitoba Hydro building, the anticipated Canadian Museum for

Human Rights (if it could ever get the federal government to be more specific about the extent of its financial support), further gentrification of Winnipeg's old warehouse district, and conversion of unused public land in St Boniface would undoubtedly help keep the flame of expansion alive. But even in good times, it seemed hard to keep the province's best and brightest at home.

Clearly Winnipeg needed more high-tech jobs and a greater ability to attract and retain cultural institutions, icons, and events. The noted new-economy specialist Dr Richard Florida insisted, in particular, on the need to expand Winnipeg's cultural life. He argued, among other things, that a more vibrant gay community would help draw increased talent and tourists to the city.

Other events

James Driskell found justice in 2005. He was the latest in an alarmingly long list of people who had served time (in his case, eleven years) for murders they had not committed. He thus joined David Milgaard and Thomas Sophonow as Winnipeggers who had gone through a similar fearful ordeal. Blocked though he and his supporters were for a while by the determined reluctance of some police to admit the possibility of error, DNA evidence ultimately proved his saviour.

One of the glories of Winnipeg is the Royal Winnipeg Ballet (RWB), and one of the glories of the RWB was Evelyn Hart, its prima ballerina. But the internationally renowned and much-decorated Hart apparently felt she was being frozen out of new roles and not being invited to dance in established works. Although the ballet company was very tactful about the issue, the fact was that Hart was pushing fifty and was hence somewhat older than those who customarily dance Juliet or the lead role in *The Nutcracker.* She left the company without notice, depriving her numerous fans of an opportunity to bid her farewell. She sought to rebuild her career in Toronto, though she also mused about opening a shop.

The Juno Awards for 2005 were held in April at the brand-new Manitoba Theatre Centre in downtown Winnipeg. It was pronounced a great success in spite of the absence of many top stars, including hometown boy Neil Young, who was recovering from brain surgery in New York City. The comedian and actor Brent Butt, star of CTV's hit show *Corner Gas,* proved a congenial and popular master of ceremonies, and Jann Arden, perhaps the most famous of those in attendance, proved characteristically gregarious, making many new fans.

KEN COATES AND GREG POELZER

The Territories

The political and administrative evolution of the Canadian North continued in 2005, at a pace that frustrated many in the region but continued to impress external observers. Nunavut struggled with the realities of self-government and territorial status. Yukon waited for a return to economic prosperity. The Northwest Territories, still enjoying the widespread benefits of the diamond and general mining boom, awaited news that the Mackenzie Valley pipeline would finally commence. Canada's growing concern over Arctic sovereignty gave the region an unexpected publicity boost, but with little direct benefit to the North. The dispute with Denmark over the ownership of Hans Island, which had begun in 2004, escalated when Canadian defence minister Bill Graham visited the tiny island in July 2005, sparking a verbal rebuke from Denmark and an escalation in national and international rhetoric about the future of the Arctic.

The North in Canadian and international affairs

The debate over Arctic sovereignty, highlighted by the slightly silly contretemps over Hans Island – a chunk of rock that neither Canada nor Denmark had taken seriously for decades – had the potential to redefine the role of the North in Confederation. Politicians happily wrapped themselves in the Canadian flag and went north to stake Canadian claims to the High Arctic. Although little of substance changed in the North, politicians from the three key national political parties spoke more openly about northern strategies and offered bold pronouncements about Canadian national interest in the region. On the ground very little changed, but northerners could see in 2005 that attitudes towards the region had started to shift. This pattern, of course, had occurred several times in the past, when external interest in the Arctic had sparked short-lived national attention to the issue. In 2005, amidst a global debate about climate change and mounting concerns about the melting of arctic ice, the sovereignty questions appeared to assume greater significance and authority.

While issues about sovereignty and arctic resources dominated the news, concern also continued about American plans to develop oil and gas resources in the Arctic National Wildlife Refuge. The ANWR lands included the calving grounds of the Porcupine caribou herd, a key resource for the Vuntut Gwich'in people of Old Crow and the surrounding region. Yukon Aboriginal political representatives, led by Lorraine Peter, MLA for Old Crow, and Chief Joe Linklater, travelled to Washington, D.C., to take their case to the American government. They secured the support of, among others, Senator Hillary Rodham Clinton and managed to stall plans – spearheaded by Ted Stevens, the Republican senator from Alaska – to open the field for exploration and development. Closer to home, Prime Minister Paul Martin spoke out in favour of halting exploration of the caribou calving grounds and promised to work to convince the Americans to back off from the project.

Yukon politics

In the absence of a federal or territorial election, Yukon politics remained comparatively quiet throughout 2005. On a sharply negative note, Haakon Arntzen, MLA for Copperbelt, was forced to resign his seat when he was found guilty of indecent assault relating to events originating in the 1970s. One of the highlights of political year came in February, when the Kwanlin Dun First Nation formally signed their land claim and self-government settlement with the government of Canada. The deal provided the Kwanlin Dun with more than 10,380 square kilometres of land, including a substantial amount of real estate inside the Whitehorse city limits, and some $47 million (minus slightly less than $15 million in negotiation costs) as part of the final settlement. The Council for Yukon First Nations had signed the initial umbrella agreement in 1993, leaving the individual First Nations to negotiate specific accords with the federal and territorial governments. The signing of an agreement that covered the territory's largest city represented a crucial step in the ongoing resolution of Aboriginal claims in Yukon.

Arntzen's resignation created an opening in the territorial legislature, and a by-election was held in November. Earlier in the year, Yukon Liberal Party leader Pat Duncan had called a leadership convention, which she contested, to provide the party with a strong leader and a fresh mandate. Arthur Mitchell ran against Duncan, as did Ed Schultz, who resigned as grand chief of the Council for Yukon First Nations in order to take part. Mitchell prevailed on the third ballot. He subsequently ran in the Copperbelt by-election and won a seat in the legislature. Schultz was replaced as grand chief by Andy Carvill.

Dawson City figured prominently in territorial political affairs throughout the year. Peter Jenkins, who was deputy premier at the time, resigned from the Yukon Party and from Cabinet in November, claiming that he could not convince the government to attend properly to the needs of his constituency. Premier Dennis Fentie responded to the resignation by pointing out that a company owned by Jenkins was $300,000 in debt to the Yukon government and that Jenkins was stalling on repayment. The government subsequently took Jenkins's firm to court over the matter. More troubling was the release of a forensic accounting examination of the financial affairs of Dawson City. It was sharply critical of the oversight exercised by former mayor Glen Everitt and his council and singled out two top officials, former town manger Scott Coulson and former treasurer Dale Courtice, for mismanagement. The report on the Dawson City fiasco, which resulted in administration of the town being taken over by the Yukon government, argued that the former politician and the administrators owed the community more than $200,000.

Yukon politics remained provocative and, at times, controversial. Former commissioner Ken McKinnon had been assigned the task of reviewing the need for electoral reform in Yukon. His final report argued that major changes were not required but that members of the Legislative Assembly needed to maintain better ties with their constituencies and that a significant improvement in decorum in the legislature was required. Many Yukoners – including some seven hundred signatories to a petition on electoral reform – claimed that McKinnon had not consulted widely enough. They asked the premier to conduct a more open investigation of the reform option, but Premier Fentie declined to pursue the matter further.

Aboriginal political affairs continued to figure prominently in Yukon. Public conflicts had arisen over matters as diverse as economic development planning and participation in planning for indigenous engagement in the Alaska Highway pipeline project. Three First Nations took steps to assume greater control over education amidst growing acknowledgement that Aboriginal students continued to do poorly in high school. Passage of the *Cooperation in Governance Act* (CGA) provided a foundation for future cooperation, however. The CGA required that the Yukon Forum meet four times a year to allow greater government-to-government interaction and to ensure that joint initiatives and matters of concern to Aboriginal and other Yukoners received a full public airing.

Northwest Territories politics

The absence of a territorial election in 2005 did not mean that the territory was without political intrigue during the year. Henry Zoe, member of the territorial legislature for North Slave and a former cabinet minister, resigned his seat in spring 2005, citing personal reasons related to a conviction for resisting arrest. A by-election was held on 18 July in the renamed Monfwi constituency, leading to the election of Jackson Lafferty in a close contest. Perhaps the biggest issue of the calendar year focused on the perpetual topic of construction of the Mackenzie Valley pipeline. The continuing contest between developers, government regulators, the territorial government and Aboriginal leaders came to a head in the spring. Pipeline developers called off engineering activity on the project, claiming that Aboriginal expectations had gotten out of control. Imperial Oil, a key partner in the multi-billion-dollar initiative, threatened to pull out entirely because of what it claimed were unrealistic demands. The Liberal government, eager to push the project forward, offered an incentive of $500 million, provided the project advanced. Government and corporate interests put together a $40-million Aboriginal training program designed to ensure that the local population was well placed to capitalize on the opportunities. However, the incentives could not breach the formidable barriers in the way of proceeding, and 2005 ended without a resolution of the pipeline project.

There was abundant evidence of the seriousness of purpose in the government of the Northwest Territories (GNWT), reflecting its recognition of serious regional challenges, the opportunities created by devolution and Aboriginal land claims settlements, and a strong sense of territorial collaboration. The government had released a ten-year strategic plan in June 2004, outlining a comprehensive strategy for collective development and setting out clear and ambitious goals for government action. The Territorial Assembly reported on its progress in fall 2005, under the four key priorities established the previous year. The central areas of emphasis for the government included environmental stewardship, improved economic activity and regional infrastructure, resolution of relations with the federal and Aboriginal governments, and assistance to individuals, families, and communities in helping themselves. The government had, in effect, established a territorial report card and committed itself to reporting on investments, policies, and results on an annual basis. The 2005 GNWT report *Self-Reliant People, Communities and Northwest Territories: A Shared Responsibility* – the first based on the territorial strategic plan – provided a comprehensive, clear and blunt assessment of government priorities and actions. The resulting portrait of government commitments was a particularly useful summary of the scale of official engagement with the lives of northerners and a clear recounting of the challenges facing the North. The report was at once empowered and worrisome, for it indicated both the major strides the NWT had taken in managing its affairs and the formidable social, cultural, economic, and environmental difficulties that lay ahead.

Nunavut politics

The Nunavut election of 2004 produced substantial change in the composition of the territorial assembly, and the following year continued a period of transition and adaptation. Paul Okalik had been re-elected to both his seat and the premiership, providing considerable continuity in leadership. The issues of Nunavut politics had become quite consistent by this juncture – still only six years after the creation of the territory – with debates focusing on housing, social and cultural affairs, language development and education (including a continuing struggle to balance instruction in Inuktitut with English competency), economic development, and distribution of jobs and opportunities between Iqaluit and the outlying communities. The latter remained a high government priority, in spite of mounting evidence that the effort to shift government offices to the smaller communities had created substantial inefficiencies and increased costs dramatically.

One of the more intriguing political discussions of the year occurred around the decision to use an inukshuk as the logo for the 2010 Olympic Games scheduled for Vancouver. Former commissioner Pete Irniq questioned the decision to give the inukshuk human characteristics. The issue was quickly defused by Premier Paul Okalik and Inuit Tapiriit Kanatami president Jose Kusugak, who expressed delight that an important Inuk image would be given international prominence through the games.

One of the most significant political events of 2005 was the signing of the Inuit Partnership Agreement in Canada by the Inuit Association and Indian Affairs and Northern Development on 18 May. The accord recognized the constitutional status of Inuit in Nunatsiavut (Labrador), Nunavik, Nunavut, the Inuvialuit Settlement Region, and southern Canada; acknowledged the special status of comprehensive land claim agreements in the area; and made special note of the fact that the honour of the Crown would be at stake in all subsequent relations with the Inuit. The accord included explicit government recognition of the important contributions by Inuit to Canada's history, identity, and sovereignty and made specific reference to federal commitments to improve the quality and standard of life for Inuit people. The high-profile recognition, plus a commitment to fostering self-reliance across the North (not restricted to Nunavut), was seen by the Inuit as a watershed development in the history of Inuit–government relations in Canada. The unique accord was signed by the minister of Indian affairs and northern development for the Crown and, representing key Inuit constituencies, by the presidents of the Inuit Tapiriit Kanatami, the Inuvialuit Regional Corporation, Nunavut Tunngavik Incorporated, the Makivik Corporation, the Labrador Inuit Association, Pauktuutit, the Inuit Circumpolar Conference Canada, and the National Inuit Youth Council.

The economy

The northern economies continued along a familiar path in 2005, with the strong performance of diamond-mining and related activities in the Northwest Territories spurring considerable exploration. Preliminary preparatory work on the Mackenzie Valley pipeline and the Beaufort Sea oil reserves continued as in the past, with no assurance of approval for the project. Promising signs in Nunavut pointed to potential mining activity, offset by the realization that substantial corporate and government investments were needed to get major initiatives off the ground.

Mining continued to show signs of strength. In the Yukon, exploration activity accounted for some $53 million in spending in 2005, the third consecutive year of growth. More than thirty projects were under active development, including properties with promising quantities of zinc, copper, tungsten, and uranium. Pending decisions on three substantial projects – Yukon Zinc's Wolverine site; the Minto copper, gold, and silver mine operated by Sherwood Copper; and Cash Minerals' promising coal reserves at Division Mountain – all had the potential to proceed to production. High gold and copper prices kept many firms active in the field and ensured a high level of exploration activity. The Yukon shipped more than $33 million in mineral products from the territory. While this remained a long way from the halcyon days when the Cyprus Anvil property at Faro was in full production, the size and diversity of mining activity sparked considerable optimism in the Yukon.

The Northwest Territories enjoyed a robust year. Mineral production remained strong, with $8 million from tungsten, $21 million from metallic shipments, and almost $1.7 billion in non-metallics, primarily diamonds. The territory produced $120 million in natural gas and

$460 million in crude oil; neither came close to the expectations of earlier years but held promise for future possibilities. Nunavut attracted a great deal of exploration, with more than $160 million spent during the year, but actual returns remained small. The economy of Nunavut did not grow appreciably during 2005, in large part because of closure of the Lupin gold mine in 2004.

Government remained the foundation of territorial economic activity. Premier David Fentie of Yukon submitted a $784-million budget early in 2005, including more than $200 million in capital spending. The overall budget exceeded the previous year's spending by more than $80 million, providing considerable stimulus for the territorial economy but sparking complaints about the spending habits of the government. The government came back for almost $41 million more late in the year, pushing the territorial budget over $800 million for the first time in Yukon history.

The general stability of the Yukon economy sparked optimism and considerable activity throughout the territory. In the capital, Whitehorse, housing prices shot up, with the average cost of an area home jumping to more than $225,000. With contractors in short supply, an insufficient number of building lots, and inexpensive mortgages, upward pressure on housing prices continued. That more than four hundred people had moved into the territory in a twelve-month period added to the demand for homes. Raucous debates ensued at the city level as residents protested civic plans to allow additional housing construction on greenbelt lands. Most of the protests proved successful, with city planners backing off their plans to open up the lands for development.

Northerners continued to enjoy substantial personal financial returns. Personal income in the Yukon rose 7.6 per cent to reach almost $41,000 (determined by GDP) in 2005, ranking second only to the Northwest Territories, where personal income equalled almost $45,000. In both jurisdictions, solid salary increases for workers in public administration provided the highest average earnings. Unemployment, except in Nunavut, remained low by national standards, with a rate of less than 5.5 per cent for the Northwest Territories as against a national average of 6.8 per cent in 2005. However, many of the highest-income workers in the North, particularly in the NWT, did not show up in territorial statistics. Transient employees in the fly-in/fly-out diamond-mining and oil and gas exploration projects typically lived in southern Canada and were not active members of northern society.

The North had a formidable economic downside as well. In Nunavut, where many people had opted out of the job search because of limited opportunities, unemployment remained extremely high, defying government efforts to stimulate economic activity. Indeed, in 2004–05 Nunavut experienced a very sharp rise in reliance on income support, with the number of cases jumping from 3,200 to almost 3,600, and more than 13,000 territorial residents showing up on the income-support rolls during the course of the year. Continued difficulties with the sale of seal pelts, which were under concerted attack by environmental and animal rights groups, reduced incomes further and made it difficult for many hunters to sustain their country food production. Median income in Nunavut stood at around $21,000 in 2005, well below rates in Yukon and the Northwest Territories; factoring in the higher costs of living in the North, this resulted in very low real incomes.

Social conditions

Northern Canada's roller-coaster demographic and social realities remained in evidence throughout 2005. Diabetes continued to pose a major health problem in the North, with the Yukon experiencing a 45 per cent rise over the four years following 2001 and the NWT recording 31 per cent growth. Importantly, the surging diabetes epidemic began to attract national attention in this period, largely because of aggressive efforts by indigenous organizations. In the Yukon, births fell almost 18 per cent from the previous year after rising almost 15 per cent in the twelve months before that. Nunavut continued to have the highest fertility rate in the country, with 2.72 births per hundred people, followed by the NWT with 2.11 per hundred – both twice the national average. The territory's sharp rise in deaths from 2003 to 2004 (up almost 19 per cent) slowed dramatically in 2005. Like the NWT and Nunavut, the Yukon ran up sizable health-care costs, with per capita spending exceeding $6,000, against a national rate of $4,400 per year.

The North reversed population losses in 2005, with the Yukon recording a slight gain through migration. All three territories had substantial population gains through births compared to deaths; the North continued to have the highest birth rates in the country. Of particular interest in the continuing search for stability was movement of non-indigenous peoples in and out of the North. In the Yukon, for example, the territory gained 316 people through migration, only to lose 109 the following year. In 2005 the net gain was 141, still inconsistent and highlighting the continued transiency of the non-Aboriginal population in the region.

Smoking remained extremely commonplace across the North (as, importantly, did the consumption of pop and junk food). In Nunavut, more than half of all residents over twelve years of age smoked regularly, considerably higher than in the NWT (36 per cent) and Yukon (30 per cent); the entire North was well above the national average of 22 per cent. The Nunavut rate, incidentally, represented a drop of more than 10 per cent over two years. Among the Inuit in Nunavut, the smoking rate was a staggering 85 per cent, with two-thirds of Inuit smoking regularly. The health effects of smoking showed up in exceptionally high rates of lung cancer, described in a Statistics Canada study as among the highest in the world. With many expectant mothers smoking regularly and many pregnancies occurring in the teenage years, it did not surprise health authorities to discover that the Inuit had infant mortality rates three times higher than the Canadian average.

Crime remained a serious problem across the North, with Whitehorse recording a series of dramatic, high-profile murders and the NWT and Nunavut crime rates continuing to rise dramatically. Even in the area of property crime, where national rates fell sharply, the NWT's increased significantly. Much of the criminal activity, including significant problems with firearm offences, related to the overconsumption of alcohol and drugs. Nunavut made significant strides in combating one of the most serious problems in its communities, teenage suicide. Suicide rates were more than ten times the national average, with thirty-seven people killing themselves in 2003. By 2005 the number had fallen to twenty-two, still high by national standards but an improvement that reflected public education campaigns and the engagement of parents and elders in efforts to save young people from suicide.

A prominent characteristic of northern public affairs in 2005 was an increasingly open conversation about the social and cultural roots of criminal and antisocial behaviour. Suicide, for example, had long been shrouded in secrecy and shame. Leaders in Nunavut in particular became far more vocal in describing their challenges and issues, decrying the influence of *palisialuk* (an Inuk word meaning 'big policeman' but referring more generally to the authority of an intimidating outside person) as a cause of Inuit distress. Lori Idlout, who organized a suicide-prevention organization called the Embrace Life Council, said bluntly, 'For the last 100 years, Inuit have just been sort of standing there and having stuff shoved down their throats.'[1] To many in the North, suicide

---

1 Bob Weber, 'Nunavut May Be Turning Corner in Fight against Youth Suicides in Territory,' NatNews-north, 17 Dec 2005.

was seen as an outcome associated with the failure to establish effective regional control.

Housing remained a serious crisis in Nunavut. The rapidly increasing population was not being matched by housing construction, and privately held homes remained rare throughout Nunavut. In particular, the territorial government took steps in 2005 to improve the private housing market in Rankin Inlet, Iqaluit and Cambridge Bay. Part of the strategy included allowing the rents of government employees to increase to market rates over a five-year period. By matching government rents to market conditions, the government believed it could gradually withdraw from the subsidized housing sector in the three largest communities, allowing it to focus its efforts on social housing in other communities. These steps proved far from adequate, however, and territorial demands for federal attention to the severe housing shortages continued.

The Nunavut housing situation contrasted sharply with the Yukon. A vibrant economy produced substantial increases in local housing stock – albeit constrained by lack of readily available land – and even sharper increases in housing prices. Whitehorse dominated the territorial housing market, as the community was home to almost 75 per cent of the territory's population. Housing prices had increased dramatically over the previous decade, from less than $150,000 in 1995 to more than $225,000 in 2005. At the same time, Yukon residents worried about unchecked urban growth and the rapid development of new housing projects. On several occasions throughout 2005, local residents protested development plans, particularly those affecting green spaces, and convinced municipal officials to abandon housing projects. As a result, the planned private sector construction of several hundred housing units was cancelled. Interestingly, similar disputes between developers and local residents also occurred in Yellowknife.

The North continued to provide examples of the opportunities available to the territories to capitalize on federal funding for regional projects. In October 2005, Whitehorse celebrated the opening of the Canada Games Centre. Despite the city's small size and remote location, it had often attracted national and international sporting events. Well in advance of the 2007 games, the opening of the centre provided the community with Olympic-sized (ATCO Ice) and NHL-sized (Northwestel Arena) ice rinks, an indoor soccer field, a running track, a play area, a swimming pool, and other sporting facilities. Few communities of comparable size in Canada could boast such impressive athletic and meeting facilities.

The North in 2005

While much of the internal debate in the Yukon, the Northwest Territories and Nunavut focused on continued and even deepening social, cultural, and economic crises, the nation's attention had begun to focus elsewhere. The continued emergence of Aboriginal governments in the North, through land claims agreements, self-government accords, and economic engagements, drew positive reviews from a nation used to seeing the North as a minor and dependant appendage of the nation-state. Increasingly as well, national debates about oil and gas reserves, pipeline development, major resource projects (particularly around diamonds), global warming, and Canadian sovereignty focused on the territorial North.

The attachment of national priorities to northern realities gave northern political affairs new-found potency and currency. Not since the days of the Mackenzie·Valley Pipeline Inquiry in the 1970s had the region attracted so much sustained attention and sincere concern. Given the turmoil occurring at the federal level – the increasingly desperate government led by Prime Minister Paul Martin signed the Kelowna Accord on Aboriginal affairs in the waning weeks of his administration – it was unclear whether indigenous and northern affairs would retain their more prominent place in Canadian affairs. What was increasingly obvious to political observers in the country was the growing sophistication and confidence of northern indigenous organizations, the assertiveness and determination of territorial governments, and mounting northern frustration with the lack of national attention to pressing social, cultural, and economic challenges.

The collapse of the Liberal minority government in the late fall of 2005 and the subsequent launch of the federal election dropped the country into a massive political campaign just as the year ended. The North seemed likely to figure more prominently in the national election than in earlier contests, with party leaders promising to visit the region and speaking strongly about arctic sovereignty and related issues. As the year ended with the polls pointing towards a Conservative minority government, it appeared as though considerable change lay in the offing. How the possible reorientation of national politics might affect the North – and the country – remained unknown. After a year of limited political activity across the territorial North, the year ended with partisan gusto as the three major political parties and the emerging Green Party moved quickly to assert their northern credentials. As 2005 drew to a close, it became clear that the next year could well see major shifts in northern and national affairs.

ROBERT DRUMMOND

Ontario

The Liberal government of Premier Dalton McGuinty reached the mid-point of its first term in office during 2005 – a milestone that was assured by its passing legislation that would establish a fixed four-year term for its mandate. The Liberals continued to struggle with the budget deficit left by their predecessors, but favourable economic circumstances enabled them to approach a balanced budget earlier than initially predicted. They faced labour relations issues in the education and health sectors, including difficult negotiations with physicians concerning the schedule of fees for their services. They pursued certain reforms in education policy and environmental protection, including extending the time students were required to stay in school, establishing protected greenbelt areas, providing incentives for recycling, and levying harsher penalties on polluters. Changes in social policy included the end of mandatory retirement at age sixty-five, a ban on smoking in all public places and workplaces, a ban on owning or breeding pit bull dogs, and a law permitting disclosure of adoption information to adoptees and birth parents.

Some of the greatest challenges the government faced were in the area of energy policy, where they were haunted by their promise to close all coal-fired generating plants by 2007. The high demand for electricity occasioned by a very hot summer led to concerns about the overall generating capacity of the province's system. There were competing calls for more use of renewable energy sources (such as wind, water, and solar power) on the one hand and more nuclear plants on the other. Continued reliance on natural gas seemed unavoidable, and the likelihood that coal-powered generation could be abandoned was increasingly in doubt.

Mr Justice Linden continued his inquiry into the events of September 1995 during the occupation of Ipperwash Provincial Park, when Native protestor Dudley George was killed. There was increasing pressure to determine the extent to which the Mike Harris government had been responsible for actions taken on that occasion by the Ontario Provincial Police. Several civil servants and police officials testified, as did then attorney general Charles Harnick. Former premier Harris was expected to testify before the inquiry concluded in 2006.

The Legislative Assembly began sitting in mid-February, continuing the first session of the thirty-eighth Parliament that had begun with the election of the Liberals in 2003. Conservative leader John Tory was nominated on 12 February to run in a yet unscheduled by-election in the seat vacated by former leader Ernie Eves (Dufferin-Peel-Wellington-Grey). The Liberals nominated a candidate on 17 February (the NDP and Green Party had already nominated candidates) and the vote was scheduled for 17 March. The House took a brief recess in early March and resumed sitting near the end of that month, by which time Tory had won his seat in the by-election.

The government brought down its budget on 11 May. Finance minister Greg Sorbara promised no new taxes or tax increases and predicted a deficit of $3 billion, down from $6.1 billion in 2004–05. He predicted that the government would balance the books by 2008–09, one year after the next election. Spending was cut by 23 per cent in the Ministry of Agriculture and Food, but an additional $1.8 billion was promised for health (although hospitals claimed that was not enough to allow them to balance their budgets without cutting services). The largest commitments, however, were made in the area of education, with a 10 per cent increase in annual funding for elementary and secondary schools, a two-year freeze on university and community college tuition, and a proposal to spend $6.2 billion over five years for post-secondary education, including operating funds for universities and colleges, student aid, and apprenticeships.

In June the House was prorogued, ending the thirty-eighth Parliament's first session. While the House was not sitting, Premier McGuinty shuffled his Cabinet. The top posts – health, education, finance, and energy – remained unchanged, but two new ministries were created, one for health promotion and another for research and innovation. McGuinty himself undertook to lead the latter ministry, while Jim Watson (formerly of consumer and business services) took on the former. Two ministers who had been the focus of opposition criticism – Harinder Takhar, for alleged conflict of interest, and Joe Cordiano, for extraordinary expense claims – retained their portfolios (transportation and economic development, respectively). The Ministry of Training Colleges and Universities, where large expenditure plans were to be implemented, went to former labour minister Chris Bentley. Marie Bountrogianni left the hot seat of Community and Social Services for the post of intergovernmental affairs minister, responsible for negotiations with Ottawa. Two new faces entered Cabinet: Laurel Broten, in Environment, and Mike Colle, in Citizenship and Immigration.

On 19 August the federal government appointed former Legislature Speaker Alvin Curling ambassador to the Dominican Republic. When the House resumed in October, a by-election was scheduled for 21 November; the Liberals retained Curling's Scarborough–Rouge River seat, electing municipal councillor Bas Balkissoon.

When the second session of the thirty-eighth Parliament was convened, Michael Brown, the Liberal member for Algoma-Manitoulin, was elected Speaker and the government presented its Speech from the Throne. Highlights of the speech included plans to reform the Drive Clean emission testing program, measures to assist in lowering the province's high-school dropout rate (including an alternative diploma emphasizing non-academic areas over standard high-school studies), and a money-back guarantee if birth certificates ordered online were not produced within fifteen business days.

Hours before the Throne Speech was delivered, finance minister Greg Sorbara resigned his cabinet post and Dwight Duncan moved to Finance from Energy; Donna Cansfield took up the latter post. Sorbara had been a director of a company, Royal Group Technologies, that was now being investigated for fraud. While he protested his innocence, the issuing of a search warrant targeting him led to his stepping down. Conservative leader John Tory called the resignation a 'body blow' to the government on the eve of the Throne Speech. Soon after the speech he moved want of confidence in the government over the Sorbara 'scandal,' arguing that the resignation should have come sooner. The challenge was easily turned back by the government majority.

During the calendar year, thirty-five public bills were passed, including an unusually high number (six) of private members' bills. In addition to the measures mentioned above, bills dealt with such issues as a requirement that hospitals report to police all gunshot wounds treated, provisions to strengthen the law around family and child support payments, and amendments to various statutes required to give recognition to the legality of same-sex marriages. The province also moved to bring its film classification law into conformity with a court decision from the previous year that had struck down some of the censorship aspects of the existing law.

On 28 November Canadian Press reported expectations that three members of the Legislature – John Baird and Jim Flaherty of the

Conservatives and Marilyn Churley of the NDP – would resign their seats in order to run in the upcoming federal election. Eventually all did so. They were joined in the federal contest by former Conservative health minister Tony Clement, who had been defeated in the 2003 Ontario election.

Education

The Liberals enjoyed a short honeymoon with teachers after their election, as they appeared likely to reverse some of the policies of the Harris government that had caused many teachers and their unions to oppose that administration strongly. By early January 2005, however, both elementary and secondary school teachers were planning to hold strike votes. On 6 January Greg Bonnell of Canadian Press quoted Emily Noble, president of the Elementary Teachers' Federation of Ontario, as saying that a work-to-rule campaign could come as early as March or April. Rhonda Kimberley-Young, president of the Ontario Secondary School Teachers' Federation, also said that strike votes were likely among her members in the coming months: 'It's really just a sign of frustration and impatience,' she said. 'They've been bargaining since the start of the school year, and we have yet to settle any teacher contracts.' In December 2004 the government had urged teachers to consider longer-term contracts of four years rather than the usual two or three. While two-year contracts were also to be offered, the province sought the greater stability of longer contracts by guaranteeing funding for a 2 per cent increase in each of the first two years, 2.5 per cent in a third year, and 3 per cent in a fourth. Teachers' union leaders, however, pointed to workload as a central concern and indicated that new teachers were leaving the profession soon after their first appointments, in part because of inadequate preparation time. By 20 January teachers in various parts of the province were threatening strike action.

By 17 February Canadian Press was reporting that elementary teachers had completed voting for strike action and that no local had voted less than 87 per cent in favour. The teachers were mainly concerned about preparation time, asking that they be given credit for 200 minutes (up from 180). Strike votes were not held at two boards whose contracts already included credit for 200 minutes of preparation time. By 9 March elementary school teachers in twelve boards (including Toronto and Hamilton-Wentworth) had begun a work-to-rule campaign in which they stopped performing administrative or custodial duties and refused to organize any new field trips or attend staff meetings. All of these previously common activities had been identified by the union as voluntary. By 21 March eighteen more boards had become involved in the campaign, for a total of thirty.

Before the House took a brief recess on 9 March, it passed legislation intended to encourage the longer-term contracts the government had described in December. In order to take advantage of the funding guaranteed for salary increases and other improvements, boards would have to demonstrate that they were using the additional money to pay for priorities such as smaller class sizes, keeping good schools open, and providing support for low-income and new immigrant students, as well as those from single-parent households. The province also agreed to provide a reopener for this framework agreement after two years. Some critics declared themselves unimpressed, saying that what would bring stability to labour relations in education was a commitment to meeting teachers' needs. Nevertheless, on 14 April the government announced it had reached a four-year framework agreement with elementary teachers. The teachers agreed to put their work-to-rule campaign on hold until they had seen how local agreements within the framework developed. Some opposition critics charged that $960-million was too high a price tag for labour peace, but government spokespersons described it as a worthwhile investment that served several education goals.

On 28 April the government promised the same monetary deal for a four-year agreement to the secondary school teachers, and by 2 May they had an agreement. Money was guaranteed not only for salary increases but also to hire new teachers. As with the elementary schools, boards would have to commit to certain provisions with respect to class size and support for at-risk students. It was also required that the boards secure local agreements within the framework by 1 June or risk losing the funding for special programs. For complete success of the agreement, it was necessary for seventy-two boards to negotiate 122 collective agreements by the deadline. By 1 June ninety-one agreements had been reached; in twenty-two cases extension had been granted for legitimate logistical reasons. In nine cases there were no agreements; the boards faced 'accelerated work-to-rule' campaigns as well as being dropped from the funding plan. Despite these holdouts, both the government and the unions predicted labour peace for the next four years. This optimism about education was enhanced in late May, when the Ontario College of Teachers announced that the teacher shortage of the past several years seemed to be diminishing, although gaps remained in some areas such as French language and the sciences. They credited falling retirement rates and fewer teachers' leaving in the early years of their careers.

A less positive note was sounded in November, when a survey of teachers conducted by the Ontario English Catholic Teachers' Association and the Ontario Secondary School Teachers' Federation found 30 per cent of teachers reporting they had experienced bullying by parents or guardians, 24 per cent by a superior, 15 per cent by a colleague or co-worker, and 40 per cent by a student. The unions asked for a change in legislation that would recognize bullying and psychological harassment as workplace hazards under the *Occupational Health and Safety Act*. Education minister Gerard Kennedy expressed sympathy for the teachers but downplayed their demands for changes in legislation.

Further bad news came in October, when it was announced that only 62 per cent of Ontario students were meeting provincial standards in reading and mathematics. While standardized testing remained a matter of controversy, no one was very pleased by the level of success in the most recent round of assessments.

In late January the province had discussed changes in the school funding formula aimed at paying for lower class sizes. The government agreed to publish by mid-September the results of its efforts to reduce class sizes. In November Education Minister Kennedy announced that more than half of elementary school classes were at or below the twenty-pupil cap.

Schools were in the news at several other points throughout the year. In April a report was issued by the Parent Voice in Education Project, calling for more formal involvement of parents in the schools their children attended. Education Minister Kennedy promised to implement the recommendations. In May the province began to make changes in line with the government's intent to raise the school-leaving age to eighteen. The education minister announced a plan to spend $158 million for applied and technical education programs that would justify keeping students in school who were headed for technical or trades employment. In order to discourage dropouts, he also announced curriculum changes that would increase practical instruction, especially in the Grade 9 applied stream. The aim would be to reduce the use of concepts that were 'too abstract,' lower the amount of material to be covered in some areas, and provide more practical examples in lessons. In the field of vocational education, the province had earlier announced in January its plans to spend $5.8 million over two years in order to create fifteen new programs to help up to 1,400 foreign-trained professionals qualify for Canadian credentials.

In August, Emily Noble of the Elementary Teachers' Federation expressed her concern that schools were becoming subject to inappropriate corporate influences, as well as fundraising by parents, that she felt could lead to privatization of education. Responses from some quarters pointed out that the funds being raised were generally for matters outside the Ministry of Education's mandate. That is, they were not supplanting but supplementing public funds. Sponsorship of such additional supports by private firms was therefore argued not to pose a danger of privatization. It is not clear whether Noble would have been reassured or confirmed in her anxiety by a statement from Janet McDougald, chair of the Peel District School Board: 'In Peel, we are open for business and open for any endeavour that would create opportunity for student learning' (quoted by Shannon Montgomery, Canadian Press, 11 Aug.).

In October the province proposed to combat childhood obesity by requiring twenty minutes of physical activity from students each day in school. Medical observers praised the plan but suggested that an hour would be a better minimum time.

School safety remained an issue, but the *Safe Schools Act,* passed by the previous government, came under attack in July when the Ontario Human Rights Commission alleged that application of the act by the Toronto District School Board (TDSB) targeted visible minorities and students with disabilities. The TDSB had actually urged the province to repeal the act, but the government had not agreed. Education Minister Kennedy indicated (as he had in 2004) that the province would prefer to 'fix' the act rather than repeal it. As late as 31 October, however, Canadian Press reported that NDP leader Howard Hampton was still calling on the government to repeal the act, calling its 'American-style zero-tolerance school policies' a total failure and suggesting they might in fact be helping to recruit students to gangs.

An approach to improving education for at least one visible minority was discussed in September, when Lloyd McKell of the TDSB told the *Toronto Star* that a 'Black-focused' school might make students of colour feel more comfortable and might lead to more effective learning. The premier declared himself uncomfortable with the idea, reflecting the difficulty many people had in distinguishing this kind of school from segregated 'separate but equal' schools in the 1950s southern United States. Proponents emphasized the voluntary nature of the suggested approach and insisted that integrated schools would still be available to those who wanted them. It was felt that a focus on African-Canadian history and experiences might be a valuable means of making education attractive to black students, although some asked why such material might not be valuable to include in *all* schools.

The post-secondary education system was also a focus of considerable attention for government during the year, particularly after the February report of the commission of inquiry headed by former premier Bob Rae, which was established in 2004. Rae recommended tuition increases, within a regulated framework, for universities and colleges of applied arts and technology (CAATs), as well as a significant increase in provincial grants to those institutions: $1.3 billion per annum to bring university funding up to the national average. Rae argued that tuition rates were not the impediment to post-secondary education that student groups argued, but rather that income levels were the problem. Thus higher tuition should be accompanied by increases in student aid – preferably in the form or grants rather than loans – and increases in aid would require added funding for post-secondary institutions.

In April the Ontario Confederation of University Faculty Associations (OCUFA) issued a report complaining of poor student/faculty ratios in the province's universities. According to the report, Ontario ranked last among Canadian provinces, with an average of twenty-four students per professor; the ideal favoured by the OCUFA was fifteen to one. To reach that standard by 2010 would require eleven thousand new hires, the report suggested, while just to retain the status quo would require a funding increase of 5 per cent to hire almost 2,650 faculty members over five years. The premier expressed some sympathy for the OCUFA position but also used it as an occasion to discuss his position on federal-provincial financial arrangements: 'Ontario, Canada's economic engine, now stands 10th out of 10 provinces when it comes to university funding. This doesn't make sense, not when we're sending $23 billion to the federal government to support higher levels of funding in other provinces' (Colin Perkel, Canadian Press, 11 Apr.).

The finances of one Ontario university received special scrutiny in late February, when NDP leader Howard Hampton called for a provincial inquiry into the sale of land by York University for a housing development on the south edge of its main campus. Reports in the *Toronto Star* had raised questions about the sale, asking whether the university had received full value for the land and whether there had been collusion between the developer, Tribute Homes, and former York board of governors member (and brother of Ontario's then finance minister) Joseph Sorbara, who had advised university officials on the sale. On 1 March the premier rejected the idea of a provincial inquiry; York later undertook its own inquiry, appointing former judge Edward Saunders as an independent third party to review the transaction. He concluded that there had been no improper dealings between Sorbara and the principals of Tribute Homes and that the price negotiated for the land was not out of line with market expectations, especially given the standards York had asked the developer to meet in designing the housing to be built in close proximity to the campus.

When the government tabled its budget on 11 May, one of the key elements of its expenditure plans was a significant commitment of funds to support universities and CAATs. The Liberals elected to freeze tuition fees through 2005–06, although in October the premier warned that tuition would probably increase when the freeze guarantee expired in September 2006. In addition they committed to invest $6.2 billion in post-secondary education over the next five years, in return for multi-year accountability agreements from the post-secondary institutions with respect to increased enrolment. Particular attention was to be paid to expanding graduate education, as well as to enhancing access for Aboriginal students, persons with disabilities, and other underrepresented groups. Student financial assistance was also targeted, with $192 million in fiscal 2005 pledged to improve access for low- and middle-income students.

Health

As always, diverse health issues occupied the government throughout the year, with particular attention to the costs of health care and the government's election campaign commitment to improve wait times for critical surgeries and other treatments.

In late 2004, physicians had rejected the government's proposal for an increase to the fee schedule under the Ontario Health Insurance Plan. Negotiations continued in early 2005, though not without some difficulties. In February the province's anesthesiologists held a one-day 'study session' at a Toronto hotel, resulting in widespread delays for elective surgeries (Canadian Press, 11 Feb.). Health minister George Smitherman accused the doctors of violating an Ontario Medical Association (OMA) guarantee that patients would not be 'held hostage' during continuing negotiations. He urged patients to make their dissatisfaction known to their physicians.

The anesthetists, on their part, called Smitherman's remarks insulting and indicated that their concern was not with the fee schedule; rather, it was with the province's inability to address the shortage of such specialists and the looming increase in the problem likely to arise from impending retirements in the profession. Dr Geraint Lewis, head of the OMA's anesthesiology section, was quoted as saying that the province would need to hire more than 450 anesthetists over the next ten years or operating rooms would close and wait times for surgery increase. Citing the province's promise to reduce wait times, he said, 'I'm here to tell you that this goal is not possible without immediately increasing the number of anesthesiologists in Ontario' (ibid.). The government's response concentrated largely on the increases promised in the fee schedule, criticized the OMA for failing to sell the agreement to its members, and said almost nothing about the alleged shortage of anesthesia specialists.

In early March, pediatricians joined the chorus of criticism, also asserting that money was not the main issue. On 3 March Canadian Press reported the creation of a new lobby group, the Ontario Parent-Pediatric Alliance, which would press the government to address what they described as a crisis in pediatric care. This crisis, they said, resulted in part from a shrinking pediatric workforce and in part from government policy incentives that were pushing pediatricians away from community care to crisis care. Spokespersons for the group described long wait lists and difficulty accessing needed programs. A child with an undiagnosed developmental problem might wait twenty-four months to see a specialist, according to a pediatrician quoted by Canadian Press. The president of the OMA, Dr John Rapin, welcomed the creation of a group that would encourage more support for children's services.

The following day the province announced that it had reached a tentative agreement with representatives of the OMA on a revised fee schedule for a four-year period. The agreement added $120 million to the deal the doctors had rejected the previous fall, but it also included key provisions such as the removal of caps on billing and a provision making the fee increase retroactive to 1 April 2004. Family doctors received a 2.5 per cent increase, while specialists received 2 per cent. The agreement also included a 'safety valve' reopener for possible financial adjustments in the final year; the contract would run to 31 March 2008. The OMA's governing council would need to ratify the deal at a meeting on 30 March; in the meantime, doctors would be able to express their views on the agreement in a non-binding telephone referendum between 22 and 28 March.

The OMA president was quoted by Canadian Press as saying that the agreement would help address the province's doctor shortage, presumably by increasing incentives for physicians to remain in practice and by attracting others to enter the profession. However, Conservative health critic John Baird was quoted as saying, 'There's nothing here on the main issue – there's not enough doctors today.' NDP critic Marilyn Churley generally praised the agreement but worried about some of the details, such as the revenue loss the government might experience by allowing physicians to incorporate their practices, thereby acquiring certain tax benefits.

On 18 March a coalition of family physicians expressed serious criticism of the deal; a survey of its 3,700 members had found that 98 per cent of respondents believed the agreement did not meet their needs. Interestingly, while the president of the group, Dr Douglas Mark, said he would be voting no in the referendum and the group withheld its endorsement, it did not direct its members to vote no. A few days later a coalition of specialists was not so reticent, urging doctors throughout the province to reject the agreement. OMA president Dr Rapin remained optimistic that the deal would be ratified.

Indeed, when the OMA governing council voted on 30 March, the deal was ratified. According to Health Minister Smitherman (quoted by Keith Leslie of the Canadian Press), the deal had the support of 74 per cent of Ontario physicians. John Baird complained that there had been no public costing of the deal and said some doctors had claimed that the agreement added $500 million (rather than $120 million) to the deal rejected in 2004. The NDP accused the government of caving in to the doctors' demands without ensuring needed reform of the primary care system. Smitherman asserted that the deal encouraged more doctors to enter family health teams with nurses and other practitioners, thus reforming primary care. In mid-April the province announced it would commit $600 million over a three-year period to build fifty-two family health teams, perhaps lending some credibility to the notion that the deal with physicians had a significant cost beyond the direct increase in the fee schedule. Both Minister Smitherman and Dr Rapin suggested that the deal was a first step in addressing unacceptably long waiting lists for tests and treatment, as well as the critical doctor shortage facing the province, and they argued that the investment was worthwhile if improvement in those areas could be accomplished.

In early April the province moved to rearrange local health-care delivery in a couple of ways. The government moved to replace district health councils with 'local health integration networks' (LHINs), in a plan the health minister described as a coordinated strategy for health-care delivery. This would take the powers of the health ministry and push them down to the community level, where important decisions about priorities would be made. The Conservative leader, John Tory, however, used a leaked cabinet document to argue that the plan was simply going to waste taxpayers' money, with no gain of improved service. Smitherman disputed the numbers Tory cited, claiming that the cabinet document was not an accurate reflection of where the government's planning now stood.

In an area more directly related to the delivery of treatment, the province also moved to consolidate surgical programs in hospitals, allowing for greater specialization and reducing the range of surgical services each hospital would provide. The LHINs would decide which hospital in each region would be the site for each type of surgery and how much funding each would get. Critics expressed concern that people would have to travel long distances to get the care they used to be able to access at their local hospital. The premier, however, described these remarks as 'blatant scare-mongering' and said, 'Of course we're going to take into account regional differences and distances and driving times' (quoted by Keith Leslie, Canadian Press, 7 Apr.).

The health minister stated his belief that there were considerable inefficiencies in Ontario hospitals that could be reduced by specialization, including high-tech diagnostic services. He cited MRI machines operating well below capacity in some areas, while others were overloaded. The government's attention to the costs of high-tech diagnostic tools had no doubt been heightened when it was led to promise $120 million in February to replace MRI and CT machines. It had also committed some $140 million to hospitals and long-term care facilities later that same month to update a variety of equipment. Despite these and other expenditure announcements for hospitals, there remained several areas in which hospital budgets apparently could not be balanced. On 2 May Canadian Press reported that hospitals in the so-called 905 area (Toronto's immediate exurban surroundings) might need several hundred million additional dollars to serve their patients in the coming year. They reported a higher acute-care bed occupancy rate than both the city of Toronto and the provincial average; they also claimed to be more efficient but they expected their extraordinary needs to be met.

The province continued to adjust in various areas to take account of changing health-care priorities. In February it promised $29.2 million to create nursing-home beds to free up acute-care hospital beds then being used for long-term patients. In April the government issued layoff notices to some 3,700 workers, two-thirds of whom it said were psychiatric hospital workers whose jobs would end but who would mainly be transferred to other employers. The Ontario Public Service Employees Union (OPSEU) accused the government of breaking its pledge to rebuild the public service, which had been significantly diminished by the Harris government. In July the government announced that it planned to close the Rideau Regional Centre in Smiths Falls by 2009. The centre served disabled adults, many of whose families mounted a protest against the government decision.

In July the government announced a program, foreshadowed in its budget in May, that aimed to reduce the number of nurses taking early retirement. The program would provide funding to allow nurses fifty-five years of age and older to spend a portion of their time on the job in less physically demanding tasks, such as mentoring young nurses, offering clinical advice, and educating patients and their families. The program was described by the premier as part of a broader plan to stabilize the nursing workforce that included hiring additional nurses. The government claimed to have hired three thousand additional nurses since coming to office, but NDP health critic Shelley Martel cast doubt on those numbers, saying that the government had no concrete data on hiring and that in some areas nurses were being laid off, not hired. Conservative leader John Tory pointed to the apparent inconsistency of the government's policy, since it had earlier established a transition fund for hospitals (to assist with budget balancing) that included more than $90 million to help defray the costs of laying off nurses. Nurses, however, applauded the move, and many said they would have sought early retirement if such a plan had not been designed.

In late November physiotherapists complained that the government was trying to reduce the amount of therapy being provided to residents of long-term care facilities. Physiotherapy had been delisted from the Ontario Health Insurance Plan (OHIP) in 2004, except for seniors and persons with disabilities in long-term care settings; in those cases the physiotherapy was thought to make it less likely that patients would have to be hospitalized. The physiotherapists argued that the province had reduced allowable treatments from 150 per patient per year to 100, and was planning to go down to forty-nine. The government said it was trying to ensure that as many persons as possible had access to treatment, but apparently it hoped to do so with no increase in cost.

Early in the year the government called on hospitals to balance their budgets by 31 March 2006, but many argued that was nearly impossible if services were to be maintained and if no new money was forthcoming from the province. The budget challenges faced by hospitals were highlighted in Sarnia on 10 August, when Bluewater Health, which operated two hospitals in Sarnia and one in Petrolia, announced plans to cut 169 employees, including nurses, technicians, and support staff, to address a $14-million deficit. In addition it would close its palliative care unit, cut operating times, and scale back laboratory and imaging department activities. Around a thousand protestors rallied outside Sarnia's city hall on the day of the announcement. Ironically, the following day the health ministry announced plans for a new hospital in Sarnia.

Much of the government's focus, apart from doctors' fees and administrative restructuring, was on the subject of wait times for surgeries and other treatments. In early April the *Globe and Mail* cited a report by Dr Alan Hudson, head of the government's wait-time strategy, who asserted that hospitals would be responsible for reducing wait times and that funding would be related to improvements. However, in late May the government announced special funding to reduce wait times for cancer treatment and cardiac surgeries, which would give hospitals an additional $154 million.

In June the Supreme Court of Canada ruled in a Quebec case that it was permissible for someone to pay privately for medically necessary care within the province (thus overturning a provincial ban on the practice) if their treatment had been significantly delayed, and especially if the delay had created additional risk to their health. The message of the case was clearly that a failure to deal successfully with wait times could undermine the whole system of national medicare. The Ontario government, which was working to reduce wait times, suggested that it was premature to expect a similar court challenge in Ontario or to predict whether the province would use the 'notwithstanding clause' of the Constitution to preserve a ban on private billing for medically necessary services. On 11 August the Canadian Press's Sheryl Ubelecker reported a call by the Wait Time Alliance, a coalition of medical specialty societies, for the federal and provincial governments to provide $3 billion to address wait times – $1 billion for more health professionals (including doctors) and $2 billion to fund patients' travel to places where care was available. In late October the government announced that a website on which patients could track wait times for various procedures would soon be up and running. Critics made the obvious point that information alone would not solve the problem. At year-end the issue of wait times remained on the agenda, both as a challenge to the health-care system and as the government's preferred index of successful system improvement.

A continuing theme throughout the year was the demand that government pay for efficacious treatments for relatively rare diseases or in cases where a decision had been made to limit government funding. The demands of parents with autistic children that government extend support for behavioural therapy beyond the age of six continued in 2005. On 2 February Mr Justice Ferrier of the Ontario Superior Court ordered the province to pay for autism treatment for three children whose parents had filed suit. The decision differed from that of the Supreme Court of Canada in a B.C. case. There the court had ruled that the choice of medical programs to be supported was within the powers of the province. The grounds for the Ferrier decision, however, were not medical but rather a requirement that the children be given treatment so that they could receive the education to which Ontario law entitled them. Parents' efforts to broaden the field on which this battle was being fought led to a complaint against school boards before the Ontario Human Rights Commission. However, on 9 February Commissioner Keith Norton ruled that the complaint could not proceed, as the issue fell not within the jurisdiction of the school boards but within that of several Ontario government ministries, where the matter was already under review. In April Madam Justice Kiteley of the Ontario Superior Court ruled that the province's refusal to extend autism therapy to children beyond the age of six was discrimination on the basis of age and disability; she ordered the province to provide the therapy. In early December the province launched an appeal of her decision.

On 2 June a number of patients with Fabry's disease – there were known to be thirty-one in the province – protested that the government was refusing to pay for an enzyme replacement therapy approved by Health Canada. Ontario would not pay for the treatment, which cost approximately $300,000 per patient per year, saying that there were doubts about its efficacy. The protesting patients asserted that the government was simply leaving them to die. The government did agree in July to pay for three new and expensive drugs for cancer treatment: one for breast cancer (Herceptin) and two for lung and prostate cancers (Navelbine and Taxotere). Shortly after the announcement was made, patients with multiple myeloma wanted to know why a new drug for their cancer (Velcade) was not being funded, asserting that Ontario was the only province not funding the drug.

On 1 September the provincial ombudsman castigated the government for refusing to fund a drug for treatment of Batten's disease, a neurodegenerative disorder that was threatening the life of a teenaged patient. The drug, Cystagon, was apparently very effective in treating the disorder but was very expensive. The family had been told incorrectly that the drug had not received Health Canada approval, but the government was paying for it to be used in treating other ailments.

Issues of this kind appeared likely to continue challenging government for the foreseeable future. In a somewhat related vein, it was reported in July that Dr Peter Anglin had established a private clinic to provide patients with cancer-treatment drugs that had been approved by Health Canada but were not yet funded by OHIP. Especially in light of the Quebec case, there was concern that this was another of the increasing private challenges to the public system. Anglin denied that his clinic was competing with the public health plan, saying that it was simply complementing it.

Numerous other health issues came to public attention during the year – an outbreak of rubella, apparently related to a community's religious objections to inoculation; an *E. coli* scare from unpasteurized milk; a dispute with Quebec about the location of a new Shriners' hospital (eventually situated in Montreal); a plan to increase the number of diseases for which newborn babies would be routinely screened; controversy over the possibility of safe injection sites for drug users; and various calls to treat gambling addiction as a medical problem, as well as a concentrated anti-smoking campaign.

Energy

The cost of electricity was a concern throughout the year as the government sought to ensure enough compensation to producers that generating capacity would be maintained or increased, but low enough costs to businesses that capital would be attracted to and remain in the province. It also faced the political difficulty of raising household electricity rates when voters had been used to subsidized rates. In late February, opposition critics warned against increasing rates, but the government moved to increase rates for businesses while providing rebates to householders. In early March the Toronto-Dominion Bank advised that electricity rates would have to rise if there was to be investment in production capacity, while the government insisted that rates had to reflect the cost of production rather than attempts to save energy.

The government continued to subsidize household rates, and in August it was announced that the difference between the cost of electricity and payments made under the regulated fee arrangements had been in the order of $113.5 million since 1 April. In October, however, the province announced that the cost of electricity had been below predicted levels and they would be providing consumer rebates (about $60 for a typical household). After an unusually hot summer in which there had been frequent concerns about the prospect of system overload and blackouts, the government announced a plan to encourage homeowners to install so-called 'smart meters.' The meters would record electricity use for particular periods so that consumers could manage their energy use more effectively. The government hoped to have smart meters installed in 800,000 homes by 2007. On 14 November, when Ontario Power Generation (OPG) announced a profit of $181 million, large businesses asked for a rebate of some of their electricity costs.

Over and above concerns with cost, the very capacity of the electricity system was a matter to which the government necessarily devoted considerable attention during the year. It had promised in the election campaign of 2003 that it would close all coal-powered generating stations before the next election, in 2007, but as the year wore on its ability to honour that commitment became increasingly in doubt. Alternative sources were pursued, and in early March the government approved eighteen sites for water-powered electricity production. Those sites would produce some 200 to 300 megawatts, replacing coal plants would require approximately 7,500 megawatts. Wind power was expected to produce perhaps another 3,000 megawatts, and the government agreed to accept proposals for wind farms on Crown lands by 1 April.

On 12 April the government indicated that it would soon announce the private energy firms with whom it would contract for 2,500 megawatts of additional power. NDP leader Howard Hampton accused the government of reneging on a campaign promise to keep electricity generation in public hands. He noted that rates had increased more than 34 per cent, from 4.3 cents per kilowatt hour when the Liberals came to power to 5.8 cents per kilowatt hour, depending on the time of use. He predicted they would go up at least 20 per cent more if private producers were encouraged. The next day the province announced it had signed a deal with a U.S. firm to build a natural gas electricity plant near Sarnia and had worked out a co-generation project with the Greater Toronto Airport Authority. In addition it announced a conservation agreement with Loblaws stores to use less power in peak periods. On 18 August OPG announced that it was committing approximately $985 million to a tunnel to drive more water through its hydroelectric generating station at Niagara Falls. On 30 November energy minister Donna Cansfield had to assure the legislature that the Sarnia plant was still on track, despite the potential bankruptcy of the U.S. partner, Calfine Corporation of San Jose, California.

On 20 April the government announced the appointment of Peter Lowe, executive director of the Canadian Energy Efficiency Alliance, as provincial energy conservation officer. Critics charged that the move would simply create more bureaucracy and was not a solution to energy shortages. The government countered that it expected Lowe to oversee implementation of particular conservation measures essential to maintaining a healthy energy system in the province.

On 28 April Canadian Press reported efforts by the government to reassure Ontarians that closure of coal-fired plants would not result in a drain of power from the system. Critics feared that this assurance depended on the creation of new nuclear plants, and energy minister Dwight Duncan refused to rule such plants out or in. He did observe that the existing nuclear plants were ageing, and that meant the province would have to confront the question of whether to replace them with new nuclear facilities. At the end of May, northern Ontario municipalities expressed concern that they not be presumed to be natural sites for the storage of nuclear waste. It was observed that Ontario was currently both the source and the storage site of most of Canada's nuclear waste. On 15 June the province admitted that it probably could not close all the coal-fired plants by 2007.

On the energy conservation front, the Ontario legislature and another ten provincial government buildings joined thirteen other downtown Toronto buildings in using deep-lake water technology to chill coolant for air conditioning. In August, as summer heat taxed the air conditioning – mostly electrically produced – of the province's homes and businesses, the premier opined that two or three more summers of curbing power use would be necessary before significant new generating capacity could come online. Shop owners were urged to keep the doors of their air-conditioned stores closed to save power, as the province feared brown-outs and a peak demand of nearly 26,000 megawatts; if only 10 per cent of stores with open doors were to close them, it was estimated that might save about 200 megawatts of power. As power demand rose, on 12 August Ontario Power Generation announced that it would probably not refurbish and restart two units at its Pickering nuclear plant, preferring to focus on two other units that were better candidates for a return to service. It also suggested that it would be better advised to devote resources and expertise to maintaining its ten other units. On the same day, the Canadian Press reported experts' opinions that energy conservation had not improved since the big blackout of 2003; while the electricity system had become more efficient and capacity had increased, the system still faced peak demand that threatened its stability. A report by the Pembina Institute in December asserted that Ontario was spending approximately

$10.5 billion on new electricity-generating capacity but only $163 million to help reduce demand for power.

In early October a study of electricity-generating sites throughout North America listed two of Ontario's coal-fired plants as among the cleanest on the continent. Some groups, including the Power Workers' Union, asked whether it made sense to close those plants if it meant importing electricity generated in 'dirtier' natural gas plants in the United States. Later that month the province was reported to be ready to approve refurbishing and restarting two nuclear reactors operated by Bruce Power at its Kincardine site. Before Bruce Power would undertake the renovation, it required an agreement from the province on the payment rate for the electricity generated; the provincial auditor general undertook to review the agreement. In late November Ontario was reported to be considering two new nuclear reactors for the Darlington power station. John Mutton, mayor of Clarington (where the plant is located), was supportive, as was Murray Elston, president of the Canadian Nuclear Association.

On 9 December a report from the Ontario Power Authority called for expenditure of some $70 billion by 2025, requiring a charge of roughly $2 billion per year to Ontario electricity consumers. It called for more renewable sources, another gas-fired plant, and up to four new nuclear reactors. The Authority projected quite optimistic numbers for renewable sources, believing that an expenditure of $14 billion to $22 billion would produce more power (13,900 to 16,100 megawatts) than would result from some $30 billion to $40 billion invested in nuclear power, which would produce 12,900 to 15,900 megawatts. Natural gas might be the most efficient producer, as the Authority predicted 10,200 to 12,500 megawatts from an expenditure of $7 billion to $10 billion. Conservation might require about $5 billion to $11 billion dollars to save between 1,800 and 4,300 megawatts. A few days later, OPG urged quick action on nuclear generating capacity, while Theresa McClanaghan of the Canadian Environmental Law Association complained that her group did not get to address power planning, as they were not behind-the-scenes proponents of nuclear expansion.

The energy portfolio was further complicated by the fact that in late March the engineers and professional staff at Hydro One, members of the Society of Energy Professionals, voted to go on strike. A major issue for the union was the employer's proposal to establish a two-tier wage and benefit structure in which new employees would get less than existing workers. Antipathy was perhaps exacerbated by the defence offered by the energy minister on 1 March of a 35 per cent increase in the salary of Hydro One CEO Tom Parkinson, because 'all performance targets

[had] been met' in 2004 (Canadian Press). NDP leader Howard Hampton accused the Liberals of saying one thing about high Hydro One salaries while in opposition and quite another once they had formed the government. The employees went on strike on 1 June, and by early July they were picketing not only their own operations but also those of Ontario Power Generation. Mr Justice Colin Campbell granted an injunction on 6 July requiring that pickets at the OPG sites allow the employees of that firm ready access to their workplace, because, he said, to prevent or significantly delay their access was to put the electricity system at risk. By late July no talks had been scheduled between the parties, and the Ontario government appointed labour arbitrator William Kaplan to mediate between them and help get them back to the table. He was not given power to arbitrate the dispute, however. By 8 September, with no end to the strike in sight, the union was reported to be planning a series of attack ads calling on the premier to settle the dispute (Canadian Press). On 13 September the parties agreed to submit the dispute to arbitration. It was presumed unlikely that an arbitrator would impose the two-tier wage structure the company had been proposing.

Another energy issue for the province during the year was an effort to increase the use of ethanol in gasoline for automobiles. In June the government moved to remove a tax exemption on ethanol and transfer the resulting revenue (some $520 million) to support new ethanol plants. In early July it was announced that three of the sites assisted by federal funds supporting ethanol production would be in Ontario, with the other two sites being in Manitoba and Alberta. Ontario intended to require that gasoline sold in the province contain 5 per cent ethanol by 2007, but on 18 August the Ontario chapter of the Canadian Petroleum Products Institute asked the government to delay implementation of the plan (Gillian Livingston, Canadian Press). Faith Goodman, vice-president of the chapter, said, 'The January 2007 timeline is overly aggressive and will likely have serious unintended consequences.' The concern was over the time needed for the gasoline industry to adjust. However, Kory Teneycke, executive director of the Canadian Renewable Fuels Association, said, 'They're trying to manufacture a crisis to try to prevent this policy from being implemented.' On 6 October the provincial Cabinet approved the plan to require 5 per cent ethanol by 2007 and 10 per cent by 2010.

Ipperwash inquiry

In late February the inquiry into the 1995 events at Ipperwash Provincial Park moved to Toronto, on the grounds that much of the testimony to come would address the involvement of Queen's Park and that it would be most convenient to arrange that testimony if the hearings moved there. It was expected that witnesses would testify that the Ontario Provincial Police (OPP) had been pressured by politicians to get the protestors out of the park. Indeed, on 8 March Robert Watts, a former federal assistant deputy minister, testified that a friend had reported to him a remark said to have been made by Premier Harris, ordering that the 'Indians' (described with an obscene modifier) be removed from the park, using guns if necessary (Canadian Press, 8 Mar.). Harris's lawyer denied the allegation, which Watts had passed on to Kettle and Stony Point chief Tom Bressette on 6 September, just before Dudley George was killed. Watts reported that his friend Leslie Currie, of the Ontario Native Affairs Secretariat, had heard the story from Julie Jai, a fellow employee of the Secretariat. Jai in turn had reportedly heard the story from Deb Hutton, an aide to Premier Harris, at a high-level meeting just before the September 6 events.

On 17 May John Carson, the OPP incident commander at the park, told the inquiry that OPP Inspector Ron Fox had informed him of a meeting he had attended at Queen's Park in which he said Deb Hutton had made clear the premier's wish that the Aboriginals be removed from the park. According to Carson, Fox had warned that there might be women and children involved, but Fox said the officials seemed to be on a 'testosterone high.' However, Carson testified on 20 June that he did not believe it had been a mistake to order the riot squad into the park on the night George was killed. He denied that political pressure had played a role in his decision, though he acknowledged he had been told that the premier was watching the incident closely. He denied in later testimony that the reputation of the OPP had been his main concern that evening.

When Inspector Fox testified, he made it clear that Harris had not directly instructed the OPP, but Fox believed it was clear that the premier wanted the Aboriginals removed from the park . A debate arose among the lawyers at the inquiry about the need to release OPP disciplinary records in order to assess any role that racism might have played in events. On 15 August Mr Justice Linden ordered the records released.

On 29 August, Scott Hutchison, a lawyer with the Ontario government, testified about his attendance at the 6 September meeting of civil servants and political officials at which Deb Hutton had represented Premier Harris. Hutchison believed it was clear that Harris wanted the protestors removed without negotiations. The meeting, he said, had a 'law and order' tone. On 31 August Julie Jai began her testimony; she denied that Deb Hutton had used an expletive to describe the Aboriginals when reporting the premier's views. However, it had appeared that a go-slow approach, earlier recommended to and approved by Attorney General Charles Harnick and Solicitor General Bob Runciman, was now being overruled. The premier apparently wanted the matter settled within a day or two and saw the matter as a law-and-order concern, not an Aboriginal issue. Government lawyer Eileen Hipfner later testified that the tone of urgency was introduced when Deb Hutton spoke. Former deputy attorney general Larry Taman then testified that Charles Harnick had changed his mind about the urgency of removing the protestors after hearing from the premier. When Deb Hutton testified in late November, she denied that the Premier had proposed using force to get the protestors out of the park; however, she received considerable criticism for her frequent assertions of a failure to recall the events about which her testimony was being sought.

Still later in November, Charles Harnick testified. He contradicted the testimony of his former deputy about having changed his mind, and asserted that he had not heard from the premier. He had sought an injunction to force the Aboriginals' removal because that was standard practice in such matters, he said. The question of whether or not the injunction should be *ex parte* – requiring no notice to the protestors – was a matter for government lawyers, not politicians, to decide. He described as absurd the suggestion that the premier had wanted the Aboriginals removed within twenty-four hours. Harnick went on to say that Premier Harris had indeed used profanity in his remarks about the removal of the Aboriginals but that his words had implied no racist intent. Moreover, Harnick denied that any call had been made for armed force to be used. Some commentators observed that he had denied in the Legislature that he had heard the remark he was now describing. Murray Klippenstein, lawyer for the George family, was quoted on 28 November by Canadian Press as saying, 'If this evidence is trustworthy, it looks like a contemptuous comment from the head of the province that is an attack on Indian people.' However, Harnick suggested that the premier acknowledged that what he had said was inappropriate. Oddly, when Elaine Todres, former deputy solicitor general, testified on 30 November she said it was Chris Hodgson, then minister of natural resources, who had used the obscene term in calling for the removal of the Aboriginals from 'his' park.

In September the time frame of the inquiry was extended into March 2006, and testimony was still expected from former Premier Harris.

The Legislature recessed on 15 December with a promise to resume in February 2006. Many of the issues that had taken up the attention of government in 2005 – energy, health care, education, the environment, and the Ipperwash inquiry – promised to remain matters of importance in the coming year.

DANIEL SALÉE

Quebec

In 2005 Jean Charest's Liberals remained unable to stem the tide of dissatisfaction they had faced almost without relief since their electoral victory two years earlier. The new government's program of neo-liberal reforms was proving much harder to sell than anticipated; opposition to it went on unabated, and in fact intensified in 2005. The rate of satisfaction with the government hovered around a rather unimpressive 25 per cent through most of the year, and declarations that this was the worst government in the history of the province continued to be made unceasingly and with unusual vehemence by almost every quarter of Quebec society. A rap song titled 'Libérez-nous des Libéraux' ('Deliver us from the Liberals'), released in late 2004 by the popular local hip-hop group Loco Locass, became a hit in 2005 and received telling accolades from the music industry as best song of the year. The lyrics raked Charest and his government over the coals for betraying Quebec's social democratic achievements of the past forty years, for selling out to the narrow interests of the private sector, and for giving in to the federal government. A crowd-pleaser, the song was heard at anti-government rallies, on picket lines, and of course at the Fête nationale celebrations on Saint-Jean-Baptiste Day, revealing in no uncertain terms the depth of social discontent with the Charest administration.

In a way, the unrest was more of the same for Premier Charest. No stranger to the perils of Quebec politics by now, the former Conservative federal minister, one of the main protagonists of the No camp during the 1995 referendum on sovereignty, had faced his share of taunts from opponents in his home province over the years. There is an inherent risk in questioning the dual orthodoxy of Quebec nationalism and the state-driven model of social and economic development that Quebecers have lived by since the days of the Quiet Revolution. Jean Charest has no doubt always been aware of it. Whether he was prepared for the widespread resentment expressed during his first two years in office was less certain. In retrospect, he obviously misconstrued the electoral support that had led him to power in 2003; it was much more about telling off the governing Parti Québécois than a ringing endorsement of the Liberals' vision of a 're-engineered' state or of their quest for new socio-institutional arrangements. The constant tug-of-war that pitted most sectors of Quebec's civil society against his government during its first eighteen months in office made that abundantly clear. Things would hardly be different in 2005.

Quite a few policy decisions contributed to this deepening of popular disgruntlement. In early January, news that minister of education Pierre Reid had signed a $10 million deal that would fully subsidize private Jewish schools raised a collective howl of indignation. It was later discovered that the Jewish community had contributed $750,000 to the Liberal party: the deal unavoidably looked like a partisan reward. The idea that ethnic private schools could benefit from state funds – as had been the case with Greek schools for years – also angered many who could not help but note that in comparison the French-Canadian majority-based private Catholic schools were only partly subsidized and the public school system was suffering from underfunding. The government backtracked and withdrew the deal amidst rumblings of internal dissent and settling of accounts within the Liberal Party.

The choice of a Montreal building site for the new super-hospital complex affiliated with the Université de Montréal was another dossier about which the government seemed unable to make a final decision. The selection process was marred by animosity and wrangling among a number of competing private stakeholders. Even Charest and his star health minister, Dr Philippe Couillard, were at odds, each favouring a different site. The health minister's view eventually prevailed, somewhat to the dismay of members of the Liberal caucus, who began to doubt Charest's leadership abilities.

Finally, the resignation of the well-liked minister of finance, Yves Séguin; the disappointing budget of his successor, Michel Audet, who with his $81 million in tax relief fell quite short of the $1-billion tax reduction per year promised during the electoral campaign of 2003; a $50-million cut to the child-care program and the decision to allow privatization of child-care services; and the seemingly haphazard restructuring of state agencies and organizations under the supervision of the president of the Treasury Board all combined to project the picture of a rudderless and inept government.

Two events, though, deserve a more in-depth examination: the student strike over changes in the government financial assistance program and the labour dispute with state employees. Both illustrate not only the gulf between the government and significant segments of the Quebec population but also societal and ideological tensions over the kind of society Quebecers should strive for, as well as the high political stakes involved in attempts to reconfigure entrenched socio-institutional arrangements.

Showdown with students

From late February to mid-April, in one of the most unyielding and disruptive confrontations with authorities in recent memory, more than half of the entire post-secondary student population went on strike to protest a cost-cutting measure outlined in the 2004 budget, designed to convert $103 million worth of student bursaries into repayable loans – nearly doubling the debt load of the poorest students. The measure was part of a broader package of changes to the province's student financial assistance and loans program, which also included linking student loan forgiveness to academic achievement, establishing income-contingent loan repayment, and a long-term project to eliminate student bursaries.

Access to affordable post-secondary education has been a bone of contention for several decades in Quebec. A mainstay of the social reforms brought about by the Quiet Revolution in the 1960s, it was something of a public trust. But as the cost of public education became prohibitive and universities were straining under significant deficits as a result and scrambling to find new sources of additional revenue, calls to shift larger portions of the cost of higher education onto the students – those who stood to benefit directly and personally from quality training – had become increasingly pressing. All the more so since Quebec's tuition fees were the lowest in Canada (60 per cent less on average) and had remained virtually frozen at their current rate for more than a decade.

While few questioned that financial assistance to low-income students was a good way of levelling the playing field, many were wondering how Quebecers could realistically afford both cheap tuition and an extensive bursary program without further increases to their tax burden – a decidedly unpopular alternative. Besides, they argued, despite the higher degree of affordability of post-secondary education in Quebec, there was no evidence that children of low-income families were more likely to go to university there than anywhere else in the country. In the end, low tuition and generous financial assistance programs seemed to benefit mostly the middle and more affluent classes whose children made up the bulk of university clientele. Should basic equity not dictate that those who stood to gain the most from a public service contribute a larger share to its maintenance?

Such arguments had little purchase with student organizations, and they strongly encouraged their members to take to the streets and oppose the government's plan. A long and successful tradition of student struggles in Quebec went back to the 1960s. Thanks to those struggles the affordability of higher education was a given to most Quebecers. In fact, to the more uncompromising elements in the student movement, anything short of free access to higher education was not acceptable. While that view was by no means shared by all students who took part in the 2005 strike action, it certainly underscored the debate, and protecting the acquired right of affordability motivated many normally unengaged and politically indifferent students to participate in several mass demonstrations, in Montreal, Sherbrooke, and Quebec City. For seven weeks exceptionally large numbers of university and CEGEP students – many of them from institutions with little or no history of student activism – boycotted their classes at some point for varying lengths of time. Many also joined picket lines and other protest events. While purposely missing classes might seem like an odd tactic that could prove self-detrimental, the intensity of the movement and the student leaders' ability to mobilize several socially and ideologically disparate and wide-ranging segments of the student population bore witness not only to their remarkable resolve but, more importantly, to that of their constituency as well. The government took note and agreed to sit down and negotiate with the students.

Some observers have argued that the strike had a depth and significance comparable to the student protests that shook and transformed Western societies in the late 1960s (*Le Devoir,* 4 April). Tactically and politically astute, the students were indeed relentless in organizing numerous marches, sit-ins at MNAs' and ministers' offices, roadblocks, and other such attention-grabbing actions that disrupted businesses and delivery of government services. In truth, the student movement was divided between radical and moderate organizations, particularly over issues of strategy and the nature of the demands to bring to the government. Large segments of the student population never joined in. As for popular support, it was more rhetorical than real and shifted almost daily as events unfolded. Public opinion polls conducted at different times during the strike revealed conflicting stances that reflected in part the confusion many may have felt about the whole issue. The population, for example, was almost evenly split over the idea of forsaking the government's promised tax relief in order to help out the students.

And while a majority, according to one poll, seemed happy to see the students hold their own ground and supported proposals that the sums cut be reinvested in bursaries (*Le Devoir*, 31 March), according to another poll, only one in four people thought the government should give in to the students.[1] Noticeable also was the apparent disinclination of the labour movement and the community sector to try to capitalize on the student action to instigate some sort of broad social opposition coalition to rein in the government's policy agenda.

The student strike certainly contributed further to negative sentiment against the government, but its transformative impact was not quite what some claimed. The students eventually succeeded in getting the government to maintain the status quo as far as financial aid was concerned, to reinstate the $103 million that had escaped them as bursaries, and to reinvest $482 million in loans into bursaries over the next five years. The government consented to this package largely because the federal government promised to inject more than $140 million through the Canada Millennium Scholarship Foundation. In the end, the Charest government got what it had wanted from the start: to minimize its outlay of new money for the financial aid program. The strike proved to be more of a zero-sum game than anything else. Funding for post-secondary education, the issue that implicitly lay at the heart of the whole affair, ultimately remained unaddressed.

Clamping down on public sector employees

Although less flamboyant in their approach than the students, the more than half-million salaried and unionized employees of the province were another significant group of stakeholders with which the government had to contend in 2005. Relations between the Charest government and the labour movement had been excessively tense from the start. One of the first things the Liberals managed to accomplish quickly once in power was a series of laws ostensibly designed to weaken unions and curtail their influence in Quebec society,[2] particularly that of public sector unions, the largest segment of Quebec's labour movement. Needless to say, there was no love lost between the government

---

1 Léger Marketing, 'Opinion des Québécois à l'égard des manifestations étudiantes,' opinion poll commissioned by Le Groupe TVA, 16 March 2005, www.zombiemedia.org/IMG/pdf/sondagetvaleger16mars2005.pdf (accessed 22 April 2010).

2 See Daniel Salée, 'Quebec,' in *Canadian Annual Review of Politics and Public Affairs 2003*, ed. David Mutimer (Toronto: University of Toronto Press, 2009), 191–96.

and its employees. Negotiations for a new contract, two years over-due, had stalled during 2004 despite a concerted effort by all the unions involved to take the government to task. In February 2005 Monique Jérôme-Forget, president of the Treasury Board, announced that she was prepared to settle before the end of autumn. That was not to be. Both parties remained unflinching in their positions, and the unions' bitterness towards the government grew steadily. Pay equity and wage increases were the principal stumbling blocks. Determined to tighten its control over state expenditures in a context of difficult public finances, the government remained unyielding. The unions, who felt they had un-justly borne the brunt of a decade's policies of state retrenchment, were no less resolute in their desire to catch up after years of frozen wages and paltry pay increases.

Although the Charest government agreed to comply with a 2004 Su-perior Court ruling invalidating a section of Quebec's 1996 pay equity act – which freed employers who already had pay equity measures in place from the obligation of adjusting to the more demanding require-ments of the law – it soon argued that the cost of compliance would be significant (more than $800 million a year in additional compensation) and limited its ability to offer the wage increases unions were calling for (12.5 per cent over three years). Given the financial situation of the province, it would have to be one or the other. The unions balked at this suggestion. They claimed that pay equity and wage increases were two separate issues that could not be lumped together: pay equity was a legal obligation of the government and a matter of social justice that had nothing to do with current contract negotiations. They kept on insisting that the government take on both pay equity adjustments and the salary increases. Pleading poverty, the government disagreed, offering noth-ing better than a freeze on wages for the first two years of the collective agreement.

For the public employees the stakes were high. If the government's position was to prevail in the current round of contract negotiations, they would fall even further behind in comparison to private sector wages. For several decades, from the days of the Quiet Revolution until the 1990s, conventional wisdom had been that Quebec government em-ployees were among the best paid of the Quebec labour force. In ad-dition to attractive remuneration, they also enjoyed enviable working conditions and highly desirable social benefits packages. By 2000, as a result of successive governments' gnawing away at working condi-tions and compensation on account of tight public finances, this was no longer the case. In 2005, data released by the Institut de la statistique du Québec revealed that the wages of public sector employees were 15 per cent lower than their private sector counterparts (both unionized and non-unionized) and 22 per cent lower if only unionized private sector workers were considered. The hackneyed image of the overprivileged public employee, the unions argued, did not hold true; it was but an ideological stratagem to garner support for the government's position. In fact, they maintained, the continued deterioration of the working conditions of public sector employees was a worrisome trend. As a career as a public employee became less attractive to the younger generation, recruitment and retention of new, quality human resources would become problematic, which in turn would jeopardize the stability, continuity, and delivery of public services.

The government remained deaf to this kind of argument. After a failed attempt at a settlement in June and inconclusive negotiations during the fall, the Liberals finally opted for special legislation. Introduced in the National Assembly on 15 December, Bill 142 was passed expeditiously the next day as *An Act Respecting Conditions of Employment in the Public Sector.* The new law – a government decree, in actual fact – was binding until 31 March 2010. It renewed collective agreements with the government employees by imposing a retroactive freeze on their wages for the first two years and nine months of the contract and a 2 per cent increase in the next four years. This amounted to an 8 per cent wage increase over the duration of the seven-year contract, or 1.2 per cent per year, which was below the average 2 per cent inflation rate experienced over the course of the previous five years. In addition to a number of provisions reducing job security and increasing workloads, the most significant measures contained in the new legislation were those inflicting severe penalties on any employee involved in a strike action or other form of work stoppage: the equivalent of two days' pay per day on strike and fines between $100 and $500; for a union leader, fines could amount to between $7,000 and $35,000 per day on strike, and between $25,000 and $125,000 for a labour organization. The government thus brought an end to the protracted contract negotiations with its employees by making, for all intents and purposes, any attempt at opposing its methods of labour management unlawful, much to the outrage and consternation of the labour movement and its sympathizers.

Meanwhile, in the opposition camp ...

The student strike and the labour dispute with public sector employees did not help the general public image of the Charest government. At the end of the year, voter intent showed the Liberals trailing by 26 percentage points behind the Parti Québécois. Yet when one considers the rather hard-nosed way in which the government ultimately dispatched its labour dispute, it is remarkable that – except for the odd left-leaning column or editorial denouncing the special legislation as abusive and contrary to established practices of labour contract negotiation – few went out of their way to defend the public sector workers, and fewer still called for civil disobedience or reprisal against the government. The Parti Québécois did what is normally expected of the official opposition in the National Assembly, but having run roughshod over public employees during its own government stints, its disapproval of the legislation seemed insincere. By Christmas Bill 142 was barely on anyone's radar screen. In contrast with Quebec's past episodes of civil unrest in similar situations, all hell did not break loose over the government's tough stance with its employees. A few segments of Quebec society – notably the business sector in its entirety – were even comfortable with the government's gesture, while others remained silent or indifferent.

The relative weakness of the parliamentary opposition accounted in part for Charest's ability to withstand and deflect the storm of resentment that his policy agenda and strong-arm governance generated during his first two years in office. The Parti Québécois was kept busy with internal difficulties of its own and was hard pressed to capitalize effectively on Charest's troubles and offer the kind of robust opposition that could bring his government down. As for Mario Dumont's Action démocratique du Québec, it kept on slipping in voter intent, from 24 per cent in January to 14 per cent in December.[3] The Gomery inquiry on the federal sponsorship scandal also helped somewhat in distracting attention from the Charest government's unpopular policies.

Although the electorate seemed prepared to put the Parti Québécois back in power, it was less clear whether the party itself was up to the job. The electoral defeat of 2003 had raised concerns internally over the leadership of former premier Bernard Landry, and a number of party luminaries, including former ministers Pauline Marois and François Legault, had started to push openly to succeed him. Others went about coaxing the Bloc Québécois leader, Gilles Duceppe, to switch to provincial politics and take over the party. Like other PQ leaders before

3 CROP, 'Évolution du climat politique au Québec, Montréal, 2009,' http:www.crop.ca/documents/Evolution%20 politique%20CROP20août09.pdf (accessed 24 April 2010)

him, Landry tried to cling to his post by catering to the more radical elements of the party, who had long insisted that the next PQ government should secede from Canada immediately upon re-election. Moderates pressed him in turn to renounce such a course of action and support holding a referendum on sovereignty – only if and when winning conditions emerged.

This perennial strategic issue of when and how to gain sovereignty had often proved lethal to PQ leaders, who would find themselves in the middle of internal squabbles between moderates and the more vocal radical wing, unable most of the time to satisfy either side and politically weakened by the tensions. Unimpressed by the 76.2 per cent support he had received in a statutory confidence vote held by delegates at the party convention on June 5, Landry resigned on the spot, a decision many observers considered impulsive and uncalled for. With a similar score, Lucien Bouchard in his day had nonetheless stayed on, and given the plummeting popularity of Charest and his government, there was really no need for the PQ to change its leader at that juncture. Landry later came to regret his action, hinting publicly in the following weeks that he might come back if he was asked. But it was too late – this was the opportunity a number of would-be successors had longed for since the general election. The leadership race was on almost immediately after Landry stepped down.

Surprisingly for a political party with a tradition of virtually crowning its leaders with little or no opposition from serious contenders, this time around no fewer than nine candidates came forward to replace Landry, including four former cabinet ministers and the former chief of staff of party founder René Lévesque. In the end, Pauline Marois, a veteran cabinet minister who had served in every Parti Québécois government since the 1980s, and André Boisclair, a young, high-profile minister in the Bouchard and Landry governments, were really the candidates to watch. On 15 November, after two days of voting by telephone, party members elected Boisclair, whose youthful appeal and moderate stance on sovereignty and socio-economic issues carried the day. Despite his declared homosexuality and disclosure during the campaign that he had been using cocaine while serving as a cabinet minister, he came out a clear winner, with 53.7 per cent of the membership vote compared to 30.6 per cent for Marois, his closest rival. The Parti Québécois, it seemed at the time, had made the right choice. Public opinion polls conducted shortly afterwards suggested that the Boisclair-led PQ would win a landslide victory over Jean Charest's Liberal Party.

Rethinking Quebec: Lucides vs Solidaires

Aside from the self-inflicted incapacity of the parliamentary opposition to pack a more effective political punch, there was another, more subtle, less tangible but in some ways more fundamental phenomenon that could explain why the Charest government escaped irremediable opprobrium. That is, disapproval of its actions was not as universal as news reports and columnists regularly suggested. It was no doubt quite vociferous – hence the impression that everybody disagreed with the government – but it did not necessarily reach as deep as opponents claimed. Parallel to the animosity against the government, within several segments of Quebec society ran policy ideals that largely vindicated the kind of socio-institutional changes it was putting forward, namely with respect to the role and presence of the state. The release of the independent manifesto 'Pour un Québec lucide' ('For a clear-eyed Quebec') on 19 October, at the height of heated negotiations with public sector employees, showed that the government was not alone in pushing for in-depth reconsideration of the so-called Quebec model of state intervention, social democratic policies, and consensus-based governance inherited from the Quiet Revolution.

The brainchild of a group of twelve opinion leaders comprising former politicians (including former premier Lucien Bouchard), academics, journalists, and businesspeople, the manifesto was a ten-page unambiguous, forceful statement with a distinctly neo-liberal perspective on what ailed Quebec and the policy directions Quebecers should embrace to ensure the province remained socially and economically vibrant. Its authors intended it as a wake-up call. They argued that Quebecers needed to be realistic about their current situation and be responsible about how to address it. Despite unprecedented growth and social change over the past fifty years, Quebec 'still figures among the 25 percent least prosperous provinces and US states' and was hampered by the highest per capita public debt on the continent. Quebecers were experiencing one of the most rapid demographic declines in the world and facing, like all developed countries, fierce economic competition from Asian countries. They had to acknowledge that those realities could have a negative impact on their quality of life if they were not prepared to do things differently – to seriously reconsider well-entrenched socio-institutional practices that were no longer adequate or appropriate to deal with the socio-economic challenges at hand. Quebec was 'losing speed,' and denying that fact or minimizing its significance would be counterproductive.

The Lucides proposed a number of solutions that, in their view, had to be implemented as soon as possible in order to put Quebec back on track. They included alleviating the burden of public debt so as 'to meet the growing health expenses resulting from an aging population' and facilitate 'massive investments in education and training.' However, students would have to realize that paying for a high-calibre post-secondary educational system 'exceeds the government's capacities'; a sensible approach demanded that the freeze on tuition fees be lifted and a student loan repayment plan proportional to income be put in place. Encouraging mastery of several languages, supporting promotion of a flexible work environment that put a premium on performance and innovation, increasing electricity rates, carrying out major tax reforms that would focus on taxing consumption rather than income, and creating a guaranteed minimum income plan also figured in the solution package suggested by the Lucides.

Although the authors of the manifesto presented it as a non-partisan document of reflection meant to engage Quebecers, they made no bones about the importance of doing away with the negative spirit of suspicion and intolerance towards change – particularly change propounded by the business sector – that, they lamented, was unfortunate and all too pervasive in Quebec society. They chastised the labour movement and associated groups for that:

Social discourse in Quebec today is dominated by pressure groups of all kinds, including big unions, which have monopolized the label 'progressive' to better resist any changes imposed by the new order. ... Judging by the way labour leaders behave today, especially in the public sector, is union action not often limited to the short-sighted protection of members' interests?

Quebecers would have to be open to proposals coming from the private sector; for one thing, such openness would not mean abandoning the Quebec model, and working together was the only way they could deal successfully with the challenges they were now facing.

The Lucides' discourse was hardly new. It had been part of Quebec's political landscape since the mid-1990s, though rarely had it expressed itself so publicly, with such transparency, and with such boldness of tone. Before the election of Jean Charest's Liberals, even hints of criticism of the so-called Quebec model had been swiftly suppressed by the intelligentsia. In a way the Lucides' manifesto marked a new step forward for Quebec's ideological right, towards self-assertion in a political and policy environment that had been customarily unsympathetic to the view it propounded. It crystallized and reflected the impatience of growing segments of the middle class with institutional practices they perceived as too rigid and holding back Quebec's economic development; with the social and political influence of vocal left-leaning stakeholders; and with what they deemed inconsiderate efforts by the latter at shooting down individual enterprise and profit-driven initiatives.

Whether such a discourse was warranted is no doubt a matter of debate. Judging from the outcry against the manifesto, it was not clear whether, when the chips were down, a majority of Quebecers would endorse it fully. Two weeks after the release of the Lucides' manifesto, a group of about three dozen individuals from the labour movement, the community sector, the media, the arts, and academia responded by proposing their own manifesto, 'Pour un Québec solidaire' ('For a Quebec based on social solidarity'). The Solidaires, predictably, contested every single statement made by the Lucides about the socio-economic challenges and issues facing Quebec society. They maintained that in spite of its declining demographics, Quebec had kept producing wealth at an accelerated rate over the past three decades; Quebec spent less on health care and controlled health-care costs better than most other jurisdictions in Canada and the United States; Quebec's public debt was not as bad a problem as portrayed by the Lucides, for only a small proportion of that debt was owed to foreign creditors; the tax burden of Quebecers might be significant – although still among the lowest in Canada for private corporations – but it paid for enviable social protection and collective services. The Solidaires contended that the Lucides' vision for Quebec was in fact far from being as clear-eyed as they pretended and was largely unacceptable, for it was premised on the erosion of hard-won social and economic rights and on an understanding of social relations defined by individualistic aims rather than collective goals, by profit for the few rather than social justice and an equitable distribution of wealth.

This debate between Lucides and Solidaires mobilized much intellectual energy among policy specialists and engaged citizens during the last months of the year. On the whole, though, it ended up being a dialogue of the deaf more than anything else. The views of each camp about the policy choices Quebec should make were so completely opposite and to a certain extent so stereotypical that a different outcome would have been surprising. The debate remained significant, however, for two reasons. First, by questioning Quebec's ways the Lucides ripped away the veil of sacredness that had long shrouded the so-called Quebec model of governance and policy choices – it had underscored the province's nationalistic movement of political and administrative assertiveness and economic development since the 1960s. In this sense the Lucides' manifesto signalled the rupture of Quebec's middle class and power elite with the very policy ideas and principles that had guided their socio-political ascent.

Second, given the sensitivities about the Quebec model, the fact that the Lucides had brought their views openly to the public was remarkable. The importance of their manifesto lay not so much in what it said but in the fact that it was uttered at all; it bore witness to the increasing political self-confidence of neo-liberal proponents and gave neo-liberal policy ideals in Quebec's public sphere the ideological legitimacy that had eluded them until then. In fact, the Lucides framed the debate largely by imposing on it their own terminology and reference points, describing themselves as the real agents of change. The Solidaires' manifesto was mostly reactive. It barely questioned the Lucides' ideological framework and merely reiterated the well-worn solutions of the left (consolidate labour laws, apply more rigorous environmental protection laws, tax wealth, increase funding for education, lower electricity rates, protect universal access to health care, maintain state presence in key sectors, etc.), proving in a way the Lucides' argument about the inability of some stakeholders to think beyond the beaten paths.

The Charest government may not, after all, have been without allies, but the Lucides–Solidaires debate called attention, perhaps more than ever before, to the ideological fault line that divided Quebec society over the fundamental policy choices it was facing.

Family feud: Quebec–Ottawa relations

'The empty chair policy has never paid off,' claimed Jean Charest in his review of the year. 'Under my government,' he went on, 'Quebec has defended with success the notion of asymmetrical federalism and has renewed the leadership role it must play in Canadian affairs for the benefit of all Quebecers who can in turn enjoy the services and positive fallouts of the agreements we negotiated with the federal government.'[4] This rather upbeat assessment of Quebec's dealings with

---

4 Translation: 'La politique de la chaise vide n'a jamais été payante. Sous mon gouvernement, le Québec a fait reconnaître le fédéralisme asymétrique et repris le leadership qu'il doit assumer sur la scène canadienne, et ce, pour le bien des Québécois qui bénéficient des services et retombées générés par ces ententes.' Office of the Premier, 'Le premier ministre dresse un bilan positif de la session parlementaire,' press release, 16 December 2005, http://www.premier-ministre.gouv.qc.ca/salle-de-presse/communiques/2005/decembre/2005-12-16.shtml (accessed 25 February 2010).

Ottawa in 2005 masked what was, by most standards, a fairly turbulent relationship through most of the year. Under the leadership of strongly autonomist ministers such as Yves Séguin in Finance, who battled Ottawa relentlessly on the question of fiscal imbalance, and Benoît Pelletier in Canadian Intergovernmental Affairs, often suspected of being a closet separatist, the Charest government continued to push for a more decentralized and asymmetrical federalism, much to the growing dismay and impatience of federal politicians who had been hoping for greater docility on the part of a Liberal federalist provincial government. Considering that both Quebec and Ottawa were being led by governments from the same political tradition, surprisingly robust jurisdictional tensions – erupting in particular over the financing of parental leave, a national daycare system, and Quebec's role in international affairs – gave the ROC cause for concern.

Wrangling over maternity and parental benefits

On 1 March Quebec and Ottawa came to an agreement in principle over the financing of parental leave. Starting on 1 January 2006, the federal government would reduce by $750 million the premiums collected from Quebec employers and employees to finance the Employment Insurance (EI) fund, thus opening the way for Quebec to impose its own dues to support and manage its new parental leave program. In addition, Ottawa was to contribute $200 million in the first year to help launch the program and $5 million a year towards administrative costs.

This agreement was hailed by the Charest government as a victory and additional proof that Canadian federalism could be flexible and profitable for Quebec. Barely a month earlier, though, federal and provincial ministers had been publicly hurling charges of intransigence and unreasonableness at each other, and negotiations looked as if they were heading towards a standstill. This was nothing new. Quebec and Ottawa had an almost decade-long history of difficult negotiations and acrimony over Quebec's efforts to implement a parental leave program that extended to self-employed workers and was deemed by all accounts more generous than the provisions of the federal EI program.

Since 1996 Quebec had been trying, with little success and much reluctance from Ottawa, to establish its own parental leave system.[5] Invoking section 69(2) of the *Employment Insurance Act,* which provided

5 Information in the following draws from Beverley Baines, 'Federalism and Pregnancy Benefits: Dividing Women,' *Queen's Law Journal* 32, no. 1 (2006): 190–223.

for a reduction in the unemployment insurance premiums that employers and employees must otherwise pay to the federal government if a province took over provision of benefits for illness, injury, quarantine, pregnancy or child care, the Quebec government had pressed the federal government to let it opt out of EI, with compensation, in order to put in place its own parental insurance program as part of its family policy. Negotiations soon reached an impasse: the federal government did not necessarily disagree with the idea of Quebec's opting out of EI, but both parties diverged significantly over a formula for reducing premiums, a transition fund, and federal taxation benefits.

Eventually Ottawa had reconsidered its initially supportive position about opting out and threatened to use its discretion to deny Quebec that possibility; it further suggested limiting Quebec's input to simply topping up parental benefits delivered under the existing EI program. The Quebec government responded by asking the Quebec Court of Appeal whether provinces had jurisdiction over maternal and parental leave and whether the federal government was exceeding its employment insurance power by offering maternal and parental leave within EI. The court ruled in 2004 that maternity and parental benefits under EI were unconstitutional, as they could not be subsumed under section 91.2A of the *Constitution Act* (1867) because they amounted to an intrusion of the Parliament of Canada into an area of exclusive provincial jurisdiction. The federal government launched an appeal to the Supreme Court of Canada in response.

When the agreement in principle was signed in early March, the Supreme Court had not yet rendered its verdict, and Quebec was unwilling to wait for it. The ruling of the Quebec Court of Appeal had strengthened its political resolve and provided the necessary support for settling with the federal government. The Quebec government succeeded in obtaining in the end much of what it had been seeking, in terms of both financial compensation and jurisdictional recognition. Despite general satisfaction with the agreement, the sceptics, mostly among the sovereignists, declined to share in the joy of victory. In their view the federal government's attitude had prevented Quebec from exercising its rightful power within its own jurisdiction and had delayed by several years implementation of a good social program that met with universal assent in Quebec – how could one argue that Canadian federalism was benefiting Quebecers? The Supreme Court decision, which finally came down in October in favour of the federal government, completely contradicting the Quebec Court of Appeal, was grist for their mill. Although Ottawa did not renege on the agreement as a result, the decision certainly opened the door a little wider for the federal government to

step further into the areas of social policy restricted to provincial jurisdiction.

National daycare program

The idea of putting together a national daycare program had been float-
ing around for some time, but it would turn out to be another bone of
contention between Quebec and Ottawa. In November 2004 the federal
government had struck an agreement with all the provinces except Quebec to establish and finance a national early childhood education program. Ottawa committed to pay the provinces $5 billion over five years
on the conditions that they be accountable to the federal government for
monies spent, conform with measurable standards and objectives, and
abide by organizational principles – quality of service, inclusive universality, access, and contribution to child development – all determined
and imposed by the federal government. Prime Minister Paul Martin
was quite candid about his government's goal: he was hoping for no
less than to create a national network of daycare centres that would be
the country's next nation-building symbol, like universal health care (*Le
Devoir,* 21 Sept.).

To Quebec the federal government's vision was unacceptable, largely
because it already had a well-integrated and affordable daycare system for which it had been spending in excess of $1 billion a year since
1998. It was not willing, therefore, to adjust its system to meet with the
federal conditions and pan-Canadian norms. The Charest government,
which was bowing out of a federal-provincial agreement for the first
time, argued that Quebec should be allowed to spend the federal sums
earmarked for early childhood education and child care as it pleased.
Quebec's adamant stance on this eventually infuriated the federal minister of transport, Jean Lapierre, Paul Martin's Quebec lieutenant, who
at one point publicly charged Minister Benoît Pelletier of being 'more
sovereignist than the sovereignists' and of being responsible for the difficult relationship between Quebec and Ottawa in a number of dossiers.

After a year-long process of negotiation, Quebec and Ottawa ultimately agreed on mutually acceptable terms on 28 October. Ottawa
basically came around to Quebec's position and committed to transfer
$1.125 billion to Quebec over the next five years, with no strings at-
tached except for an indefinite requirement to use the money for the
general welfare of families. The Charest government had ultimately got
its way, but not without frustration and tension on both sides over, once
again, Quebec's administrative leeway and autonomy. While Ottawa's

attempts at shaping local policy in areas of provincial jurisdiction irked the Charest government and upset its idea of decentralized federalism, Quebec's insistence on closely guarding and controlling any policy field for which the constitution acknowledged provincial primacy tended increasingly to rub federal politicians and observers in the ROC the wrong way. Indeed, many felt that the Martin government had again given in too easily to the federation's spoiled brat.

Quebec's role in international affairs

In January 2004, as he was taking over as prime minister, Paul Martin had openly entertained the possibility of designing with the Quebec government a policy defining the nature and extent of provincial representation in international organizations to which Canada belonged. This did not fall upon deaf ears in Quebec City. Since the 1960s Quebec governments had always unequivocally striven to maintain a distinct presence on the international scene. They had been guided in that by what was known in Quebec as the Gérin-Lajoie doctrine (after its proponent Paul Gérin-Lajoie, minister of education in the Lesage government). It held in essence that Quebec was entitled to represent itself abroad and to conclude international agreements in areas of exclusive provincial jurisdiction. On the basis of that doctrine, Quebec had developed over the years an efficient and relatively extensive diplomatic machinery, with trade offices and general delegations – virtual embassies in some cases – in several key cities and capitals of the world. All this was much to the annoyance of successive federal governments, who invariably insisted that Ottawa was perfectly capable of representing Quebec's interests abroad, and that in any case it was preferable that Canada speak with one voice on international issues. Although with time Ottawa came to tolerate Quebec's proactive approach to international affairs, the history of Quebec-Ottawa relations abounded with instances of intergovernmental discord over Quebec's role in international matters that might affect its interests.

Excited by Martin's unexpected overture, the Quebec government laid out its vision of what proper provincial representation in international organizations should entail. In line with the Gérin-Lajoie doctrine, it insisted on five basic points:

(1) Quebec must have access to all information and must be involved in helping plan the Canadian position before any negotiations; (2) Quebec must be a full member of Canadian delegations and must solely be responsible for appoint-

ing its own representatives; (3) Quebec must have the right to speak for itself at international forums when topics under its jurisdiction are being discussed; (4) Quebec's right to give its consent before Canada signs or declares that it is bound by a treaty or agreement must be recognized; (5) Quebec must have the right to present its positions at appearances by Canada before the arbitration bodies of international organizations when Quebec or its interests are at stake.[6]

The Quebec government required in addition that the mandate of the Canadian Commission for UNESCO be amended so that Quebec would have sole responsibility for consulting Quebec civil society.

This was more than what the Martin government was prepared to contemplate. In part perhaps because it had been seen as too accommodating on the parental leave and daycare program issues, the federal government was much less given to compromise when it came to ensuring that Canada's national unity appeared unquestionable in international venues. After stalling for months before engaging his Quebec counterparts on this question, the federal minister of foreign affairs, Pierre Pettigrew – also a Quebecer and once executive assistant to former Quebec Liberal Party chief Claude Ryan – did his utmost to dampen any hope Quebec might have of enhancing its international presence. This triggered an outburst of federal-provincial enmity that raged in the press and in political circles, both in Quebec and nationally, throughout September and October. Pettigrew dismissed the Gérin-Lajoie doctrine as obsolete and out of tune with the political imperatives that globalization imposed on national states like Canada. Because of globalization and its attendant high-stakes competition between states, he maintained, it was essential that Canada speak with one voice and not appear divided and therefore weak. Pettigrew also acknowledged that he was concerned that increasing Quebec's room for independent manoeuvring in international affairs might lead to unmanageable situations for Canada, were 'Quebec sovereignty fanatics' to come back to power in Quebec City. His view was echoed with approval in virtually all the national media outlets in English Canada.

Quebec could not disagree more. As Monique Gagnon-Tremblay, minister of international relations put it, 'Some like to assume that Canada must speak with a single voice on the international stage and that this voice must be that of the federal government. Such an assumption

---

6 Monique Gagnon-Tremblay, 'Who dares speak for Canada abroad? We do,' *Globe and Mail*, 3 October 2005. Madame Gagnon-Tremblay is the Quebec minister of international relations and minister responsible for La Francophonie.

is a misunderstanding of the very nature of the Canadian federation. The voice of Canada is also the voice of the provinces.'[7] At the year's closing, the dispute over Quebec's role in international affairs was still largely unresolved.

Annus horribilis?

Jean Charest's positive year-end assessment of his government's accomplishments notwithstanding, 2005 was not an easy year. The historic all-time low of a 20 per cent satisfaction rate at mid-year must have taken its toll. But with two more years to go in his mandate, there was still plenty of time to turn things around. Mr Charest must have wagered on that, as his government stayed the course on most policy decisions in spite of its unpopularity. The government's satisfaction rating improved slightly during the fall months to close in December at five percentage points above the disastrous showing recorded at the end of spring. Its firm and unabated stand against the federal government had probably helped a little.

The fact is that after two and a half years in office, Charest had succeeded in implementing a good deal of the neo-liberal policy agenda that got him elected. The labour code had been revised and relaxed, much to the benefit of employers, the labour movement had been tamed, public sector unions were now in check until 2010, the province's budget was balanced, the Quebec model was losing its lustre, and it looked as if, with some tenacity, Canadian federalism could be made to work a little more to Quebec's advantage. Much remained to be done, particularly with respect to the health-care system and revamping of public infrastructure. And it was far from clear as the new year dawned whether Quebecers would be able to stomach more of the changes Jean Charest seemed bent on bringing to the socio-institutional arrangements they had lived by for several decades. The years ahead were bound to be interesting times.

---

7 Ibid.

RICHARD WILBUR

New Brunswick

The year began on a sombre note with the death of former Liberal premier Louis J. Robichaud, who died of cancer on 6 January in a hospital near his birthplace, St Antoine, Kent County. Among the dignitaries attending the state funeral in Moncton on 11 January were Prime Minister Paul Martin, Premier Bernard Lord, and former Liberal premier Frank McKenna, as well as Robichaud's cabinet colleagues from his tumultuous years in office from 1960 to 1970. That decade, probably the most significant in New Brunswick's 200-year history, saw the introduction and implementation of the Program of Equal Opportunity, which transformed the province's taxation, social, and education structures. 'For this he was vilified,' noted a front-page editorial in the *Telegraph-Journal,* which added that 'the English-language press, including the Telegraph-Journal, raised grave concerns about the wisdom of his government's policies and the seriousness of their consequences. We were wrong, and he proved it by winning two more terms of office' (7 Jan.).

The legislative sessions

The on-again/off-again sittings of the fifty-fifth legislature, caused mainly by the Lord government's determination to protect its one-seat majority, resulted in an unproductive and divisive spring session. During its brief sitting in December 2004, the government had agreed to reassemble for two weeks in January to pass the remaining capital estimates. This schedule was interrupted by Robichaud's death and funeral; when the members met again a week later, the sitting hours were extended to allow time, as one reporter put it, 'to get through the legislative wish list of both parties' (Moncton *Times & Transcript,* 18 Jan.).

They gathered once more in late March to hear finance minister Jeannot Volpe's budget address. Rather than cut taxes, he adjusted provincial income tax brackets to keep pace with inflation. He said it would save taxpayers $11 million that year, depending on their income level, and was part of the government's election promise of 2003 to cut personal income taxes by 5 per cent before 2007–08. Liberal leader Shawn Graham argued that such measures 'won't help individuals worried about how they were going to afford' the 9.7 per cent increase in power rates requested by New Brunswick Power (*Daily Gleaner,* 31 Mar.). In Graham's words, 'For every dollar that Bernard Lord takes out of New Brunswickers' pockets, Jeannot Volpe today is giving back one cent' (ibid.). The NDP leader, Elizabeth Weir, predicted that the government would be getting back the $11 million it stood to lose on the tax reduction by more than tenfold in revenue growth.

The budget also predicted savings of $24 million by cutting about two hundred civil service positions and reducing non-clinical health jobs in such areas as laundry services, food preparation, housekeeping, finance and payroll, information technology, and administration. According to David Rouse, president of Canadian Union of Public Employees Local 1252, which represented health-care workers, 'It's the erosion of health care. Hospitals are now barebones as far as services go' (*Telegraph-Journal,* 31 Mar.). Liberal leader Graham, on the other hand, tentatively agreed to the cuts if the government could show that patient safety would not be affected.

On 1 April Liberal finance critic Michael Murphy claimed that the government had made a multi-million-dollar windfall from high car insurance premiums, an issue that had nearly defeated the Tories in the 2003 election. He accused the Lord government of allowing 'global insurance corporations to wreak havoc on our families, the young and the old.... They protected their friends in the insurance industry.... They will collect $3.45 million in revenue from New Brunswickers in 2005–06. That compares to $2.3 million in 1999' (*Telegraph-Journal,* 1 Apr.). On 8 April, a day after a Liberal non-confidence motion was ruled out of order by the deputy Speaker, Kelly Lamrock, the Liberal house leader, announced that his party was withdrawing from the informal pairing agreement that allowed cabinet ministers and other members to be absent from the House on pressing political or personal matters. A week later, with NDP leader Elizabeth Weir out of the country, the government's slim majority was sufficient for it to pass the motion approving the budget.

Members returned to the House on 24 April after their Easter recess to examine departmental estimates. On 27 May Liberal house leader Lamrock engaged the premier in a heated debate by accusing him of 'pandering to Conservatives across the country' in preparation for entering the federal political field. Lord denied the accusation: 'I can assure [my constituents] that I am here to stay' (*Daily Gleaner,* 28 May). Answering Lamrock's criticism that the government had cut university grants, the premier reminded the House of a new bill that would reimburse students up to $10,000 of their tuition if they stayed and worked in the province. The premier's decision not to extend the term of the auditor general, Daryl Wilson, beyond its eight-year limit so he could complete his annual report prompted a strong editorial from the *Telegraph-Journal* on 7 June. Noting the public's perception that New Brunswick Power was 'a sore point for the government and that Mr. Wilson's review might not be welcome,' the editorial said, 'the government has cut short all attempts to look into how the utility failed to secure a contract (from Venezuela) for orimulsion fuel, a mistake that could wind up costing taxpayers dearly.' Shortly before rising for the summer, the government introduced legislation that would guarantee that a large percentage of the federal gas rebate promised by the Martin government would go to rural communities. Among the few bills passed was one approving a narrow decision by the Saint John city council giving the Irving interests a huge property tax break for a liquefied natural gas facility.

The long session was the final one for NDP leader Elizabeth Weir, who had indicated in 2004 that it would be her last. Her departure deprived the House of its most consistent critic since her historic first win in 1991, when she became the first elected female leader of a provincial political party. At a party leadership convention in late September, Allison Brewer, 'an openly gay social activist and founder of the province's Morgentaler abortion clinic' was chosen over two other candidates, winning 62 per cent on the first ballot (*Telegraph-Journal,* 26 Sept.). In mid-October Premier Lord announced Weir's appointment as chair of the new Energy Conservation Agency. As one astute political reporter put it, 'In one move, Premier Bernard Lord has defused a political foe and added a spark plug to his government' (*Telegraph-Journal,* 14 Oct.). The Saint John Harbour seat held by Weir was not to be vacant for long. In contrast to long delays in setting other by-election dates, Premier Lord acted quickly, staking his party hopes on a popular local figure, Saint John's deputy mayor, Michelle Hooton. The winner on 14 November, Liberal candidate Ed Doherty, a local eye doctor, received more votes than all three of his rivals, with 55 per cent; Hooton was a distant second with 27 per cent. The result left Premier Lord with the same delicate balance in the house: a majority of one.

On 6 December, against the backdrop of a federal election campaign, the third session of the fifty-fifth legislature opened with Lieutenant-Governor Herménégilde Chiasson reading a Throne Speech that contained many promises, an unusual number of them based on recently completed or about-to-be-completed studies. These included new approaches to forest practices, agri-land enhancement, technology innovation, pre-kindergarten and post-secondary education, Aboriginal education and housing, and responses to the Commission on Legislative Democracy, including one to 'modernize the Right to Information Act,' which carried a full-page edited version of the Throne Speech. More specific promises pledged to increase the minimum wage to $6.60 an hour before 2007, to create a 'new, more effective body known as Elections New Brunswick,' and to establish a commission on the future of New Brunswick universities. Elaborating on the Throne Speech, Premier Lord said the province could have a pre-kindergarten program for four-year-olds by September 2007. This proposal drew criticisms from some daycare operators, including the president of the New Brunswick Day Care Association, Linda Gould, who said that the proposed program could result in luring the best-trained workers from licensed facilities because of higher salaries. In a procedural move that had not been used since 1983, opposition leader Shawn Graham ended his official reply to the Throne Speech by proposing an amendment calling for immediate action, including rebates on home heating oil and specific completion dates for three highways in the northern sector.

On 11 December Finance Minister Volpe introduced the *Fiscal Responsibility and Balanced Budget Act,* which required the government to report annually on whether the books were balanced and whether the ratio of debt to gross domestic product had been cut. He explained that such measures would 'allow for final results to be available prior to elections, should the government adopt the measures of the Commission on Legislative Democracy for fixed election dates beginning October 2007 and every four years thereafter' (Moncton *Times & Transcript,* 8 Dec.). He dismissed opposition financial critic Mike Murphy's call for penalties for governments or cabinet ministers who failed to balance the books.

New Brunswickers struggling with low or minimum wages got the government's attention on two occasions. In September, while attending a caucus retreat in rural Albert County, Premier Lord announced that families not on social assistance and with gross incomes of less than $45,000 would get a one-time cash rebate on their home heating oil. He estimated that the program would help about 37,000 families and would cost $6 million. In mid-December the minister of training and employment development, Margaret-Ann Blaney, announced that the minimum wage would increase by twenty cents on 1 January, double what the government had promised. She added that another jump would occur in July and that by 2007 the basic hourly wage would be $7.10 an hour. About 15,300 workers would be affected (*Telegraph-Journal,* 16 Dec.).

On Friday, two days before Christmas, the Legislature adjourned after Premier Lord unveiled a support program for the troubled forest industry, which had been plagued by permanent closures, temporary layoffs, and strikes. The plan, costing $250 million and spread over five years from 2007 to 2012, would eliminate the 0.3 per cent large corporation capital tax imposed on companies with more than $5 million in capital. It would also reduce pulpwood royalties by 25 per cent and increase funding for tree planting on both private and Crown lands by 25 per cent. Despite the fact that the plan would need legislative approval and would not go into effect immediately, the industry reacted positively. Jim Irving, president of J.D. Irving Ltd, the largest forestry operator in the province, said it was good 'for the forest industry to have this support in this very difficult competitive market we are in.' He added that he would have liked to see energy costs addressed (*Telegraph-Journal,* 23 and 24 Dec.)

Summing up the legislative sessions that dragged on through the year, a perceptive *Telegraph-Journal* editorial of 20 December said:

it makes no sense for the 'fall' sitting...to begin so close to the Christmas and New Year holidays. New Brunswickers would be served better by a true fall sitting, one that begins just after Labour Day and lasts until Christmas....What we have seen this session is a different kind of co-operation, with Liberals and Conservatives taking a not-very-intensive approach to politics that yields not-very-impressive results. From the sidelines, it looks as though both parties are just going through the motions.

The economy

The grim plight of the pulp and paper mills

With the levels of the Canadian dollar and world oil steadily rising and increasing competition from Latin America, New Brunswick's forest industry, with its eighteen thousand jobs and sole dependence on export markets, had been in trouble for months. The lone exception was the largest player, the Irving interests, who announced in late January that their Saint John mill had stopped making newsprint in December, shifting to 'higher-end materials like glossier paper used in flyers and magazines.' The change came after 'a multimillion dollar investment' and would mean no job cuts for the 350 mill workers (*Telegraph-Journal,* 25 Jan.).

When contract negotiations at the Finnish-owned UPM mill at Miramichi broke down in December 2004, seven hundred workers walked out. The company, the largest direct and indirect employer in the region, cited poor market conditions, high fuel costs, and a rising dollar as the reasons for closing its kraft pulp and coated paper mills. It also stopped buying wood and laid off workers at its ground pulp mill. On 29 July the company and the union issued a brief statement that talks would resume 'under a media blackout' (*Telegraph-Journal,* 15 Aug.). An agreement reached on 13 August received union members' support even though four hundred workers would not get their jobs back. Mill production resumed in mid-September, but in December the company announced a three-month shutdown that would start 1 February and affect about five hundred workers. Union officials said they had expected the usual Christmas closure but did not know it was going to be for three months. They acknowledged that the layoffs were not related to the strike: 'The reality is that the pulp and paper industry in Canada is in a crisis' (Moncton *Times & Transcript,* 8 Dec.).

Workers who showed up on 4 August for their regular shift at the Smurfit-Stone container mill in Bathurst were stunned to learn that the mill would close immediately because of 'a drop in demand for cardboard due to an exodus of manufacturers to places outside North America' (*Telegraph-Journal,* 5 Aug.). Its workforce of 267 contributed an estimated $13.3 million a year to the small city's economy. The closure was even more surprising because the owners had announced the previous September that they would be investing $3.8 million in order to diversify the mill's product line.

On 12 October Fraser Papers announced the sale of its paperboard mill in Edmundston to Quebec-based Cascades Inc., the nation's largest boxboard manufacturer. Three days later the new owner said it would be closing the mill and moving the operation to other facilities in Quebec and Ontario. One hundred jobs would be lost. Fraser Papers, which had been Edmundston's economic mainstay for the past eighty-eight years, would be left with a payroll of 375 workers employed at a magnesium bisulphate paper mill, a groundwood mill, a co-generation plant, and an effluent treatment facility (*Telegraph-Journal,* 15 Oct.).

For much of the year the St Anne–Nackawic mill, forty kilometres north of Fredericton, which had closed in September 2004, was frequently in the news. A legal battle was launched by sixty former employees, who sued their former employer, Parsons & Whittemore Inc. of New York state, for the CAN$13.4-million shortfall in their pension plan. The American firm, which owed the New Brunswick government more than CAN$35 million, had declared bankruptcy, resulting in a situation that threatened to defeat government efforts to reach a deal with a new consortium that wished to buy the idle plant. On 18 August court documents revealed that an agreement was imminent; the consortium, headed by the Aditya Birla Group of India and Tembec Inc. of Quebec, offered to pay the government $20 million to buy out its interests in the mill. The American owners would recover CAN$35 million in loans made on their first claim on receivables, inventory, and equipment (*Telegraph-Journal,* 19 Aug.). A week later a court judgement approved a three-way deal, and the frustrated would-be pensioners withdrew their lawsuit after government assurance of partial compensation (*Telegraph-Journal,* 19 Aug.). In November Premier Lord and business minister Peter Mesheau joined the new owners' representatives to officially reopen the mill, which was expected to employ about 225 unionized workers, compared to the four hundred it had when it closed. Production was expected to resume in January. Rather than producing high-quality photographic paper, the mill would be refitted to make dissolving and specialty pulp used in the manufacture of rayon (*Telegraph-Journal,* 8 Nov.).

Farming and fishing

The two other traditional components of New Brunswick's resource-based economy, farming and fishing, got less media coverage, but that did not necessarily support the adage 'No news is good news.' Farmers' objections to proposed increases in provincial laboratory and veterinary services got a positive response inasmuch as vet fees were increased by 12 per cent instead of the proposed 50 per cent, but the original increase announced for laboratory fees would stand. In an announcement, the agriculture, fisheries and aquaculture minister, David Alward, revealed that the province expected to collect about $132,000 in fees in 2005, compared to $66,000 the previous year (*Daily Gleaner,* 9 Apr.). In June the Legislature gave first and second reading to a bill requiring farmers to pay an annual fee to the government that would be placed in a dedicated fund and remitted to the New Brunswick Federation of Agriculture. Its current membership fee of $12.50 would increase to a range of $150 to $250, or slightly lower than a similar fee in Prince Edward

Island. Alward said that future membership would be 'voluntary' but that farmers refusing to join the federation would not receive a farm registration number, used to access fuel tax exemptions, farm licence plates, and subsidized lab and vet services.

In June the owners of a controversial pig farm in Kent County quietly surrendered their operating licence after a long battle with the neighbours, who objected to the manure from the farm's ten thousand hogs, the resulting smell, and the possible pollution of nearby waterways. Despite large protests that included mailing manure samples to MLAs and occupying government offices, Premier Lord had refused to close the operation, saying that such a move was up to the owners. In 2002 the province had announced that it would spend $1.5 million to help the farm reduce its potent manure smell. When the farm's licence had come up for renewal in June 2004, it was for eighteen months only, on condition that a new manure treatment plant be installed.

In July New Brunswick's 880 cattle producers made their first shipment of live cattle since the United States had imposed a ban on all Canadian cattle two years earlier, following the discovery of an Alberta animal inflicted with mad cow disease. Before the ban, 80 per cent of New Brunswick cattle were exported to the United States.

The lobster fishery, the mainstay of the fishing industry since the cod collapse of the early 1990s, continued to decline in the Gulf of St Lawrence and Northumberland Strait, where New Brunswick boat licences dominated (571 out of just over 800). Prices also tumbled. By contrast, the several hundred Bay of Fundy fishermen continued to bring in good catches, especially during their winter season, from mid-November to the end of March. The herring fishery suffered a severe administrative blow in August, when the Department of Fisheries and Oceans announced a 40 per cent cut in the Bay of Fundy quota. Fraser MacLeod of Connors Bros, whose plant at Blacks Harbour was the world's largest, said, 'Quite frankly we don't believe this is supported by science' (*Telegraph-Journal,* 10 Aug.). By contrast, a spokesman for the Maritime Fishermen's Union said that fishermen 'have been saying for years that too much herring is being caught. This is something everybody expected.... We can't do to the herring what we did to other fish' (ibid.).

Massive consolidation in the salmon aquaculture industry aroused concerns. What had begun with ninety-plus independent growers in the late 1980s was reduced in 2005 to a mere handful, after the largest player, Cooke Aquaculture, bought Heritage Salmon from the Weston Group and began talks to take over another major competitor, Norwegian-owned Stolt Sea Farms (*Telegraph-Journal,* 23 Dec.) Earlier, lobster fishermen had tried a boycott to stop Cooke from establishing a massive site (the size of seven football fields) at Haley's Cove, one of the last great stretches of untouched Fundy coastline between Saint John and the U.S. border. A company spokesperson said the large site was needed 'if it's going to compete with countries like Chile, where workers are paid a fraction of those in [Canada] and the farms are even bigger' (*Telegraph-Journal*, 25 July). Two weeks earlier, New Brunswick's representative in the federal Cabinet, Andy Scott, had announced that the salmon growers would be getting 'a $20-million bailout' to cover losses incurred since 2001 because of diseases (*Telegraph-Journal*, 11 July). By the year's end no money had been received because the two levels of government could not agree on how much each would contribute (*Daily Gleaner*, 9 Nov.).

Other segments of the economy present an uneven picture

As Canada's most rural population, New Brunswickers are acutely aware of the state of their roads and travel costs. Hence their keen interest in highway construction, insurance premiums, and gasoline prices. In February Premier Lord revealed details of agreements in which the Brun-Way Group, composed of Atcon Construction of Miramichi and SNC-Lavalin of Montreal, would be paid $540 million to complete twinning of a thirty-kilometre stretch of highway known locally as Suicide Alley, from its high accident rate. They would also operate and maintain the entire 275-kilometre stretch from the Quebec border to Longs Creek, west of Fredericton, until 2033. Ottawa would contribute $200 million of the $543.8 million deal, while the consortium would receive $18.8 million a year (*Daily Gleaner*, 8 Feb.; Moncton *Times & Transcript*, 10 Feb.).

A new province-wide car insurance plan that went into effect 1 January brought lower rates, but according to Roland Godin, the consumer advocate for insurance, 'many drivers are still too scared to claim minor accidents' (*Telegraph-Journal*, 23 May). Godin's office was established in March, after high premiums had become the biggest issue and nearly defeated Premier Lord's Tories in 2003. Appearing before the New Brunswick Insurance Board in June, Godin said that 'one thousand dollars a year for insurance often means the difference between being able to own a vehicle or not' (*Telegraph-Journal*, 29 June). He noted that the insurance industry had enjoyed 'incredible profits' in 2004. In November Attorney General Brad Green said that bodily injury claims had decreased by 44.3 per cent since the government placed a $2,500 cap on this type of claim (*Telegraph-Journal*, 4 Nov.).

By mid-year the Lord government was struggling to cope with rapidly fluctuating gasoline prices and promised to introduce legislation to allow a regulated gas market. In September, long-distance truckers blocked a number of highways. Within hours some grocery stores in the northern areas reported running out of fresh produce, farmers were short of animal feed, and gas stations were shutting down. As police prepared to remove the blockade, the truckers ended their protests. What did not end was the wild fluctuations, mostly upwards, in gasoline prices.

High gas prices and the rising Canadian dollar were being blamed for another flat tourist season, with numbers down for the fifth straight year (*Telegraph-Journal,* 29 Aug.). However, two unusual events, one in the dead of winter, lured thousands. More than five thousand visitors from as far away as London and California showed up in mid-February for Plaster Rock's annual pond hockey tournament (*Telegraph-Journal,* 18 Feb.). On the Labour Day weekend, an estimated eighty thousand gathered outside Moncton for a Rolling Stones concert (*Telegraph-Journal,* 6 Sept.).

The hub city experienced another increase in the number of people working at its numerous call centres when Asurion Canada announced in late August that it would add 300 employees to its existing staff of 350. It would also receive a provincial loan guarantee of $900,000 (*L'Acadie nouvelle,* 26 Aug.). In July Bathurst, hard hit by its mill's closure, learned that ClientLogic, which handled service calls for Rogers Wireless, had met its target of hiring 350 people during its first year of operation – qualifying for the government's grant of $7,000 per job – and that it planned to add another 235 by the year's end (*Telegraph-Journal,* 31 Aug.)

On the other hand, textile factories established in depressed northern communities continued to fail. In March the owner of Sunshine Mills announced its immediate closure, despite several millions in direct grants and guaranteed loans since the plant opened in Tracadie-Sheila in 2002. More than a hundred local people lost their jobs. In nearby Pokemouche, Atlantic Yarns Inc., which had received a total of $64 million in loans, laid off two hundred workers in December for a month and closed another facility at Atholville, near Campbellton, affecting another two thousand (*Daily Gleaner,* 17 Dec.).

In August, Saint John residents were awakened by loud blasts. They watched as five giant cranes were deliberately demolished at Saint John Shipbuilding and Dry Dock, marking the end of an industry that had existed almost as long as Canada's oldest incorporated city. Over the past eight decades 149 vessels had been built at the yard, many by its current owner, the Irving family. Its last big contract was Canada's frigate program, which had been completed in the early 1990s (*Telegraph-Journal,* 29 Aug.).

A few days earlier, at the resort town of St Andrews, another event further emphasized the changing industrial climate. More than a thousand people gathered in the local arena to protest against proposals to build one and possibly three liquefied natural gas (LNG) utilities in nearby Maine, ventures that would see mammoth tankers using a narrow channel in Canadian waters (*Telegraph-Journal,* 23 Aug.). Both the local MP, Greg Thompson, and federal Liberal cabinet minister Andy Scott, as well as Premier Lord, urged Ottawa to follow their lead and oppose the plan. However, at year's end Canadian senior officials remained silent as project proponents went through the various levels of the U.S. government seeking approval (*Telegraph-Journal,* 25 Aug.).

Three dominant sectors: energy, health, and education

Energy

Orimulsion and refurbishing the Lepreau nuclear facility were frequent media topics throughout the year, but one issue remained paramount: rising electricity rates. How could the utility raise rates by a total of 5.9 per cent in a single fiscal year without regulatory review? 'It's a good question,' energy minister Bruce Fitch acknowledged early in March after New Brunswick Power officials explained that the increase above the 3 per cent level was legal 'because of legal and regulatory changes that split the utility into five independent business units last fall' (*Daily Gleaner,* 3 Mar.). The next day Premier Lord said he thought New Brunswickers 'can afford New Brunswick Power's proposed rate increases of nearly 10 percent...I'm not saying it is going to be pleasant...but...can [they] afford not to pay the price of the cost of producing electricity' (*Times-Telegraph,* 4 Mar.). The 3 per cent hike went into effect 31 March, prompting Liberal leader Shawn Graham's comment that 'the provincial government's mishandling of the Orimulsion fuel deal got New Brunswick Power into the financial mess' (*Daily Gleaner,* 1 Apr.).

Two months early, the recently appointed CEO and president of New Brunswick Power, David Hay, revealed that the utility was withdrawing its lawsuit against two Venezuelan fuel producers after failing to serve the necessary legal papers (*Daily Gleaner,* 2 Feb.). It had already spent $340,000 in legal fees, plus $750 million to refurbish the Coleson

Cove generating plant near Saint John so it could handle Orimulsion. On 7 June Hay announced a 3 per cent increase effective 7 July, the third in sixteen months (*Telegraph-Journal*, 7 June). He said the latest increase was necessary because the Public Utilities Board (PUB) had refused the utility's application for a 4.5 per cent increase retroactive to 1 April. On 9 September Hay told homeowners to expect a 14 to 16 per cent increase by April 2006: 'it is something that we have to do to be fiscally responsible' (Moncton *Times & Transcript*, 1 Oct.). On 21 December the PUB sought a compromise by ruling that industrial users would have to pay 'a larger part of the average 11 percent increase that New Brunswick Power is seeking in 2006–2007 and residential users should pay less' (*Telegraph-Journal*, 22 Dec.).

In July the Lord government was stunned to learn through the media that despite earlier assurances by Andy Scott, New Brunswick's representative in the Martin government, that Ottawa would share the cost of refurbishing the aging Lepreau nuclear plant, Scott had confirmed rumours of no deal. Noting that three Ontario reactors and one in Quebec all needed major repairs, he said 'there was a fear that provinces would see this as a subsidization of power and they would ask why the federal government was off-setting the costs for one province over another' (*Telegraph-Journal*, 14 July). Two weeks later Premier Lord announced that the government 'has decided to accept the risk and proceed with a $1.4 billion refurbishment of Lepreau's single nuclear power plant' (*Telegraph-Journal*, 30 July). No details of the agreement worked out with Atomic Energy of Canada Ltd were released. The premier said he agreed with the assessment by New Brunswick Power's board that AECL's price was too good to refuse compared with an earlier option from Bruce Power, which was too expensive and 'not worth the extra protection that Bruce would provide in case something goes wrong' (*Telegraph-Journal*, 30 July). That extra protection included a performance guarantee, which was not in the AECL deal.

Health

The most beleaguered yet determined member of Premier Lord's cabinet was undoubtedly his health minister, Elvy Robichaud, a former high school principal who in 1999 had scored an historic breakthrough in the strongly Liberal area of Tracadie-Sheila, in the Acadian peninsula. His department's decision in 2004 to close or drastically reduce the services of several hospitals had been fiercely and continually challenged through the media and by sit-ins and threats of legal action throughout the year. Nevertheless, in late February he announced in Edmundston, where he was giving details of new medical equipment slated for the local hospital, that the 'new Provincial Health Plan will go ahead as planned this spring' (*Telegraph-Journal*, 25 Feb.). The response of hundreds of Caraquet residents was to block a key highway and demand that their hospital not be downgraded to a community health centre. They remained there for several hours, despite the RCMP helicopter hovering over them, leaving only when a fierce winter storm struck (*L'Acadie nouvelle*, 2 Mar.). After an injunction to prevent further loss of services was rejected by the Court of Queen's Bench, they continued to stage protests around the peninsula and even at the Legislature – all to no avail. On 1 May the last of the protestors ended a thirty-two-day occupation of the hospital after receiving promises that no equipment, bedding, or instruments would be removed from what was now a community health centre – one that lacked both obstetrical and surgical facilities and had thirty-eight fewer employees (*Telegraph-Journal*, 2 May).

In the Upper St. John River Valley, opposition to downgrading of the Woodstock hospital and plans to build a new one further north, near the tiny community of Waterville, at a cost of $78.3 million produced no sit-ins and few demonstrations, but a lawsuit was launched similar to the one attempted by Caraquet citizens. When Robichaud unveiled his departmental estimates before the Legislature in late January, he said $29 million would be spent on the new facility in 2005 and that upon completion in 2007 it would provide services for forty thousand citizens in the region. He added that the government was closing or downgrading five hospitals in the area to make way for the new one (*Daily Gleaner*, 1 Jan.).

In April Premier Lord defended the hospital plan, arguing that while 294 beds would be eliminated, the largest item in the current health department budget was the $64 million 'added solely to cover wages to help lure more doctors and nurses to the province' (Moncton *Times & Transcript*, 11 Apr.). In August Robichaud revealed that under a new contract, doctors would earn 20 per cent more over the next three years (*Telegraph-Journal*, 10 Aug.). Meanwhile, Moncton's civic officials welcomed news that the province would spend $2.7 million to upgrade the Université de Moncton and the Dr Georges-L. Dumont Hospital to accommodate a new medical training plan, which would see twenty-four Université de Sherbrooke students in its four-year program starting in September 2006 (*Telegraph-Journal*, 25 July).

Education

Throughout much of the winter and into the spring, the province's 7,600 teachers and thousands of students and parents watched as the teachers' negotiating team tried to reach a contract agreement with the Lord government. The teachers, without a contract since February 2004, had rejected a conciliation board's recommendations for a 12 per cent raise over four years. Talks broke off on 8 February, and on 16 March the membership voted 97 per cent in favour of a strike, which legally could begin within a week. Rather than take that step, they withdrew from extracurricular activities (*Daily Gleaner,* 13 Apr.). On 29 April the two sides reached a 'joint proposed agreement' after the province offered to create an additional 125 teaching positions and establish a joint action committee and a $2.5-million fund to address classroom composition. The next day the tentative agreement was rejected by the board of directors of the New Brunswick Teachers' Federation (*Telegraph-Journal,* 30 Apr. and 2 May). Finally, on 30 May, exactly fifteen months after their previous collective agreement had expired, the membership agreed by a vote of 65 per cent to accept the terms of a new one. It included a 13 per cent wage increase costing $115 million over the next four years and changes to classroom composition (*Telegraph-Journal,* 1 June).

In November Premier Lord and Fredericton Liberal MP Andy Scott jointly announced a major funding program for New Brunswick's two francophone institutions. École Sainte-Anne and Centre communautaire Sainte-Anne in Fredericton and the Centre scolaire et communautaire Samuel-de-Champlain in Saint John would share more than $27 million over the next three years. Earlier the federal language commissioner, Dyane Adam, in her sixth annual report, had praised New Brunswick's bilingual efforts, noting that the province had made the biggest gains in 2004 respecting the *Official Languages Act.* Statistics showed the province tied with Quebec for the most bilingual students – 48 per cent (*Telegraph-Journal,* 1 June). Somewhat ironically, a 5–4 decision by the Supreme Court of Canada in mid-December ruled that the City of Saint John was not obligated under provincial law to conduct its legal proceedings in French. The case had been instituted by a Moncton lawyer, Mario Charlebois, who in 2001 had won a similar case, forcing the City of Moncton to translate its bylaws and provide more bilingual services (*Telegraph-Journal,* 16 Dec.).

Two records were set in individual bequests to universities during the year. In January the Irving family donated $2 million to fund two chairs in journalism, at the Université de Moncton and at St Thomas

University (*Telegraph-Journal,* 14 Jan.). In August the University of New Brunswick announced details of the largest bequest it had ever received. The estate of its former president Dr Colin B. Mackay donated $3 million for scholarships and bursaries for students attending the Saint John campus, and a similar amount to the law faculty in Fredericton (*Telegraph-Journal,* 3 Aug.). In October Margaret McCain, chancellor of Mount Allison University, announced details of a $5-million donation, the largest single gift from a living individual in that institution's long history. She said that she and her husband, Wallace, hoped that their contribution to construction of a new student centre would make campus life 'dramatically different' from when they had studied there in the 1950s (*Telegraph-Journal,* 15 Oct.).

PETER E. BUKER

Prince Edward Island

The year 2005 in PEI was one of stable economic activity and continued initiatives in agriculture, forestry, and the island's ecology. While no key legislative changes occurred, a plebiscite was held on electoral reform. There were significant new infrastructure improvements, financed by the federal government, and the provincial government initiated a 'renewal' program in the public service that saw many job changes and cuts.

The economy

The PEI economy grew by 2 per cent in 2005, up slightly from the previous year; the total provincial GDP was $4,142 million at market prices. The all-items consumer price index rose by 3.2 per cent and energy prices were up 15.7 per cent compared to 2004. On 1 September the Island Regulatory and Appeals Commission raised the price of regular gasoline to a record-setting $1.35 a litre; September's average prices for gasoline and heating oil were $1.21 and 83 cents respectively.

Statistics Canada estimated a 0.2 per cent year's increase in PEI's population to 138,113 as of 1 July 2005; 7 per cent of this change was due to natural increases (births minus deaths), 43 per cent to net international migration, and 50 per cent to net interprovincial migration. Total employment rose 1.9 per cent from 2004, to 68,200. The average unemployment rate dropped half a percentage point, to 10.8 per cent, and labour force participation increased by the same amount, to 68.5 per cent. The public service sector accounted for 28.7 per cent of total employment on PEI in 2005.

Manufacturing shipments rose 5.1 per cent from the previous year, to $1,486.7 million, much of the growth being attributable to fish processing and chemical manufacturing activity; the total value of manufacturing shipments was $932.4 million, mostly due to the manufacture of food products. Manufacturing employed 10 per cent of PEI's workforce, the third-largest employment sector after the retail trade and public sectors. Exports increased by 19.9 per cent, to $772.8 million, with only forestry products shipments showing a decrease; 65 per cent of exports were of agricultural and fishing products. Overall the agricultural sector improved, with total receipts for 2005 of $364.4 million. Market prices for potatoes increased, largely because of a Canadian and America-wide voluntary reduction in seeded acreage; in 2005 the PEI acreage was decreased to 95,500 from 106,000 acres in 2004. Total fish landings decreased 2 per cent, to $163.7 million, and lobster landings declined 7.1 per cent.

The value of the indicators used to measure tourism remained approximately the same as in 2004, with some increases in provincial park visits, number of tourists arriving by air and cruise ships, and rounds of golf played. Visits to national parks and historic sites decreased, traffic arriving by ferry declined, and visits to tourist information centres were down. The measurement of tourism on PEI was altered in 2005 to record non-resident and resident visitation over a twelve-month period, in keeping with a change in how tourism was measured at the national level.

In March Air Canada, the only air carrier offering winter service to PEI, decided to cancel part of its service from Charlottetown Airport because of the PEI government's decision to subsidize a summertime air service (which started 28 June) by its competitor WestJet. The province guaranteed WestJet's first $300,000 in revenues – a target that was met, so the province did not have to pay – and contributed approximately $200,000 towards marketing the new flights. In September WestJet decided to expand its air service to PEI to year-round. Northwest Airlines introduced a daily direct flight, commencing on 1 July, between Charlottetown and Detroit. Tourists travelling by air increased by 11 per cent in 2005, and total air passenger traffic to and from PEI increased 12.2 per cent over the previous year.

There was a 6.2 per cent decrease in housing starts in 2005, to 862, while non-residential construction increased by 24.1 per cent over the previous year to $116.8 million. This included the Jean Canfield federal building, the Wellness Centre in Summerside, the Maritime Electric generator plant, and construction on the University of Prince Edward Island (UPEI) campus. Statistics Canada estimated that total investment on PEI had increased 6.2 per cent from 2004, to $768.3 million; public sector investment increased 32.5 per cent, to $145.6 million, and private sector investment increased 1.5 per cent, to $622.7 million.

Total provincial revenues in the 2004–05 fiscal year were $1,065.3 million, of which 40 per cent was from federal transfers. Total expenditures were $1,097.4 million, a decrease of 2.6 per cent from the previous fiscal year. The deficit for the fiscal year 2004–05 was $32.1 million, and net provincial debt was up 2 per cent from the previous fiscal year, to $1,276 million or approximately $9,260 for every islander.

On 4 May the provincial treasurer announced that Dominion Bond Rating Service (DBRS) had confirmed PEI's credit rating of A (low) for long-term and R-1 (low) for short-term borrowing. Those ratings were a consequence of moderately improved fiscal performance and expectations of narrowing deficits over the next few years, assisted by cost constraint measures introduced in the 2005–06 budget. DBRS reported that the debt-to-GDP ratio would rise only modestly, to 36.2 per cent in 2005–06 from 36.1 per cent in the prior year, and that the province's debt-to-GDP ratio had fallen 38.7 per cent from two years before.

Fiscal events

With funding from the PEI Adaptation Development Agricultural Production Technology (ADAPT) Council, the new Atlantic Beef Products Inc. plant in Albany got a traceability system working in late October. The system recorded each animal and the time and date the beef was processed, measures important to food safety as well as for increasing capacity through determining meat cuts. The plant was processing cattle from all three maritime provinces, with approximately 80 per cent of the animals coming from Prince Edward Island; it had a full-time workforce of more than sixty and an annual payroll of $2.5 million. The ADAPT Council also funded a new optical grading system – the first of its type in Canada – for W.P. Griffin Inc. in Elmsdale, PEI, which similarly allowed tracing back to the field from which the cow had come.

In January provincial funding was given to the PEI Certified Organic Producers' Co-op to promote their products in a wider marketplace. The first meeting of a PEI convivium of the slow food movement was held in May. In June the PEI ADAPT Council announced financial support for PEI agri-tourism, an infant industry on the island regarded as an important tool in diversifying the agriculture sector. On 13 June the PEI Department of Agriculture, Fisheries and Aquaculture, in cooperation with the Department of Tourism, distributed the 2005 *Fresh Produce Directory* through Island newspapers and the Web, listing more than fifty farms that sold directly to consumers.

On 1 April a major addition to the Prince Edward Island Food Technology Centre to accommodate the Atlantic Natural Products Development Initiative was officially opened. The expanded capacity was to develop innovative technologies to extract high-value natural products from agricultural and marine bio-resources. Major funding came from a $4.9-million contribution from the Atlantic Canada Opportunities Agency (ACOA) Atlantic Innovation Fund and $1.5 million from the province.

The not-for-profit corporation PEI BioAlliance Inc. was formed in March 2005 to facilitate collaboration and growth within the network of individuals and organizations dedicated to building the bioscience-based economic sector. On 28 October a strategy was announced by Premier Binns and ACOA minister Joe McGuire that aimed to increase bioscience research and development expenditure from its current level of $15 million to $40 million, to increase private sector employment from four hundred to a thousand, and to increase private sector revenue from $60 million to $200 million by 2010. A state-of-the-art greenhouse, a key component of the Atlantic Canada Network on Bioactive Compounds (ACNBC), was officially opened on 10 November. The ACNBC, a pan-Atlantic collaboration of independent researchers, universities, industry, and government agencies based in the Faculty of Science at UPEI, was investigating the health benefits of wild rosehips and wild blueberries.

On 27 April $121.5 million in infrastructure funds was announced, to be managed under a 'one-committee, three-program' governance framework involving cooperation among the three levels of government and invested in PEI communities over the following five years. The three programs were the Canada-PEI Municipal Rural Infrastructure Fund (MRIF) – $54 million, representing equal investments by the three levels of government; the Canada Strategic Infrastructure Fund (CSIF) – $30 million, representing a $15-million investment by the government of Canada; and a $15-million investment program financed by the government of PEI and the Federal Gas Tax Fund – $37.5 million invested by the government of Canada over five years. On 22 November the federal and PEI governments signed an agreement that would invest gas tax revenues in communities across PEI as part of the New Deal for Cities and Communities. The money was earmarked for environmentally sustainable municipal infrastructure over a five-year period; fiscal year 2005–06 investments were to be $4.5 million. On 13 October the ACOA minister and the premier provided details of the first thirty-four projects funded by $14.6 million from the Canada-Prince Edward Island MRIF.

In October the City of Charlottetown, partnered with a private bus operator, launched its first public transit system. Erection of the Jean Canfield Building in Charlottetown, 'one of the most environmentally friendly buildings ever constructed by Public Works and Government Services Canada,'[1] commenced in the summer of 2005. On 8 November the federal and provincial governments announced infrastructure funding to support the second phase of construction of Summerside's $28.5-million Wellness Centre, a multi-purpose 'non-traditional' recreational and business facility. The federal government committed $3 million on top of the PEI government's previous $3.1 million. An athletic facility for major amateur events was also planned in support of PEI's hosting of the 2009 Canada Summer Games.

On 2 February the government asked for expressions of interest from the private sector for establishing an oilseed extraction and biodiesel manufacturing plant in Prince Edward Island. On 22 April it was announced that Hydrogenics Corporation, based in Mississauga, Ontario, and the PEI Energy Corporation, funded by the federal and PEI governments, would lead a consortium of industry and government partners to develop Canada's first wind/hydrogen demonstration village. Its purpose was to show how wind energy and hydrogen technologies could work together to offer clean and sustainable energy solutions across a wide range of applications. On 23 September it was announced that the Canadian Wind Energy Institute (CanWEI), funded partly by the province but mostly by the federal government, would open at North Cape the following year. CanWEI was to focus on four areas of wind power generation: testing and certification, research and innovation, industry training and public education, and technical consultation and assistance. On 30 September the provincial government gave approval to the PEI Energy Corporation to proceed with final design and development of a thirty-megawatt wind farm at the eastern end of the island.

Politics and the legislature

PEI had seen, as in other parts of Canada, much public controversy surrounding the federal Parliament's passing of Bill C-38, the *Civil Marriage Act,* in June. The first same-sex marriage was performed in PEI in August.

A plebiscite on electoral reform was held on 28 November in which two-ballot, mixed-member proportional representation was proposed.

1 See http://www.tpsgc-pwgsc.gc.ca/medias-media/af-fa/2008-08-08-01-eng.html.

Premier Pat Binns set the winning threshold for this controversial proposal at 60 per cent; however, only an approximate 33 per cent of islanders actually turned out to vote – far lower than the normally high voter turnout in provincial elections – and of those voters, only 36 per cent supported the change. The low voter turnout occurred despite earlier polls by the Commission on Prince Edward Island's Electoral Future that had indicated a strong intent to vote by islanders.

The collapse of Polar Foods in 2003, the largest fish processing company on PEI, continued to dog the Binns government. In his report released on 13 January, provincial auditor general Colin Younker determined that provincial losses from the debacle had been $31 million, and in February he suggested that the province had possibly contravened the *Companies Act* by allowing payments to Polar Foods shareholders. In October it was revealed that the RCMP had been called in to investigate and in November a forensic audit of Polar Foods was made public. Central to the report was the issue of payments made to shareholders while the company was losing money; the recommendation was to seek legal advice.

On 13 May it was announced that the herring seiner exclusion zone had been restored to the historic 25-fathom line by the federal government in recognition of the need to protect herring stocks, the lobster habitat, and PEI's inshore fishery. On 3 November the Supreme Court of Prince Edward Island ruled that the provincial government's lawsuit launched on 23 February, challenging the constitutional authority of the federal fisheries minister to manage the fisheries under the *Fisheries Act,* could proceed. The federal government had applied to PEI's Supreme Court in May to have the case dismissed.

Premier Binns established a thirteen-member Task Force on Student Achievement in February 2005, with a mandate to examine current educational research, consult with educators, seek public input, and recommend strategies to improve student achievement. By July more than six hundred individuals and groups had provided input into the public consultations; the report had not been released, however, by the end of the year. On 22 February the PEI government announced that it would make $2.5 million available for construction of a new school for French first-language students in West Prince. On 12 October Premier Binns chaired the twelfth meeting of the Council of Atlantic Premiers in Mill River, PEI; the premiers discussed skills training and post-secondary education and prepared for the upcoming First Ministers' Meeting on Aboriginal Issues.

The *Renewable Energy Act,* passed in the autumn 2004 session of the Legislature, was proclaimed on 22 December 2005, with the exception of one section requiring utilities to obtain 100 per cent of electrical energy from renewable energy sources by 2015; the act approved three sets of regulations governing key aspects of renewable energy development in the province. The report *Recommendations for Regulation of Construction and Demolition Debris Sites in PEI* was completed by the Environmental Advisory Council and released by the minister of environment, energy and forestry on 1 June. The construction and demolition disposal site at Hazelbrook had been in the news in January and February because of a smouldering fire and its effects on surrounding air quality. The same day the minister tabled the Public Forest Council's report *Woodlands Hold Our Island Together* in the Legislature; it was the culmination of extensive consultations over the winter in an effort to determine government's role in the management and conservation of public and private forest lands across PEI.

On 6 January 2005 the provincial government released the Public Forest Council's 2004 *Report on Ground Hemlock,* which contained recommendations for solving an array of problems and concerns surrounding the harvesting of ground hemlock in PEI. The province reached an agreement on 13 December with the Environmental Coalition of Prince Edward Island to manage 800 hectares of public land under a ten-year lease agreement; the Macphail Woods Ecological Forestry Project in Orwell would administer the lands to demonstrate sustainable forest management and restore native Acadian woodlands. The Wildlife Conservation Fund, intended to assist community-led projects supporting wildlife and wildlife habitats, was transferred on 9 December from the Department of Environment, Energy and Forestry to a committee representing wildlife conservation groups that directly contribute to the fund. On 25 August the province confirmed that it had contributed $300,000 to the Nature Conservancy of Canada to purchase Boughton Island, one of PEI's most important and beautiful offshore islands. A book, *Memories of Boughton Island: From Memory Only,* was also published in 2005.

On 17 March the provincial government announced its Workforce Renewal Program. This program offered incentives to provincial employees to volunteer for early retirement and provided severance payments. The premier said the objective was to reduce spending by an estimated $25 million and renew programs. More than 700 provincial public servants voluntarily left and an additional 330 were laid off, of whom 225 were rehired in vacated positions. Other provincial government cuts were made in the budgets of the Dental Health Program, the Human Rights Commission, the Confederation Centre grant, other cultural and heritage grants, and sports and recreation grants. The Georgetown Youth Centre, the Brackley Beach and Poole's Corner visitor information centres, and Strathgartney campground were also closed. It was announced on 7 October that, effective 1 April 2006, the minimum wage in PEI would increase from $6.80 to $7.15 following a recommendation by PEI's Employment Standards Board.

On 16 September Premier Pat Binns led Trade Team PEI – jointly sponsored by the PEI and federal governments and made up of trade officials and representatives of Island companies – to Hainan, PEI's sister province in southern China, to explore business opportunities in biotechnology, information technology, construction, and educational services. A delegation from Hainan arrived in PEI on 18 September.

Effective 1 August, amendments to the *Tobacco Sales to Minors Act,* its title now changed to the *Tobacco Sales and Access Act,* resulted in stronger legislation around accessibility to tobacco products. The new act restricted venues where tobacco products could be sold and focused particularly on places where young people might be present. The mosquito-sampling program, begun two years before to monitor the species of mosquitoes most likely to carry West Nile virus, continued in the summer of 2005.

The Speaker of the Legislative Assembly announced on 29 March that Karen Rose, PEI's first information and privacy commissioner, was resigning; Rose had been appointed to a five-year term in November 2002. An offshoot of the Department of Health, the Department of Social Services and Seniors became officially functional as of 8 November, with Chester Gillan being sworn in as minister. The newly designated department was part of a reorganization of PEI's health and social services system; its creation was anticipated to save $9 million annually. On 7 December a Seniors' Secretariat was announced by the provincial government; it would work with government departments and the province's seniors' groups, with a mandate to support policy initiatives that would improve the quality of life and promote public education efforts for and about Island seniors.

The Legislative Assembly resumed its second session of the 62nd General Assembly on 6 April; the provincial treasurer, Mitchell Murphy, delivered the budget address on 7 April. The third session of the Legislature opened on 16 November.

In early March Premier Binns wrote to the prime minister to protest the direction of recent discussions between Transport Canada and Northumberland Ferries Ltd concerning ferry service between Wood Islands, PEI, and Caribou, NS. There was a fear that Transport Canada was intending to reduce its subsidy, raising worries about the sustainability of the ferry service. On 22 March a new five-year agreement was negotiated between Northumberland Ferries and Transport Canada that satisfied the provincial government. A five-year federal funding agreement was signed between the province and the federal government in November to improve and expand PEI's regulated early learning and child-care system, focusing on children under the age of six.

Other events

On 29 March twelve anti–seal hunt protesters – Paul Watson and eleven crew members from the Sea Shepherd Conservation Society – were arrested by the RCMP on the ice between the Magdalen Islands, Cape Breton, and PEI. They were charged with being within a half-mile of sealing activity without permits. On 9 December the protesters lost their legal challenge to Ottawa's right to restrict their movements during seal hunts, claiming that their right to freedom of expression was being violated. At the end of 2005 the protesters were still waiting to face charges of violating federal regulations.

Several PEI natives distinguished themselves nationally in sports. On 28 July a twenty-five-year-old Charlottetown woman, Kirstin Roe, swam sixteen kilometres, crossing the Northumberland Strait from Cape Tormentine, NB, to Borden-Carleton, PEI, in seven hours and forty-five minutes. Her swim raised money for AIDS PEI and the Stephen Lewis Foundation. In August Jared Connaughton won two gold medals at the Canada Games in Regina for the 100- and 200-metre sprints; he was PEI's first ever Canada Games double gold medal winner. Mark MacDonald of Kingston, PEI, broke a six-year record for wins in Canadian harness racing, with 644 wins in one season. PEI native Brad Richards was named to the Canadian Olympic hockey team in December.

On 7 March the premier and the minister of community and cultural affairs announced the recipients of the first Volunteer Recognition Awards at a ceremony in Montague. Honoured for their service to others were Rosemary Batchilder of Georgetown, David Boyce of Poverty Beach, Ron Erickson of Summerside, Donna Lewis of Brooklyn, Arlene Power of Stratford, Elaine Smith of Hunter River, and Bob and Carolyn Bateman of Charlottetown. The 2005 recipients of the Order of Prince Edward Island were announced by Lieutenant-Governor J. Léonce Bernard; the recipients were Angéle Arsenault, OC, of Summerside, Leone Bagnall, CM, of Hazel Grove, and Derek Key, QC, of Summerside.

Rainbow Valley, a landmark Cavendish theme park that had been a cultural icon for Island children and tourists since it opened in 1969, was closed on 5 September 2005, despite public opposition based on both sentiment and concern by tourism operators. Parks Canada bought the 39-acre site for $2.7 million; it was to become a nature park as part of the PEI National Park. Developer Matthew Jelley announced plans to build a new $4-million theme park across the road from the old Rainbow Valley site.

A Charlottetown restaurant, the Noodle House, and its owners, Tommy and Lina Ko, made national news. The restaurant – located just a few doors down from the Charlottetown police station – and its clientele had been subject to snowball attacks, threatening gestures, and other harassment by local high-school students over a five-year period. There was widely publicized community disgust with the harassment and attempts to make amends; the Kos, however, eventually sold their business and moved away from PEI.

The City of Charlottetown's 150th anniversary of incorporation was on 17 April. It was celebrated with various festivities and events, funded in part by a $237,950 contribution from the Atlantic Canada Opportunities Agency.

George Key, former member of Summerside Town Council, mayor of Summerside, and leader of the Progressive Conservative Party of PEI, passed away on 3 July. Gary Robichaud, a teacher and leader of the Island New Democrats since 2002, announced his resignation as party leader on 23 June; he died on 8 September of lung cancer.

The International Adult Literacy and Skills Survey (IALSS) was released on 9 November. It indicated that, compared to 1995, literacy had increased slightly on PEI. Compared to the rest of Canada, PEI showed slightly more literacy in the highest information skills and slightly lower literacy at the skill level of people who cannot read or who can deal only with the simplest and clearest of material.

The *PEI Wind Atlas,* an online interactive map identifying areas with the best potential for future wind energy development, was released on 12 October as part of the provincial government's Renewable Energy Strategy. The Department of Environment, Energy and Forestry published its new *Prince Edward Island Atlas* on 17 August. Based on aerial photography and ground analysis from the 2000 Land Use Inventory, the atlas provided detailed information about natural and human-made land features.

At the Tourism Industry Association of Canada's 2005 annual meeting in Quebec City in late October, Rodd Hotels and Resorts captured one of their most prestigious awards, the APR Media Ltd Business of the Year Award, Multiple Unit.

Toronto lawyer Jacki Lewis raised awareness and more than $41,000 for breast cancer by circumnavigating PEI. She completed her twenty-three-day 'Kayak for the Cure' trip on 25 July, in a pink kayak purchased for the journey. On 18 September the Terry Fox Run across the Confederation Bridge marked the twenty-fifth anniversary of the Marathon of Hope; it attracted more than 13,000 participants and raised funds for cancer research.

On 27 September Jeffery E. Lantz, an Island lawyer and a former attorney general of Prince Edward Island, was appointed a provincial court judge, filling the position left vacant by the retirement of Judge Ralph C. Thompson on 21 October. After a long investigation, in December an arrest was made for the July 2002 murder of Chrystal Beairsto.

ROBERT FINBOW

Nova Scotia

The winds of change were felt in Nova Scotia politics with Premier John Hamm's impending retirement. For the first time since Robert Stanfield in 1967, a sitting premier was departing without serious scandal or condemnation from politicians or pundits. While Hamm's rule had few milestone achievements and was marked by many reversals and compromises, the Conservatives' credibility as a governing party had been restored, despite their failure to retain a majority. Indeed, collegial cooperation among parties allowed Hamm's minority regime to be among the most durable and productive in Canadian history, a clear contrast to the Liberal minority government's travails in Ottawa. Yet changes in the demography and composition of the province, especially with urbanization and an increasingly diverse population, left the Nova Scotians divided in their political goals and loyalties as never before. A three-party competitive system made for interesting manoeuvring amidst the adjustments required for Nova Scotia to be competitive in the new, globalized economy of the twenty-first century.

And change was evident in the economy, buffeted by fuel costs that seriously affected public finance, consumer well-being, and economic prospects. Adjustment to new industries proceeded. Research in Motion, the profitable maker of Blackberrys and other mobile communications devices, announced local operations, complete with major construction, at several sites. This increased Halifax's stature among investors, helping create a strong base for the high-tech sector.

Nova Scotia continued to try to punch above its weight in a globalized world. Notably, Halifax was selected as the official Canadian bid city for the 2014 Commonwealth Games. As the province marked the 400th anniversary of the French settlement at Port Royal and the grim 250th anniversary of expulsion of the Acadians from the Annapolis Valley, Nova Scotia sought to become a welcoming destination for a diverse population. New government programs would attract, acclimatize, and retain immigrants to address long-term population decline. These and other issues made headlines as the province adjusted to new political, economic, and cultural realities.

Politics

Premier Hamm announced his retirement after six years as premier, and the Conservative party searched for a new leader, to be selected in 2006. Even his opponents in the House acknowledged Hamm as respectful and statesmanlike, not given to the mean-spiritedness so common in public life. Federal Conservative deputy leader Peter MacKay, who had endured a high-profile romantic break-up with fellow Tory MP Belinda Stronach when she crossed to the Liberal ranks, was touted as a replacement but decided to remain in Ottawa. Leadership candidates included former finance minister Neil Leblanc, former president of Maritime Life Bill Black, and current immigration minister and Cape Breton fiddler Rodney MacDonald. Leblanc, who promised to take a tougher line with the opposition, was seen as the front-runner, and the debates focused on his record as a minister. The low-key campaign was overshadowed by federal political dramas that lead to a winter election call. Nova Scotia's federal political loyalties remained in flux; Tory leader Stephen Harper was unpopular, but local Tories worked to bring the party to power nationally.

Despite a civil tone among the three provincial parties, the continuing threat to the minority government created intrigue. Although he flirted with the idea in the spring, Hamm sought to avoid an election as soaring fuel prices weakened the party's poll numbers, despite the premier's own favourable ratings. The government gained versus the opposition NDP early in the year but the polls showed a spike in NDP support in summer, to 30 per cent, although the three parties still split the vote. The government had positive ratings, so a majority was not out of reach, though the low popularity of federal leader Harper did not help. The NDP benefited from Darryl Dexter's steady leadership and strong personal support; he was the top choice among voters to be premier. But later polls showed softening of the NDP position. Uncertainty bred caution: none of the parties sought an expeditious trip to the polls when they also faced demands on finances and volunteers from a federal election campaign.

Liberal fortunes under new leader Francis Mackenzie were mixed as spillover from Liberal scandals in Ottawa contributed to weak poll numbers. Mackenzie's own performance as leader, handicapped by lack of a legislative seat, was criticized for inconsistency, and his personal ratings trailed. Veteran MLA Michel Samson was selected to lead the party in the House when former leader Danny Graham left to be with his ailing wife. The House probed Liberal Party trust funds allegedly built on kickbacks from companies, notably the liquor corporation, through government contracts in the 1970s. Drawing parallels with the federal Gomery inquiry on sponsorship funds, which resulted in the Martin government's repaying the public treasury, both ministers and NDP MLAs called for an investigation to determine whether the Liberals should repay funds to the province. Liberal spokesmen suggested that a $1.3-million payment in the 1990s had covered all funds raised illegally through toll-gating payments for shelf space at the liquor corporation, and that new legislation on party finances should not apply. The Legislature's investigation, due to be reported on in 2006, considered whether the party should be allowed to use those funds in any future election.

No comparable scandal afflicted the current government. However, there were suggestions that lack of transparency and openness in the government's conduct of its business perhaps limited the ability to scrutinize deficiencies in policy and practice. For instance, the government frequently dallied in responding to freedom-of-information requests from public and press, despite high fees. After a dramatic standoff between police and the parents of a toddler, leading to the child's removal by the Children's Aid Society, opposition MLAs noted the government's failure to convene a mandatory advisory committee to review legislation in that field. But the Conservatives' performance did not weaken their standing with the public; they survived their only electoral test when they held on to the Chester–St Margaret's seat in a by-election.

Politically charged issues included the Commonwealth Games bid. This major undertaking would transform Halifax's sports and recreation infrastructure with $500-million investments in facilities, including a stadium that could attract football or soccer franchises in the future. Organizers planned to use military land at Shannon Park in Dartmouth as the central site for sports venues and athletes' accommodations. The province was divided between advocates and cautious critics. Boosters predicted that visitors and expenditures would bring up to $2 billion in stimulus, but opponents feared cost overruns and long-term debt for the province.

Hamm created an Office of Immigration headed by a cabinet minister, Rodney Macdonald. The declining birth rate and continued out-migration by the young were creating concerns about population replacement, and the province sought to double its intake of immigrants from abroad and create the means to keep them in the region, energize society, and sustain the economy. The province was seeking 3,500 immigrants per year and hoped to persuade 70 per cent to remain long-term residents. The controversial Nova Scotia Nominee Program fast-tracked potential entrepreneurs, charging them $28,000 for sifting through red tape and another $100,000 for a six-month work term to integrate them into Nova Scotia business life. But there were concerns about transparency, since the names of companies handling the paperwork and serving as mentors were kept confidential and they were not required to apply for tendered contracts (*Daily News,* 23 Oct.).

The legislature

The minority conservative government survived two legislative sessions. The spring session was productive, with the enactment of thirty-one bills, including six introduced by the Opposition. A controversial mental-health reform act was delayed by opposition resistance. There was also tension between the NDP and the community services minister. The party introduced a motion to cut his salary to one dollar while the minister made accusations about the conduct of an opposition critic. The NDP withdrew their motion, which had been designed to embarrass the minister for his allegedly poor performance, when it became clear the government might fall, triggering an election. That was as close as the province got to a motion of no confidence.

The spring budget focused on spending in education, health, infrastructure, and debt repayment. With education as its theme, the budget included provisions to increase school board budgets, renovate schools, hire specialists, limit class sizes up to Grade 2, support African-Canadian, Mi'kmaq, and special needs students, and experiment with preschool programs. Critics suggested that the modest programs lacked vision and left Nova Scotia close to the bottom in funding per student among provinces. Health spending included funds to treat autism in its early stages, check newborns for hearing problems, recruit new nurses to rural areas, boost health promotion, and acquire diagnostic equipment. The budget addressed the infrastructure deficit with increased spending, mostly for highway upgrades. The finance minister projected a surplus of $63 million.

The budget generated mixed reaction from business, which welcomed the pledge to study the impact of regulations on business competitiveness and performance in the province, which it hoped would alter the bureaucratic mindset and turn 'red tape into smart tape' (*Chronicle-Herald,*

27 Apr.). Business also welcomed extension of the film tax credit, elimination of the business occupancy tax, cuts in corporate taxes, and an increased threshold for small business taxation. However, the lack of income tax cuts and insufficient debt reduction worried some commentators.

The opposition criticized the budget for a lack of vision, and the NDP initially indicated its concern that tax breaks to large companies were taking precedence over the needs of families. Others complained that not enough had gone into community services, social supports, or university tuition and student debt relief. Critics also noted that significant increases were planned in the budgets of the executive council for the intergovernmental relations office, the immigration ministry, the public service commission, and the treasury and policy boards, and for physical improvements to the office of the Speaker of the House. This continued a trend of rising spending under the Conservatives since Hamm had taken office, running against stated principles and fiscal need in a province with sustained high debt loads (*Chronicle Herald,* 3 May).

However, chastened by the previous election, which had brought a minority government, and fearful of provoking another electoral contest, which the public did not want, all the parties collaborated to avoid a confrontational vote on the budget or other confidence issues. The NDP in particular did not want to risk another defeat when on the brink of power, as had happened when a hasty confidence vote in 1998 gave Premier Hamm his first majority (*Chronicle Herald,* 16 May). Despite dissatisfaction over the lack of new spending on education, the $6-billion budget easily received final approval. It passed with support from the NDP, which noted with approval spending to reduce healthcare wait times, provide breakfast for low-income schoolchildren, aid families with autistic children, help low-income diabetic patients, and purchase new MRI machines. The Liberals voted against the budget, citing inaction on pressing needs in education, health, rural development, and social assistance. By year-end, high prices for natural gas had boosted the province to a $78-million surplus, with revenues up $113 million over estimates but with a charge of $28 million for a pension valuation adjustment. Most of the surplus was dedicated to debt reduction as the province sought to improve its fiscal picture after years of increasing debt.

The spring session saw more debate over the volatile price of gasoline. Many independent gasoline retailers claimed they would be forced out of business because of unsustainable pricing by the oil refiners and their retail chains. The government sought a bill allowing Cabinet to negotiate on regulation with retailers and suppliers. However, the Opposition rejected such a blank cheque. The Legislature passed the *Petroleum Products Pricing Act* after much debate and study in committee, but many details remained to be worked out. The act proposed five zones for regulated pricing, to prevent the closing of more small rural retailers. However, the government delayed implementation of these measures. Critics suggested that the large oil companies and bureaucratic resistance had dissuaded government action, but the intricate nature of the gasoline business also made a regulatory solution difficult. It was not clear that regulation would keep prices down or allow independent retailers to survive, though this was important to a government reliant on rural votes (*Cape Breton Post,* 15 June).

All the parties introduced bills to control the spread of video lottery terminals (VLTs), which were being blamed for rising gambling addiction. The Liberals sought a ban, the NDP advocated a plebiscite, and the Tories aimed to reduce the numbers of gambling machines in bars and restaurants. Eventually the number of VLTs was reduced by one-third, hours of operation were cut off at midnight, the rate of play was slowed, and a card-reader system was proposed to allow limits on daily wagers in an effort to control problem gambling. In addition, the province pledged education efforts to address the gambling addiction that had caused distress for so many families.

Few other issues emerged in the spring. The government proposed measures to improve sustainability, promising to increase the number of protected wilderness areas. The NDP pressed the government on health-care wait times, especially for mental health services, when it appeared that actual wait times were being fudged. Overall there was little talk of serious scandal. The Opposition criticized secret bonuses to senior bureaucrats and the government pledged to make them public. MLAs criticized the government when it announced some $240,000 in bonuses for deputy ministers and other top civil servants as the session ended, leaving the ministers out of reach of opposition questions and criticisms (*Daily News,* 30 April).

In the fall one of the more controversial topics was regulation of all-terrain vehicles (ATVs). This issue pitted recreational and commercial ATV enthusiasts against environmentalists concerned about ecological damage from ATV use in woodlands and wetlands and on beaches and dunes. There was also concern from law enforcement and medical practitioners over health and safety risks, especially for young drivers. The rural-based Conservatives sought to allow children under fourteen to drive small ATVs if they and their parents took safety training, which went against a task force recommendation and medical representatives' concerns. An ATV accident then claimed the lives of two teenage girls, changing the tone of the debate. In a compromise between the Conservatives and the NDP, the House made safety training and insurance mandatory and banned those under fourteen from driving, except on small ATVs in closed spaces, with safety gear, and with parents and paramedics present (*Chronicle Herald*, 30 Dec.).

MLA salaries generated embarrassing controversy. The all-party internal economy board secretly proposed an increase in tax-free non-receipted travel and gas and postage allowances, as part of the MLAs' package for communications and constituency costs. The secret deliberations drew public criticism, and the increase was postponed in response to the backlash, which was heightened by the high fuel costs the public was forced to bear. The people's representatives were scheduled to receive raises of 2.9 per cent in 2006; Premier Hamm noted that they were among the most poorly compensated in the country. The salary of about $55,000 included roughly $18,000 tax-free; the premier proposed eliminating this tax-free status while studying the possibility of increased compensation. All but one MLA backed the premier's move, with the lone holdout suggesting that transparency was required sooner. Critics sought full openness for the internal economy board to restore public confidence in the system (*Chronicle Herald*, 11 Nov.).

Finally, fuel prices caused concern among MLAs faced with public expressions of hardship from high gasoline and heating costs. The Opposition wanted an early legislative session to deal with this, but the government delayed its energy plan until the regular fall sitting. The Conservatives rejected a Liberal member's bill to delay Nova Scotia Power's rate hike requests and to limit NSP to one rate hike annually. A Liberal proposal to deal with NSP more effectively, by strengthening or replacing the Utilities Review Board, was also thwarted. The NDP presented a petition from more than thirty thousand citizens demanding a fair electricity price, and an NDP MLA pushed amendments requiring the utility to produce yearly plans to reduce public demand for power. The NDP also sought removal of the HST on home heating oil and adjustments to taxes on gasoline to ease costs for consumers. The government eventually agreed to increase its low-income heating oil rebate by $50 to $250, which was small, given the price hikes. The government pledged $28 million for home energy efficiency and energy rebates. A $170,000 study was ordered to consider the feasibility of regulation.

Other bills were more quietly enacted, including mental health legislation, measures to speed up arbitrations in labour disputes, and a bill permitting the province to seek compensation from tobacco companies for the health-care costs of seniors with smoking-related illnesses. Major grocers and retailers rekindled the debate over Sunday shopping, criticizing the rural-based Tories for limiting their right to compete with smaller stores, which had exemptions for the traditional Sabbath day.

In the end, despite a consistently precarious minority and having to fight numerous battles, Premier Hamm survived the session by working with the opposition, in stark contrast to the conflicts that lead to the end of Paul Martin's Liberal government in Ottawa. In the process, his government may have set a record for longevity and effectiveness among minorities in Canada and its provinces. But there were signs that this collaborative approach would not continue as the government House leader proposed changes to procedures limiting debates and sitting days and referring more bills to committees. The changes would give the government the right to invoke closure and impose limits on debates over estimates. He defended the measures as improving efficiency, but the Opposition expressed concerns about accountability.

The economy

High energy costs made 2005 a difficult year. Prices for gasoline rose significantly, increasing costs for drivers. Gasoline sold for around $1.40 a litre in the fall after supplies were disrupted by Hurricane Katrina in the Gulf of Mexico. Oil prices drove up the costs of heating fuel by as much as $500 per family. Facing increased costs for fuel at its generating plants, the province's privately owned electrical utility asked for a 15 per cent rate hike, even though rates had already risen 6 per cent in the spring. This increase would increase the price of essentials such as electric heat. The request added to public criticism of Nova Scotia Power, which was already under fire because 100,000 people had been left without power after a November storm (a report released earlier cleared NSP of blame for a similar outage in 2004). A proposed 30 per cent electricity price hike for major users such as Stora Enso threatened the survival of such industries. The utility targeted sustainability to improve its public standing, announcing plans to clean up emissions at the Lingan generating plant.

High energy costs gave impetus to new commercial windmills; some twenty-three were operating by year's end. Meanwhile, investors considered new ways to revive and clean up Nova Scotia's dirty coal to keep that moribund sector afloat. Xstrata Coal won the rights to restore the dormant Donkin Mine. Offshore gas production opportunities were boosted by high energy costs, despite disappointing estimates of off-shore supplies; new exploration activity was minimal. Keltic Petroleum announced a $5-million plan for a liquefied natural gas (LNG) and pet-rochemical plant (with electrical generation capacity) in Guysborough County; an environmental review was expected to conclude soon. Con-struction began on Anadarko's LNG project at Point Tupper. Overall the sector had mixed and unexciting results.

Overall economic performance was weak, with employment up only 0.5 per cent, versus 1.4 per cent nationally. Manufacturing em-ployment was down, despite defence contracts for IMP and L-3 Elec-tronic Systems in the aerospace sector. Four hundred people were laid off from the TrentonWorks railcar plant, with the high dollar and costs undermining competitiveness and jobs being transferred to Mexico. There were some increases in retail jobs despite weak consumer de-mand for autos and other big-ticket items. The health sector grew somewhat. The provincial unemployment rate approached national averages and was at its lowest level since the mid-1970s. Housing was mixed, with high resale levels driven by low interest rates, but new housing starts were down 2 per cent, despite an increase in rural construction.

The development of a big-box suburban shopping complex at Dart-mouth Crossing and continued work on the ambitious harbour cleanup created construction employment in Halifax Regional Municipality. A $100-million hospital was announced for Truro, with school and high-way upgrades also adding employment. New or ongoing major con-struction projects included utility and infrastructure systems, natural gas pipelines, community college and university expansion, and broad-band and wireless upgrades. The Halifax airport (renamed for former Premier Stanfield) expanded, with a revamped terminal, retail outlets, and U.S. pre-clearance facilities. Travellers were frustrated by runway resurfacing, which lead to extensive weather-related delays at the height of tourist season.

Despite increases in neighbouring provinces, Nova Scotia exports were down by 4 per cent, with decreases in all major sectors, including fish, lumber, and pulp wood. The finished paper and natural gas sectors were worth more because of higher prices, despite weak demand. Se-curity concerns, high gas prices, and the rising Canadian dollar meant the fewest American tourists in twenty-five years. Officials worried that a new U.S. regulation requiring passports for cross-border travel would compound this problem, as few Americans held passports. This situa-tion was compounded by termination of Scotia Prince service between

Yarmouth and Portland, Maine. New services linking the province to Boston and Portland were touted for the following tourist season.

Labour relations had a tumultuous year, led by the Canadian Broadcasting Corporation (CBC), which locked out its workers in the summer. Gypsum miners were on strike for much of the year in a dispute with their American employer. It was a bitter strike, with use of replacement workers and injunctions against the picketers, but the matter was in arbitration at year's end. Also as the year closed, Stora Enso faced a strike after twenty months of negotiations had failed to resolve core issues; to deal with fluctuating markets for paper products, the company planned to lay off one hundred workers and was seeking concessions on contracting out. Stora closed for nine days at Christmas and faced a strike after 100 per cent of workers rejected its latest contract offer. The premier rejected a call from local mayors for the Legislature to reduce Stora's electricity costs to prevent closure. The company claimed the plant had not turned a profit for several years. Other plants did close, including Glace Bay Fisheries, with a loss of 150 jobs, as the fish processing sector continued to face restructuring and downsizing.

Intergovernmental relations

The province was frustrated by delays in securing compensation owed under an intergovernmental accord on offshore revenues. The $850 million, which had been held up in parliamentary negotiations that tied it to approval of the Kyoto protocol, was finally received and applied to the province's massive debt. The premier regarded this payment as a positive result of his assertive 'campaign for fairness' against equalization clawbacks on offshore revenues. The province struck a deal worth more than $1 billion to retain offshore royalties without loss of equalization payments. Hamm estimated that the province received nearly $200 million more than it might otherwise have received prior to his efforts. He considered this a significant achievement, since Ontario premier Mike Harris and other leaders had opposed concessions to Nova Scotia and Newfoundland, and Saskatchewan was complaining that its resources were not being given equal treatment. Critics warned of problems as the federal government moved from rules-based equalization transfers to side deals with individual provinces. Ontario and other provinces rejected this as 'equalization plus' and sought their own accords, which threatened to undermine the principles governing the transfers. In the same vein, the province benefited from federal adjustments to the

Canada Health and Social Transfers (CHST), which had an equalizing effect but irked richer provinces that were facing funding shortfalls.

The province offered qualified support to the minority Liberal government's federal budget but complained of lack of funds for higher education. This concern was a longstanding one, given the large number of post-secondary institutions and high percentage of out-of-province students at Nova Scotia colleges and universities. The province pushed for a dedicated transfer in higher education to help it grapple with the funding complexities of this unique situation, which had forced tuitions to rise to highest in the country. Nova Scotia would benefit from a per student rather than a population-based formula but would meet resistance from other provinces less reliant on external students to sustain enrolments.

Overall the federal political situation benefited the province, as the Liberals and Tories both promised significant spending to attract voters in this swing province, whose few MPs were suddenly crucial to the formation of a government. The Liberals completed a seven-year deal for infrastructure financing with the province. While support for infrastructure was welcome, the province also wanted Ottawa to consider returning more of the gas taxes collected in Nova Scotia for use in improving local roadways. The province and its municipalities eventually reached a municipal gas tax agreement that funded environmentally sustainable infrastructure; some $145 million was to be used in fifty-five municipalities under this intergovernmental agreement.

Nova Scotia joined in a five-year intergovernmental agreement to fund daycare in the province. The agreement was challenged by the election call, as the Conservatives agreed to continue this arrangement for only one year, preferring assistance to families to help with private child-care costs. Premier Hamm rejected claims from other premiers that the provinces would lose revenues under the Tory plan, suggesting that Stephen Harper had committed to the funds already in place, despite the one-year stipulation. The province and federal government cooperated on a $61-million commitment to twin two narrow highways with high accident rates. Improved funding was offered for health care, but concerns remained about inflated drug costs.

Locally, the province faced criticism over inequity in its transfers and spending in education when it attempted to introduce a transparent, consistent approach. School boards in Cape Breton faced major cuts because of declining enrolments, while the urban school board in Halifax felt underfunded by about 50 per cent. The Halifax board charged that the rurally dominated government did not appreciate the challenges it faced as the largest and most diverse board in the province. Cape Breton Regional Municipality also complained about underfunding of the provincial-municipal equalization system, suggesting that Premier Hamm should apply his fairness principle within the province so CBRM would not have higher taxes supporting more modest services than other communities (*Cape Breton Post,* 5 Feb. and 21 June). The minister of municipal affairs, Barry Barnet, pointed out that CBRM received 50 per cent of the equalization pot with only 12 per cent of the provincial population (*Chronicle-Herald,* 16 Aug.).

Nova Scotia hosted the annual meeting of provincial ministers of the environment, and an issue of importance to local industry took centre stage. The ministers pledged to drastically cut mercury emissions from coal-fired electrical generation, which remained important in this province. As its share, Nova Scotia agreed to cut emissions from 150 to 65 kilograms in 2010. The provincial minister agreed that reductions were feasible but NSP promised only to 'study' the proposals, which could require substantial adjustments to its generating facilities. The ministers pledged ongoing cooperation to move Canada in directions supportive of both competitiveness and sustainability (*Chronicle-Herald,* 28 June).

Mi'kmaq people who had attended residential schools expected to share in the federal government's $2-billion settlement package. Some two thousand Mi'kmaq and Maliseet had passed through such schools in Nova Scotia and New Brunswick, where evidence showed years of physical, sexual, and emotional abuse. The Mi'kmaw Kina'matnewey education agreement was extended for five years, giving First Nations control of the curriculum in band schools and $145 million in federal funds.

The Supreme Court of Canada ruled that Mi'kmaq loggers had to obtain permits to cut trees on Crown land, limiting some of the impact of the earlier landmark Marshall decision. Courts also heard cases where Métis persons sought rights under the Marshall decision to hunt and fish for food or ceremonial purposes, though those remained pending (*Chronicle Herald,* 23 Dec.). Indian Brook First Nation inked an interim deal with Ottawa and the province on fisheries, despite criticisms that they had undermined Aboriginal rights; two bands, at Bear River and Paq'tnkek, refused to sign the deal. The First Nations community welcomed contracts and potential benefits from the tar sands cleanup and the Commonwealth Games bid.

PETER NEARY AND MELVIN BAKER

Newfoundland and Labrador

The year 2005 began in Newfoundland and Labrador with a ban in effect against the display of the Canadian flag at provincial government buildings. Imposed by Premier Danny Williams in December 2004, after he had walked out of talks in Winnipeg on the revision of the 1985 Atlantic Accord, this action played to mixed reviews across the country. Prime Minister Paul Martin told reporters in Montreal on 5 January that the Canadian flag 'should not be used as a lever in any federal-provincial negotiations' (*Globe and Mail,* 6 Jan.). The flag flap brought a flood of media comment and a 7 January op-ed piece, 'We're Mad as Hell,' by Premier Williams in the *Globe and Mail.* Having made his point, he then closed down the media circus: on 10 January the maple-leaf flag was restored at provincial buildings.

Meanwhile, events were in train to get the stalled Atlantic Accord talks moving again. In a letter made public on 14 January, Paul Martin ventured that the offer already made to the province honoured his 2004 election promise about increased offshore revenues. Williams rejected this, but when he, Martin, and Premier John Hamm of Nova Scotia met in Ottawa on 28 January, an agreement in principle was reached. Premier Williams returned home to a rapturous reception at St John's airport, declaring that 'a defining moment in the history of Newfoundland and Labrador' had arrived (Executive Council, News Release, 31 Jan.). In Toronto on 3 February, he told the Empire Club of Canada that his province's success would be 'Canada's success' (Executive Council, News Release, 4 Feb.). Newfoundland and Labrador was destined to be 'prosperous, vibrant and self-reliant' (ibid.). 'Danny Millions,' as the premier was nicknamed, had become 'Danny Billions' (*Globe and Mail,* 3 Feb.).

The full sixteen-year agreement was signed in St John's on 14 February. Under its terms the province would keep 100 per cent of its offshore revenues without clawback while it was eligible for equalization. Should it cease to qualify for equalization in the second eight years of the agreement, it would still qualify, on a sliding scale, for offset payments under the Atlantic Accord. The agreement also provided for a $2 billion up-front payment, covered all new provincial offshore projects, gave the province a 'most-favoured' status in relation to any other offshore resource agreements the federal government might make, and included a joint review procedure (Executive Council, News Release , 31 Jan.). Subsequently the province was kept on tenterhooks by the possibility that the agreement might fall victim to the dissolution of Parliament, but this fear was not realized: on 29 June , Bill C-43, which covered the agreement, received assent. Then, on 5 July, natural resources minister John Efford presented Premier Williams with a ceremonial cheque for $2 billion. Perhaps the best measure of the premier's success was that by this date several other provinces had launched noisy campaigns of their own for sidebar deals with Ottawa.

The celebratory mood carried over into the twelve-page (single-spaced) Speech from the Throne, read by Lieutenant-Governor Edward Roberts on 15 March at the opening of the second session of the forty-fifth General Assembly. In remarks released the same day, Premier Williams said that the government's 'three main priorities for building a better future' were 'investing in our culture; growing and diversify-ing our economy; and fulfilling our social responsibilities' (Executive Council, News Release , 15 Mar.). The hallmarks of the government would be 'economic growth and diversification' (ibid.). Legislation passed during the session included an amended *Automobile Insurance Act,* a *Smoke-free Environment Act,* and *An Act Respecting the Practice of Medicine in the Province.*

The budget speech, delivered by finance minister and president of the Treasury Board Loyola Sullivan on 21 March, announced a 4 per cent increase in overall expenditure, from $4.06 billion in 2004–05 to $4.24 billion in 2005–06, with spending increases planned in health care and education. The deficit projected for the year was $492 million, down from $759 million in 2004–05. Fully 37 per cent of the province's rev-enue for the year would come from the federal government. The pro-vincial government's purpose, the minister said, was to balance 'fiscal responsibility with a social conscience' (*Globe and Mail,* 22 Mar.). In November, in releasing the 2004–05 audited public accounts, Sullivan observed that the province still had a long way to go to reach a 'sustain-able and sound fiscal footing' (Department of Finance, News Release , 29 Nov.). At $11.9 billion and growing, it still had the highest per capita public debt of any province. Also in November, Auditor General John L. Noseworthy reported that, among the provinces, Newfoundland and

Labrador had the highest net debt as a percentage of gross domestic product (60.8 per cent), the highest interest costs as a percentage of total revenue (21 per cent), and the lowest credit rating. It also had an unfunded pension liability of $3.93 billion and growing.

On 11 April the legislative session took a boisterous turn when about 130 angry fishermen staged a demonstration in the public gallery to protest a two-year Raw Materials Sharing (RMS) pilot project introduced in the lucrative snow crab fishery on 2 March. This had the effect of preventing fishermen from selling to the highest bidder. Premier Williams said that the province would stick with its plan, which was based on a commission report and broad community consultation. On 26 April forty vessels and crew converged on St John's and blocked the entrance to the harbour; two days later, after an injunction had ended the blockade, hundreds of crab fishermen were turned away by police when they attempted to enter the public gallery. The Liberal and New Democratic Party members left the House in protest, but Premier Williams was undeterred and acted swiftly and decisively when one of his own members, Fabian Manning (Placentia and St Mary's), spoke out against government policy. Manning was first dropped as a parliamentary secretary and then, on 4 May, expelled from the government caucus. But compromise was now in the air, and on 10 May the government named Richard Cashin, one of the founders of the provincial fishers' union, to chair a review committee on the RMS scheme. In December the committee recommended that the project be abandoned in favour of other measures.

More drama followed on 24 June when a free vote was taken on a bill to facilitate restructuring by Fishery Products International of part of its North American Marketing and Value-Added group into an income trust. The bill carried on both second and third readings by 22 to 17, with the majority including twenty of twenty-six Progressive Conservative members in the House at the time, as well as Judy Foote (Liberal, Grand Bank) and NDP leader Jack Harris (Signal Hill–Quidi Vidi). But the premier and five other PCs voted against it, as did nine Liberals, NDP member Randy Collins (Labrador West), and the now independent Fabian Manning. Absent from the House was former Liberal premier Roger Grimes, who had resigned effective 1 June as leader of the Opposition and member for Exploits. Two hours after his resignation became official, Premier Williams announced a by-election for 23 June in Exploits, which had voted Liberal in every election since 1989. His timing was impeccable – Progressive Conservative Clayton Forsey handily carried the seat.

Important appointments made during the year included:

- Gary Gorman, chair of a newly created provincial Business Advisory Board;
- Ed Martin, CEO and president of Newfoundland and Labrador Hydro and Churchill Falls (Labrador) Corp. (CFLCo);
- LeeAnn Montgomery, the province's first commissioner of lobbyists;
- Ed Walsh, chair of the Public Service Commission; and
- David Gale, deputy minister of a newly created Public Service Secretariat.

In December a federal-provincial panel, appointed under the Atlantic Accord and chaired by businessman Harry Steele, recommended that Max Ruelokke be made chair and CEO of the Canada–Newfoundland and Labrador Offshore Petroleum Board (Williams had wanted St John's mayor Andy Wells and the federal government had favoured former provincial Liberal cabinet minister Rex Gibbons). On 4 February Newfoundland native Lieutenant-General Rick Hillier became chief of defence staff in Ottawa. Effective 15 March broadcaster and author Bill Rowe resigned as the provincial representative in Ottawa.

During the year the government issued discussion papers on its innovation strategy, immigration, and a proposed energy plan. On 7 July it released *Foundation for Success: White Paper on Public Post-Secondary Education* and in December named Irish professor emeritus John Kelly and John L. Davies of Anglia Ruskin University, England, to conduct a study into possible futures for Sir Wilfred Grenfell College, Memorial University's campus in Corner Brook.

Both before and after the House of Assembly adjourned on 24 June, Premier Williams undertook a busy round of regional, national, and international conferences and meetings. In February he went to Washington for the New England Governors' Conference and met with Canadian ambassador Frank McKenna. In May he led a delegation of more than ninety people from forty-seven firms and organizations to the thirty-sixth Offshore Technology Conference in Houston, Texas. From 10–12 August he attended the Council of the Federation meeting in Banff, Alberta, and was chosen to chair a newly formed committee on energy. On 28–29 August in St John's he hosted the twenty-ninth annual Conference of New England Governors and Eastern Canadian Premiers. On 16–17 September he welcomed Taoiseach Bertie Ahern for a celebration of the developing connection between the province and the Republic of Ireland. '

On 8 November the premier shuffled five sitting cabinet members and on 21 November the House of Assembly resumed sitting. The Liberals were now led in the legislature by Gerry Reid (Twillingate and Fogo) and the party had called a leadership convention for 9–10 June 2006. The provincial NDP was likewise in transition, Jack Harris having announced on 28 October that he would step down as party leader when a successor was chosen.

The federal political scene in the province in 2005 was also dynamic. On 24 May a by-election was held in the riding of Labrador to fill the vacancy caused by the death of Liberal MP Lawrence O'Brien. Given the uncertain parliamentary situation facing the Martin minority government, the contest attracted a national cast of campaigners, but the voters remained true to their previous party choice, and Todd Russell, president and CEO of the Labrador Métis Nation, joined the Liberal caucus in Ottawa.

In the fall of 2005 the country was abuzz with stories about John Efford, whose medical problems had kept him away from Ottawa since 19 May. In September he stepped down as minister of natural resources but remained in the Cabinet as regional minister for Newfoundland and Labrador. On 12 November the *Globe and Mail* called him the 'minister in absentia,' but on 15 November, when he was finally able to attend a Cabinet meeting, he was applauded. On 22 November Efford announced that he would not be a candidate in the next federal election, whereupon Premier Williams promptly thanked him for his many services to the province. In early December, after a federal election was called for 23 January 2006, Conservative leader Stephen Harper made a foray into the province and promised that a Conservative government would take control of fishing resources extending beyond Canadian territorial limits if a satisfactory arrangement could not be reached through the North Atlantic Fisheries Organization.

Economically the province continued to advance in 2005, but there were also notable setbacks. With the price of oil rising in the world, the petroleum industry powered ahead, St John's having come somewhat to resemble the North Sea oil ports of Aberdeen and Stavanger. In April Chevron Canada Resources and three other companies reached an operating agreement for the development of the Hebron–Ben Nevis site, in the Jeanne d'Arc Basin, and plans were likewise in train for the expansion of work at the Terra Nova field and for the exploration of the Orphan Basin. In November Husky Energy reported that its White Rose project was in production and in the same month it became publicly known that the resource available at Hibernia was about 20 per cent bigger than previously thought. Ottawa owned 8.5 per cent of the Hibernia project, but following the February Atlantic Accord settlement, the province made plain that it still wanted this asset turned over to it.

By contrast, Newfoundland and Labrador was hit hard by the 2005 downdraft that beset the Canadian pulp and paper industry. On 27 July Abitibi Consolidated announced the closure of both its mill at Stephenville, in October, and the No. 7 paper-making machine at Grand Falls–Windsor, possibly by year's end. The provincial government subsequently entered into intense negotiations with the company, but at the end of the day Abitibi remained on the course it had set in July. In the wake of all this, the government established a task force to address the impact of the closure on the Bay St George area.

On 31 March the Royal Air Force ended a sixty-two-year connection with Goose Bay, Labrador, thereby casting further doubt on the future of 5 Wing Goose Bay, a key local employer. The proposed harnessing of the Lower Churchill River to produce electricity was in and out of the news in 2005 (as it had been for many years), but this possibility remained elusive. In December considerable media attention was drawn to a paper by economist James Feehan and historian Melvin Baker that detailed the questionable origins of the renewal clause in the 1969 Churchill Falls Agreement between CFLCo and Hydro-Québec. Under this clause, the price of power available to Hydro-Québec, already at a bargain basement rate in today's terms, was scheduled to drop in 2016 for a period of twenty-five years.

Culturally, the high point of the year was the official opening by Premier Williams on 29 June of The Rooms – the name is derived from that of traditional fishing premises – built at Fort Townshend in St John's to accommodate the provincial art gallery, museum, and archives. Newfoundland native and media personality Rick Mercer was emcee for the opening, which featured a live art event and a variety of musical and other evocative treats. In July The Rooms was back in the national news for a quite different reason when Gordon Laurin was let go as director of the Art Gallery of Newfoundland and Labrador, an event that made waves in the art community across Canada.

In September the National Gallery of Canada honoured Newfoundland and Labrador artist Christopher Pratt with a retrospective exhibition of his work. Known for his intense and disturbing realism, he was also the designer in 1980 of the provincial flag, a colourful abstraction. For some years the 'pink, white, and green,' an older emblem, had often been seen in the province, and in 2005 a campaign to make it the provincial flag attracted media attention – but to no avail.

Newfoundland-born actor Gordon Pinsent was also honoured during the year when the province gave his name to the arts and culture centre in his native Grand Falls–Windsor, as part of that community's centenary celebrations. Newfoundland and Labrador writer Lisa Moore was a finalist for the 2005 Giller Prize for her novel *Alligator.*

On 2 July history was re-enacted when Americans Steve Fossett and Mark Rebholz took off from St John's in a replica Vickers Vimy, heading for Clifden, Ireland. In 1919 the first non-stop transatlantic crossing by air had been made over the same route by British pilots John Alcock and Arthur Whitten Brown.

2005 also brought important developments in the province's evolving relationship with its Aboriginal peoples. On 22 January at Jens Haven High School in Nain, Labrador, the Labrador Inuit Land Claims Agreement and an agreement for the creation of the Torngat Mountains National Park Reserve of Canada were signed by federal, provincial, and Aboriginal leaders. The same day Premier Williams apologized to the Inuit on behalf of the government for the closure of the northern Labrador communities of Nutak and Hebron in 1956 and 1959, respectively. On 23 June royal assent was given to the federal act authorizing the land claims agreement. It took effect on 1 December 2005, when the government of the new territory of Nunatsiavut began functioning.

On 28 April representatives of the Miawpukek First Nation, located 224 kilometres south of Gander, and the provincial and federal governments signed the Miawpukek First Nation Self-Government Framework Agreement and announced an agreement for the transfer of land from the province for the expansion of the existing Samiajij Miawpukek Reserve.

But the year also brought continuing friction. In February some residents of the Mushuau Innu First Nation reserve at Natuashish, where Innu had been resettled from Davis Inlet, petitioned the band council for its resignation. Labrador and Aboriginal affairs minister Tom Rideout called on the federal government to investigate the expenditure of public monies at the reserve where, the *National Post* claimed later, 'all the deadly pathologies' that had afflicted Davis Inlet had survived 'intact' (*National Post,* 19 Dec.). In July researchers at Memorial University's education faculty released a report, invited by the community, titled *Recommendations for an Effective Model of Innu Education.*

Notable Newfoundland and Labrador figures, resident and non-resident, who died in 2005 included:

- Frank Duff Moores, the province's first Progressive Conservative premier (1972–79);
- William Doody, a member of the Moores cabinet and then a senator;
- Sam Drover, who sat in the first post-Confederation cabinet;
- Noel Murphy, a physician, legislator and mayor of Corner Brook;
- Grace Butt, founder of the St John's Players;
- singer Dick Nolan, celebrated for 'Aunt Martha's Sheep';
- Edgar Baird, forester and community leader; and
- writer and musician Alice Story, a magnetic piano accompanist of silent films.

Four crew members were lost when the *Melina & Keith II* sank in September, three fishermen from Belleoram died at sea in November, and Gordon Simmons and Carl Neal were killed when a Canadian Coast Guard MBB-105 helicopter crashed into the ocean off the Burin Peninsula on 7 December.

2005 was an exceptionally eventful year in Newfoundland and Labrador, and was recognized as such both there and beyond. Above all, the year belonged to Premier Danny Williams. Having settled a new deal on the Atlantic Accord, dodged the bullet of dissolution in Ottawa, accepted a ceremonial cheque for $2 billion, taken a seat away from the Liberals, bid farewell to Roger Grimes and John Efford, and spoken graciously of the exiting Jack Harris, he was king of all he surveyed. Not since the heyday of Joey Smallwood, the first post-Confederation premier, had the province seen such a commanding political figure.

Obituaries

ATKINSON, THEODORE (TED) (5 May, age 88). First horse-racing jockey to win more than $1 million in a single season.

BALTZAN, MARCEL (MARC) (1 January, age 75). Physician, former head of the Canadian Medical Association, pioneer in kidney research; officer of the Order of Canada.

BARTLEY, LES (15 May, age 51). Professional lacrosse coach.

BASFORD, RONALD (31 January, age 72). Former minister of justice who led the movement to abolish capital punishment in Canada.

BAZAY, DAVID (30 October, age 66). CBC journalist.

BELLOW, SAUL (5 April, age 89). Author of *The Adventures of Augie March* and *Herzog;* Nobel laureate, Pulitzer Prize recipient, and three-time recipient of the National Book Award.

BESSETTE, GERARD (21 February, age 84). Author and professor; recipient of the Governor General's Award for *Le cycle.*

BIGELOW, WILFRED GORDON (27 March, age 91). Heart surgeon known for his role in development of the artificial pacemaker and for using hypothermia in open heart surgery; officer of the Order of Canada and member of the Canadian Medical Hall of Fame.

BOCHNER, LLOYD (29 October, age 81). Stage, TV, and film actor.

BONNER, ROBERT (12 August, age 84). Lawyer, corporate executive, and former attorney general of British Columbia.

BOYLE, HARRY (22 January, age 89). Novelist, playwright, CBC executive, broadcast regulator; officer of the Order of Canada.

BRONFMAN, EDWARD (4 April, age 77). Businessman and philanthropist; member of the Order of Canada.

BROTT, ALEXANDER (1 April, age 90). Violinist, conductor, and composer; member of the Order of Canada.

CADIEUX, LEO (11 May, age 96). Former minister of defence and ambassador to France; officer of the Order of Canada.

CADMAN, CHUCK (9 July, age 57). Independent member of Parliament for Surrey North.

CAMERON, BILL (12 March, age 62). Journalist for Global, CityTV, and CBC television.

CAMERON, EARL (13 January, age 89). Former news anchor of CBC's *The National.*

CARDINAL, HAROLD (3 June, age 60). Author, lawyer, teacher, and Aboriginal leader.

CARISSE, TERRY (22 May, age 62). Award-winning country musician.

CHAPMAN, JEFF 'NINJALICIOUS' (23 August, age 31). Writer, urban explorer, and founder of the zine *Infiltration.*

CLAIR, FRANK (3 April, age 88). Professional football coach.

CLARK, GERALD (age 88). Journalist and editor.

CLOUTIER, MAURICE GASTON 'GUS' (29 August, age 70). Canada's longest-serving parliamentary sergeant-at-arms.

CÔTÉ-LÉVESQUE, CORINNE (19 October, age 61). Author and broadcaster; widow of René Lévesque.

CULLEN, BUD (5 July, age 78). Judge, member of Parliament, and former immigration minister.

D'AMICO, JOHN (29 May, age 67). NHL linesman and Hockey Hall of Frame inductee.

D'AMOUR, DENIS 'PIGGY' (26 August, age 45). Rock guitarist.

DOODY, C. WILLIAM (27 Dec., age 74). Newfoundland and Labrador politician and senator.

DOOHAN, JAMES (20 July, age 85). Actor famous for the role of 'Scotty' in the original *Star Trek* television series.

DROVER, SAM (20 June, age 93). Member of Newfoundland and Labrador's first provincial government.

EGAN, SEAN (29 April, age 63). Associate professor of human kinetics and mountain climber.

ELLIOT, FRASER (26 January, age 83). Corporate lawyer and philanthropist; member of the Order of Canada.

FAVREAU, MARC (17 Dec., age 76). Actor and poet.

FARNON, ROBERT (22 April, age 87). Musician, conductor, music arranger, and composer.

FEDAK, WASYLY (10 January, age 95). Primate of the Ukrainian Orthodox Church of Canada.

FILION, GÉRARD (26 March, age 95). Quebec businessman and journalist; companion of the Order of Canada.

FRITH, ROYCE (17 March, age 81). Politician, diplomat, and senator; member of the Order of Canada.

GARBER, HOPE (7 Sept., age 81). Singer and actress.

GOLD, ALAN BERNARD (15 May, age 87). Former chief justice of the Quebec Superior Court and the mediator who brought an end to the Oka crisis in 1990; officer of the Order of Canada.

GRANGE, SAMUEL (26 August, age 85). Justice of the Ontario Supreme Court.

HARRINGTON, RICHARD (11 October, age 94). Photographer; officer of the Order of Canada.

HICKE, BILL (18 July, age 67). Professional hockey player.

HISLOP, GEORGE (8 October, age 78). Pioneering gay rights activist.

HOLE, LOIS (6 January, age 72). Politician, businesswoman, author, educator, and former Lieutenant-Governor of Alberta; member of the Order of Canada.

HONDERICH, BELAND (8 November, age 86). Newspaper publisher and executive; officer of the Order of Canada.

HORNER, REGINALD 'RED' (27 April, age 95). Professional hockey player.

HUNTER, ROBERT (1 May, age 63). Journalist, politician, and co-founder of Greenpeace.

JENNINGS, PETER (7 August, age 67). Journalist and sole anchor for ABC News from 1983 to 2005; member of the Order of Canada.

JEROME, JAMES (21 August, age 72). Judge and former Speaker of the House of Commons.

KEATING, CHARLES (22 November, age 72). Former director of Shaw Communications; member of the Order of Canada.

KERR, BEN (17 June, age 75). Musician, street performer, and perennial Toronto mayoral candidate.

LABINE, LEO (25 February, age 73). Professional hockey player.

LAMBERTS, HEATH (22 February, age 63). Actor; member of the Order of Canada.

LEE, DAN (15 January, age 35). Animator who created the title character in *Finding Nemo*.

LEVINE, NORMAN (14 June, age 81). Novelist and poet.

MAZURIN, ALEXIS (20 October, age 27). Original host of CBC's Radio 3.

MCADOREY, ROBERT (BOB) (5 February, age 69). Radio and television broadcaster.

MCCALL, CHRISTINA (27 April, age 70). Author and political journalist.

MCCRAIG, J.R. 'BUD' (11 January, age 75). Chairperson of Trimac Corporation and co-owner of the Calgary Flames; member of the Order of Canada.

MCDONALD-HYDE, DOROTHY (11 November, age 59). Chief of Alberta's Fort McKay First Nation and one of Canada's first female elected chiefs.

MEERWALI, ZAID (15 August, age 33). Iraqi-Canadian kidnapped and then murdered in Baghdad.

MOORES, FRANK (10 July, age 72). Second premier of Newfoundland and Labrador.

NOLAN, DICK (13 December, age 66). Singer, songwriter, and guitarist.

PARENT, MIMI (14 June, age 80). Artist.

PASHBY, THOMAS (24 August, age 90). Ophthalmologist and former chairperson of the Canadian Standards Association; member of the Order of Canada.

PATTERSON, TOM (23 February, age 84). Journalist and founder of the Stratford Festival; officer of the Order of Canada.

PEDEN, DOUGLAS (11 April, age 88). Athlete and Olympic basketball player.

POLIE, NORMAN 'BUD' (4 January, age 80). Professional hockey player, coach, and general manager.

ROBICHAUD, LOUIS (6 January, age 79). First Acadian to become premier of New Brunswick; companion of the Order of Canada.

RUSSELL, ANDY (1 June, age 89). Trapper, conservationist, author, and filmmaker; member of the Order of Canada.

SHIBICKY, ALEX (9 July, age 91). Professional hockey player.

SMITH, ERNEST 'SMOKEY' (3 August, age 91). Last surviving recipient of the Victoria Cross.

SUTTER, LOUIS (10 February, age 73). Father of six NHL players.

TAUBE, HENRY (16 November, age 89). Chemist; Nobel Prize laureate.

TREMBLAY, KAY (11 August, age 90). Stage, film, and television actor.

TROIANO, DOMENIC (25 May, age 59). Rock guitarist.

TURNER, ROBERT (BOB) (7 February, age 74). Professional hockey player.

VERNON, JOHN (1 February, age 72). Stage, film, and television actor.

VERREAU, RICHARD (6 July, age 79). Tenor; member of the Order of Canada.

WATERS, ALLAN (3 December, age 84). Founder of the CHUM Ltd media empire.

WELSH, JONATHAN (27 January, age 57). Actor who played one of the first openly gay characters on television.

WHITE, EDWARD (ED) (26 August, age 56). Professional wrestler.

WHITE, ONNA (8 April, age 83). Choreographer and dancer.

WOJTYLA, KAROL JÓZEF (POPE JOHN PAUL II) (2 April, age 84). Supreme pontiff of the Catholic Church.

YOUNG, SCOTT (12 June, age 87). Sportswriter, novelist, and journalist.

Election table

British Columbia, Thirty-Eighth Provincial General Election, 2005

Political party	Votes received	Percentage of popular vote	Candidates elected
B.C. Conservative Party	9,623	0.55	
B.C. Liberal Party	807,118	45.80	46
B.C. Marijuana Party	11,449	0.65	
Democratic Reform B.C.	14,022	0.80	
Green Party of B.C.	161,849	9.17	
New Democratic Party of B.C.	731,783	41.52	33
Independent	16,152	0.92	
Other affiliations[1]	10,347	0.59	
Rejected ballots	11,962		
Total (valid votes)[2]	1,774,269	100.00	79

Source: Elections B.C.

[1] B.C. Youth Coalition, Bloc B.C., Libertarian Party, British Columbia Party, Social Credit Party, B.C. Unity Party, Communist Party of B.C., Emerged Democratic Party of B.C., Freedom Party, Moderates, People's Front, Platinum Party, Reform B.C., Sex Party, Western Canada Concept, Refed B.C., Work Less Party, Your Party, no affiliation.

[2] Voter turnout was 58.19 per cent.

Index of names

Index of subjects